Remapping 'Crisis': A Guide to Athens

T0302928

Remapping 'Crisis': A Guide to Athens

Edited by

Myrto Tsilimpounidi

and

Aylwyn Walsh

zero books

Winchester, UK
Washington, USA

First published by Zero Books, 2014
Zero Books is an imprint of John Hunt Publishing Ltd., Laurel House, Station Approach,
Alresford, Hants, SO24 9JH, UK
office1@jhpbooks.net
www.johnhuntpublishing.com
www.zero-books.net

For distributor details and how to order please visit the 'Ordering' section on our website.

Text copyright: Myrto Tsilimpounidi and Aylwyn Walsh 2013

ISBN: 978 1 78099 605 9

All rights reserved. Except for brief quotations in critical articles or reviews, no part of this book may be reproduced in any manner without prior written permission from the publishers.

The rights of Myrto Tsilimpounidi and Aylwyn Walsh as editors have been asserted in accordance with the Copyright, Designs and Patents Act 1988.

A CIP catalogue record for this book is available from the British Library.

Design: Stuart Davies

Printed in the USA by Edwards Brothers Malloy

We operate a distinctive and ethical publishing philosophy in all areas of our business, from our global network of authors to production and worldwide distribution.

CONTENTS

List of Images

List of Tables

Acknowledgements

We would like to extend thanks to several people who have been instrumental in getting this volume to publication. In particular, to Costas Douzinas, who provided encouragement in early phases. Thanks also to research mentors from our institutions for their constant guidance. Critical reflection has been welcomed at a range of formal and informal gatherings.

The chapter authors are to be praised for their willingness to contribute to the volume, as well as their patience working through drafts. Their many conversations in the process of putting the book together have helped tremendously. Individual street artists and interview subjects are gratefully acknowledged for the rich material they provide.

Early career scholars do not always enjoy the degree of generosity and support we have gained in the preparation of this volume, and for that Myrto thanks the University of East London, and Aylwyn thanks the University of Lincoln.

We appreciate the efforts of those at Zero Books for taking the book on. Thanks too, to all individuals who have supported the work both near and far. Although we have endeavoured to ensure accuracy, any mistakes remain our own responsibility.

Notes on Contributors

Vassilis Arapoglou (M.Sc., PhD, LSE) is assistant professor in social inequalities and social exclusion at the department of sociology of the University of Crete as well as a tutor at the Greek Open University. His research and teaching concentrates on the critical analysis of urban social problems and policies, migration, inequality and forms of belonging. He is editor of *European Urban and Regional Studies*.

Konstantinos Avramidis is a chartered architect (TEE/TCG) as well as a researcher. He is currently undertaking a PhD at the University of Edinburgh. He combines research, through writings either individually or jointly, with active professional practice, through projects both independently and as a collaborator. He holds a Diploma in Architecture from the Aristotle University of Thessaloniki and a postgraduate degree in Interdisciplinary Theory and Design of Space (MSc) from the National Technical University of Athens, where he has taught as an assistant at architectural design studios. His design work has been awarded, published and exhibited. Konstantinos has also published on themes related to spatial theory and design, emphasising on wall inscription and graffiti.

Bleeps.gr has done irrelevant studies from 1999 till 2003 when he moved to UK where he enrolled in a two-year course in painting at the Royal College of Bristol. His passion to express philosophical and political thought has found its medium through street art. Bleeps and his collectives keep themselves to the more "underground" scene although found acclaim from major media around the globe. He is based in Athens.

Leonidas K. Cheliotis is Chancellor's Fellow in Law at the School of Law, University of Edinburgh, having previously been a Lecturer and founding Deputy Director of the Centre for Criminal Justice at the School of Law, Queen Mary, University of

London. He completed his MPhil and PhD degrees at the Institute of Criminology, University of Cambridge. He has been elected to visiting positions at the Centre for the Study of Law and Society, School of Law, University of California, Berkeley, and the Centre for Criminology, Faculty of Law, and University of Oxford. He is also an Associate Editor of the European Journal of Criminology. His most recent published work on Greece concerns conditions of imprisonment and prisoner health, the politics and experience of immigration detention, and urban security.

Zacharoula Christopoulou was born in Athens. She studied History at the Aristotle University of Thessaloniki, where she developed an interest in cultural perceptions of war and conflict. After moving to England, she completed an MA in Comparative Literature at the University of Kent. Her MA dissertation was entitled: 'Historical Trauma and Women's Literature: Remembering Fascism in Carmen Martin Gaite's *The Back Room* and Christa Wolf's *Patterns of Childhood*.' Currently, she is in the process of submitting her thesis in Literature and Memory of the First World War at the University College London. Her research interests involve First World War, Literature and Trauma, Cultural History of War, Political Myth, the Fantastic.

Orsalia Dimitriou is a practicing architect and a researcher. She holds a Diploma in Architecture Engineering from NTUAthens and an MA in Art and Architecture and from UPC, Barcelona. She is currently a PhD Candidate at the department of Visual Cultures in Goldsmiths University of London and her thesis is focusing on public space, democracy and social movements using as a research method both theory and visual media. Her research interests include design as a political tool, urban insurgencies, grassroots practices, theatrical and ephemeral interventions in urban space, participatory design and social sustainability. Orsalia is currently teaching architectural design and contextual studies in the architectural department of

Central Saint Martins, London.

Costas Douzinas is Professor of Law and Director of the Birkbeck Institute for the Humanities, and visiting professor at the University of Athens. He is a regular contributor to *The Guardian*, and author of many books in the field of human rights, ethics and the law. Major recent books include *Human Rights and Empire* (2007), and his current book is *Philosophy and Resistance in the Crisis*.

Theofanis Exadaktylos is Lecturer in European Politics (EU External Relations) at the School of Politics, University of Surrey since 2011. He is also Research Associate with the Hellenic Observatory of the London School of Economics. He previously held a post with the University of Exeter where he completed his PhD. His research agenda focuses on issues of Europeanization of national foreign policy from a public policy perspective, the external relations of the European Union and the changes to EU foreign policy the Treaty of Lisbon brought about. His recent book is edited with Claudio M. Radaelli (2012) *Research Methods in European Studies: Research Design in Europeanization* by Palgrave/Macmillan. His most recent publications reflect upon the impact of the European financial crisis on political trust, policy implementation, and institutional change in the EU and the Member States.

Konstantina Drakopoulou studied Archaeology and Art History at the National and Kapodistrian University of Athens. She holds a master's degree in Art History from the Aristotle University of Thessaloniki and the Freie Universität Berlin, and a PhD from the National and Kapodistrian University of Athens. She has worked as an art historian for the Hellenic Ministry of Culture and Tourism and participated in various research programs at the University of Athens. Konstantina is currently writing a book about the graffiti scene in Greece.

Philip Hager (BA Patras, MA Goldsmiths, PhD RHUL) is Associate Lecturer in the Department of Performing Arts,

University of Winchester and the Department of Drama, Goldsmiths, University of London. His work examines the politics of theatre and performance in post-war and contemporary Europe. He has published on the politics of modern Greek theatre and the movement of the squares, and has presented papers in UK and international conferences on performances and spectacles of citizenship and democracy in contemporary urban settings. He is currently working towards a co-edited volume on the performances and spectacles of crises, capitalism and resistance staged in Europe.

Yannis Kallianos has recently finished his PhD in the Department of Social Anthropology in St Andrews University under the title: "The Subversion of Everyday Life: An Anthropological Study of Radical Political Practices. The Greek Revolt of December 2008." His thesis was focused on eighteen months of fieldwork amongst antiauthoritarian and self-organized groups in Athens and examines the revolt of 2008 as a series of subversive practices against everyday regularities, authority and power relations. Currently, he is conducting research on conflict and social change in Athens, Greece. He extends gratitude to Myrto Tsilimpounidi, Pafsanias Karathanasis and Dionisia Aggelopoulou for their suggestions and comments in the process of writing this chapter.

Pafsanias Karathanasis is a PhD candidate of Social Anthropology in the University of the Aegean, located in the island of Lesvos on the eastern border of Greece. His academic and research interests focus in the areas of urban studies and concentrate in the study of the material and visual culture produced through contemporary cultural and sociopolitical practices in the changing urban public spaces. He has done research mainly in the cities of Nicosia (Cyprus) and Athens (Greece) and through his work he explores the production and construction of urban space/landscape and the contestations in the socio-spatial formation of public spaces.

Georgios Karyotis (PhD, University of Edinburgh) is a Lecturer in International Relations at the University of Strathclyde and Secretary of the Greek Politics Specialist Group (GPSG) of the PSA. He is the section editor for the *Journal of Contemporary European Research* and convenor of the interdisciplinary group Strathclyde Conflict and Resolution (SCAR). His research interests include securitization theory, European migration policy, terrorism, political behavior, austerity politics, and South-Eastern Europe politics. Among others, he has published articles in the *British Journal of Political Science, Cooperation and Conflict, International Political Sociology* and the *Journal of Peace Research.*

Margarita Komninou is a PhD candidate in Sociology at the University of Edinburgh. Her research interests focus on the politics and ethics of consumption. She has also been involved in collaborative research on policing protest in the UK.

Thomas Maloutas is professor of Social Geography at Harokopio University and Director of the National Centre for Social Research (EKKE) in Athens. He works on sociospatial change in metropolitan areas with particular focus on Athens. He recently published 'Contextual diversity in gentrification research' (*Critical Sociology*, 38/1, 2012) and co-edited, with K. Fujita, *Residential segregation in comparative perspective. Making sense of contextual diversity* (Farnham, Ashgate, 2012).

Orestis Pangalos is an architect, currently completing his PhD on graffiti as a culture and as an art form in the public space, and the position of graffiti practitioners within the dynamics of social and political power. Orestis is a graffiti writer himself since 1993, and the publisher of the first graffiti magazine in Greece (Balbida Ektonosis Pieseon - Pressure Expansion Valve, 1997-2001). Aside from graffiti and editions, recent activities include lecturing and teaching for the art history and the art classes in the Faculty of Architecture (Polytechnic School of Aristotle University) of Thessaloniki, for the Cultural

Studies courses of the Postgraduate Program of Museology, giving open lectures at the two art museums of the same town, as well as exhibiting installations to the public.

Dimitris Skleparis is a PhD Candidate and part-time Teaching Assistant at Queen Mary, University of London. His research focuses on the securitization of migration and asylum in Greece, the role of EU policies, governmental and non-governmental actors, and security professionals in this process, and the individual and collective migrant acts of resistance that emerge as challenges within this context.

Myrto Tsilimpounidi is a social researcher and photographer. Her research focuses on the interface between urbanism, culture, and innovative methodologies. Past work explores the impact of migration on societal changes through an empirical investigation of cosmopolitan theory. Current projects focus on street politics, landscapes of belonging, and the new aesthetics of crisis in Southern Europe. Myrto is a post-doctoral fellow at the University of East London and the executive director of Ministry of Untold Stories. Recent publications include 'Performances 'in crisis': what happens when a city goes soft?' for *City* and 'The disappearing immigrants: hunger strike and invisible struggles' for *Journal of Theory in Action.*

Aylwyn Walsh is a performance studies scholar working on the arts and social change. She is currently developing practice-led research in women's prisons in the UK. Aylwyn is a lecturer at the University of Lincoln and artistic director of Ministry of Untold Stories. Recent publications have included work on arts in healthcare for the *Research in Drama Education* and the *Journal for Applied Arts and Health*; on street art in *Journal of Arts and Communities* and research on women in prison appears in *Contemporary Theatre Review.*

Sappho Xenakis is RBUCE-UP Marie Curie Fellow at the Centre for Sociological Research on Law and Penal Institutions (CESDIP)/Université de Versailles, France. She studied

International Relations at the London School of Economics and holds a DPhil in International Relations from the University of Oxford. Her research on Greece focuses on the politics of crime and punishment in the country: in addition to the volume *Crime and Punishment in Contemporary Greece: International Comparative Perspectives* (co-edited with L.K. Cheliotis), her published work addresses trends in political violence, urban security challenges, policy against organised crime, normative hybridity and perceptions of corruption, and patterns of state and public punitiveness from a political economy perspective.

Marilena Zaroulia is Senior Lecturer in Drama and Program Leader of the MA Popular Performances at the Department of Performing Arts, University of Winchester. Her research focuses on contemporary performance and cultural politics and post-1989 British and European theatre. She is currently working on a monograph studying the relation between British theatre and Europe since 1989 and co-convening 'Inside/Outside Europe: Performances of Capitalism, Crises and Resistance', an interdisciplinary, collaborative project studying performances of crises and crisis as performance in contemporary Europe.

Foreword

Intellectuals in a Time of Crisis

Costas Douzinas

Surprise and concern has been expressed in Greece about the lack of interventions by mainstream intellectuals resisting the destruction of the social bond, the humanitarian crisis and the rise of fascism as a result of the measures imposed on the Greek people by the troika of IMF, EU and ECB. Intellectuals and academics on the Left have rallied to the defence of dignity and well-being of the population but have been excluded or marginalised by the established media. It is characteristic that some of the most important academic analyses of the crisis have been published outside Greece. The present collection is the best representative of this growing genre that finds greater interest in London or Paris than in Athens or Thessaloniki.

The deafening silence of mainstream intellectuals, a normally voluble and visible tribe, alerts us to wider concerns about the existence, role and responsibility of intellectuals. What is the responsibility of intellectuals at a time of crisis? Let me start with a brief history. The term intellectual was first used in France during the Dreyfus affair. Alfred Dreyfus, a French Jewish army officer was accused by anti-Semitic nationalists of spying for the Germans. The Anti-dreyfusants coined the term 'classe intellectuel' to discredit prominent supporters of Dreyfus as decadent, anti-nationalist and Jewish. The Dreyfusants such as Emile Zola (who penned the famous 'J'Accuse' article) and Julien Benda, later the author of *Trahison des Clercs* in a masterful reversal adopted the term 'intellectual' for their cause and a new militant identity was launched.

In English, the term appeared for the first time in 1914, in quotation marks, imported by the circle of Romain Rolland and the opponents of war in France. It was used for the anti-war stance of Bertrand Russell and Walter Lipmann in his early left wing period. After the war and the Russian revolution, the term became generalised, replacing the older 'men of letters'. Intellectuals are what the French do, say the English. England has tried to keep Parisian ideas and fashions out of its shores in the same way that it quarantined pets to prevent the introduction of rabies. When Birkbeck College launched its Institute for the Humanities in 2004 with a series of lectures celebrating the life and work of Jacques Derrida (Douzinas, 2007) an Observer commentator responded in an article entitled 'What have intellectuals ever done for the world'.

Noam Chomsky in his 1967 famous essay 'The responsibility of intellectuals' wrote that it is the responsibility 'of intellectuals to speak the truth and to expose lies. This, at least, may seem enough of a truism to pass over without comment. Not so, however. For the modern intellectual, it is not at all obvious.' For Chomsky, the role of intellectuals is to 'speak truth to power' (1967). From almost the opposite side of the spectrum Judge Richard Posner published *'Public Intellectuals': A Study in Decline* (2002). Posner's claim is quite accurate on the surface. Intellectuals have progressively become extremely specialized in their field of expertise. This coincided with the huge increase in media presence and its hunger for copy. The combination of the two processes means that today intellectuals tend to speak about issues they know very little about and when they opine about wider political and social issues outside their area of professional competence they become 'false prophets'.

Let us combine the decline of intellectuals with the question of responsibility. The death of the intellectual coincides with the rise of the expert. The first generation of intellectuals were committed to of social justice and equality, resistance to racism and colonialism, opposition to war. They tended to be philosophers, well-known artists and authors, something that gave them public recognition and respect. They were representatives of radical enlightenment, speaking only partly as experts and to a much larger extent as spokespersons of a normative universalism and a political version of truth. For these public intellectuals, truth is not the objective outcome of cognitive processes but a domain of struggle one enters armed with moral principles, historical awareness and political categories which judge, criticise and resist. Truth and the universal do not mirror reality but are strategies to change it. This is the truth that Chomsky promotes and Posner derides.

Great intellectuals are not people who exercise 'responsible' critique. Their inspiration is Socrates with his persistent critique of *doxa* – common sense – and his courage. 'Courage does not require knowledge of certain things', says the general Nicias in the dialogue *Laches*, 'it is a species of knowledge of what is to be dreaded or dared either in war or in anything else.'[1] Courage does not call for empirical knowledge but for moral knowledge of self, of the good and beautiful and it is disclosed by *parrhesia* – fearless speech. It sets the natural ends of action and frees man from natural and social fears.

But this type of intellectual declined and perhaps died by the 1990s for a number of reasons. Intellectuals are now almost exclusively identified with University employees. The terms intellectual and academic have become synonyms. The grand cognitive fields of philosophy, history, letters, law have broken up into a myriad of disciplines and sub-disciplines. University life under state policies and funding priorities has become increasingly solitary, intellectually isolated strictly controlled and managed for policy compliance and economic impact. The idea of the Renaissance person, someone with encyclopaedic knowledge, moral rectitude and aesthetic discernment has passed away with the last great central European Jews (Einstein, Bloch, Derrida, Hobsbawm) and the Sixties generation of French intellectuals.

Specialisation and professionalization coincided with the emergence of post-politics and the attack on democracy as a form of life. This fear of democracy was first publicised by the Trilateral Conference. For Samuel Huntington, the problem with democracy lies with 'value-oriented intellectuals', who nurture an 'adversary culture' opposed to the pragmatism of 'policy-oriented intellectuals' (Crozier et al., 1975). They push for excessive democratic activity, challenging leadership and authority. But these jeremiads were becoming already obsolete at the time of their writing.

The new intellectuals/academics (the terms have become interchangeable) are experts in small fields. Their main function is to advise governments on policy and comment in the media. They exercise what Jacques Lacan has called the 'discourse of the University'. The supposed complexity of modern government and the heights of scientific sophistication mean that proper objective advice given to policy-makers helps solve problems. The role of intellectuals/academics is to offer tools, to become instruments of government. Let me give you a specific example of this approach from my current bête noire, the dominant view about the EU.

Academic propagandists for the Union argue that popular participation is undesirable because it is 'ignorant irrelevant and ideological'. Princeton Professor Andrew Moravcsik claims that 'social Europe is a chimera' and democratic participation should be discouraged because it 'runs counter to our consensual social scientific understanding of now advanced democracies work' (2002, p. 618). Economic and scientific expertise is not open to debate and voting. Indeed all democratic participation and mobilization is expensive, counter-productive and gives the impression that there may be more than one solution to problems that have objectively right answers. The great advantage of the Union is that it is so 'boring' that people do not care about it.

And it is this type of approach that the media have adopted towards the intellectual/ academic hybrid. Two types of intellectual/academic are evident today: the Prof/prop and the Prof/entertainer. Those in the first category, typically economists and psychologists, opine about statistics and psyche, the two main domains of power's intervention and control. They offer sound bites that mostly confirm the banal or the point the journalist wants to promote. They offer props for the argument rather than evidence for it. The entertainers, mostly historians, present series on the glory of Greece or the British Empire that mix the simplistic with the fanciful. Media dons mix claims to academic expertise that gives them a certain status and expertise with usually well-disguised establishment normative or political claims. In a situation of conflict, objectivity tends to become the best disguise for ideological partisanship.

But the idea that ideology has ended and politics was about the management of economics has come to an abrupt end in the years of the crisis. The deep social rifts and conflicts have surfaced with violence and this is the terrain where intellectuals/academics must ply their trade. In a situation of conflict, objectivity tends to become the best disguise for ideological partisanship.

And yet after Michel Foucault, Chomsky's 'speaking truth to power' is harder to support. The belief that power and knowledge are external to each other involved in a zero sum game is no longer convincing. In his article 'What is Critique', Foucault suggested that critique means developing *l'art de n'être pas tellement gouverné* (1990). He associates critique with resistance to governance and with acts of desubjectification, relative detachment from the demands of biopolitical power. This is how he put it in the seminar 'defending society':

> The role of the one who speaks [the intellectual in our context] is not that of legislator or the philosopher between camps, the

> figure of peace and armistice… To establish oneself between adversaries at the centre and above them, to impose a general law on each and to found an order that reconciles: this is not what is at issue. At issue is the positing of a right marked by dissymetry, the founding of a truth linked to a relation of force, a weapon truth and a singular right. The subject that speaks is a warring – I wont even say a polemical – subject (2004, n.p.).

Edward Saïd, following Foucault, revised Chomsky's understanding of the responsibility of the intellectuals. Saïd writes in *Representations of the Intellectual*.

> The intellectual is endowed with a faculty for . . . articulating a . . . philosophy or opinion to, as well as for, a public. And this role has an edge to it, [involving] someone whose place it is publicly to raise embarrassing questions, to confront orthodoxy. Someone whose raison d'être is to represent all those people and issues that are routinely swept under the rug (1996, p. 3–24).

The expert's role is to make us forget that the subject is warring, placed on the battlefield, surrounded by enemies, and to keep telling us about our common interests and the country's rescue.

For Saïd in his Reith lectures, on the other hand, the intellectual is a present-day Robin Hood who gives voice to those who would not be heard otherwise. This is the European tradition of the intellectual but not that of the academic or the expert. This type of intellectual has jettisoned the responsibility of knowledge or power for the irresponsibility of struggle. In English or French, 'responsibility' is etymologically linked with 'response'. You are responsible when you respond to a (moral) demand. The demand may come from power or from the other. When responsibility is defined as consent to the commands of power it is not moral. The moral attitude is irresponsibility. Moral responsibility responds to the demand of the excluded and the poor.

In periods of intense crisis the pressing need to take sides comes to the surface and trumps neutrality. The claim to objectivity, always a little problematic, can no longer be sustained, and becomes itself a ground of confrontation as the conflicts amongst economists and constitutional lawyers show. As the world is moving towards a state of permanent crisis the engaged intellectual and the committed media are coming back. And as we know, exceptional situations are the best guide for understanding normal times.

This volume pursues the classical virtues of *parrhesia* and *andreia* at a period of crisis. My hope is that this and similar initiatives will revive again the somewhat lost honor of the intellectual.

Introduction

Myrto Tsilimpounidi & Aylwyn Walsh

In the last two years, there has been a glut of new writing that engages with the era of highly charged political change that seems, at its core, to be about re-working the notion of democracy from an ideal to a practice. Scholars, journalists and commentators have churned out reflections on the so-called 'Arab Spring', the Occupy movement, and unrest across Europe. These important books seek to make sense of the breadth of the ways an urban politics of protest and revolt now characterises cities from Oakland, California to Istanbul, Turkey, and Rio de Janeiro, Brazil. There is commonality, from Slavoj Žižek's *The Year of Dreaming Dangerously* (2012), Paul Mason's *Why It's Kicking Off Everywhere* (2012), to Judith Butler and Athena Athanasiou's *Dispossession: The Performative in the Political* (2013), in the ways these authors draw on fleeting moments in order to question the ethical, philosophical and practical implications of democracy.

This collection is rather more focussed in its attempt to draw on specificities in the unfolding present of the streets of Athens; and as such, overlaps with questions about the nature of the political sphere. Yet, its scope allows for contributors to engage with empirical details that testify to the lived reality of life in a state of 'crisis'. The chapters investigate specific manifestations of what is called 'crisis' in Europe, and while the fiscal crisis inevitably inflects the examples, the authors demonstrate that the notion of 'crisis' is more likely to be present in social and ethical encounters that have implications far beyond the immediate moment.

As such, the authors of these chapters have mapped the pressing issues in the state of austerity. This mapping is, in itself, an attempt to 'deal with' crisis, but without being able to predict or define its terms. The 'remapping' of our title implies a conscious re-working of what once seemed solid. Lez Smart says that 'mapmaking is an endless quest for perspective' (2004, p. 10), characterising mapping as a means of exploring but also making an account of the exploration. Such stories that give accounts help set co-ordinates for how others might discover the territory in the future. Mapping is thus not only about landmarks but also imagination. In this light, maps 'form one of the ways by which society has sought to represent, record and communicate its world' (Smart, 2004, p. 11). This remapping project attempts to revise and reveal the assumptions and prejudices that may have determined which terrains were mapped, and what landmarks, stories or spaces were included in the hegemonic blueprint. 'Remapping Athens' is, therefore, a critical collection of shifting landscapes, border-crossing stories and the emerging possibilities. This volume attempts to engage with multiple research approaches and a range of disciplinary perspectives, including urban studies, geography, sociology, law and international relations as well as performance studies.

Remapping 'Crisis' aims to insert a critical gloss to the narratives of protest and social movements in the age of austerity and to offer a social analysis grounded in empirical research in Athens. The contributors include innovative methods of analysis of everyday social worlds, such as inviting critical engagement with readers through using images. As a whole, the volume attempts to forge a new critical discourse that relies on a wide range of urban and social research methods – thereby broadening the scope of analysis of 'crisis' from an economic phenomenon to one that fundamentally alters social realities. The book provides a Southern European perspective on the wider concerns of social movements. As such, it is an important and timely contribution to the study of social movements and the rise of direct civil action in pursuit of democracy. In this milieu of social change, Athens is its muse. The contributors in the volume are all, by and large, involved in articulating a range of positions that respond to, define, and problematize the ways economic crisis has impacted on and resulted in the social and political spheres in Athens. The book is timely for several reasons. Firstly, it is written in the wake of the crumbling of the mirage of a unified European Union. The current economic 'crisis' has evolved at such speed and with unexpected consequences that were neither predictable, nor avoidable. There have been several books in Greek on this matter, but the task of this volume is to widen the issues to an international audience – particularly since the zeitgeist of social movements, protests and activism as alternative ways of inhabiting cities requires fresh perspectives, and new research approaches.

Athens in Crisis

The city charts a spatial dimension through and within which untold stories are made visible. This edited volume considers 'crisis' in Athens as a passage to radical openness through which we might imagine the ways a specific social, political and economic crisis alters the notion of a fixed city. Collectively, the chapters seek to interrogate the gloss of nostalgia that pervades reporting on Greece and her crisis; whilst simultaneously throwing up questions about the limitations of discursive borders, perils of nationalism, euro-skepticism and the neo-liberal mass media on the characterization of Athens' hubris. Its tone is both polemical and emphatic: avoiding the Sisyphean task of articulating a contemporary city in the terms of its past.

The context of a single city provides a lens through which to consider some of the pressing questions of our milieu regarding culture, transnationalism, activism and their terrains. Each section provides a snapshot of a city at a time of emergence – in the instant of social change and in the moment of a crucible of cultural, social and ethical reforms. Contributors offer a range of perspectives on Athens and her future. The complexities and precarity of the city are explored with interdisciplinary rigor – raising multiple questions, provoking arguments that cut across themes and sections in order to paint a multi-layered picture of this contradictory urban crisis. It is an urgent and timely investigation into the space in which the dissenters and renegades can shake up grand narratives and carve up specified discursive frames. Streets, walls, and meeting places offer the hum of theories yet to be enunciated.

With the 'marble city' at the center of its gaze, the questions raised by contributors locate its thrust within wider arguments about social movements, the limits of 'democracy', urbanity and social change. A city is a living organism consisting of the 'hard city' one can map through roads, buildings, public spaces, and the 'soft city' of inhabitants, multiple belongings, and imagining desires. This book is an account of the process of softening the urban fabric, or the extent to which the 'soft city' informs, interplays, and eventually remaps the 'hard city'.

Why Remapping?

For the purpose of this analysis a map is used as a symbolic multi-layered metaphor in certain ways: to highlight relationships between individuals, groups and communities; to represent the power dynamics that construct and reconstruct social borders; to define 'home' and feelings of 'belonging'; to foreground social gaps, contradictions and non-places; to outline bridge building and social change processes. Mapping moulds new relationships between spaces and lived experiences and the social dynamics that form dialogue around them. Map-making is closely linked with the way we perceive the world that surrounds us and the current characteristics of our historical moment; and therefore a choice structure for charting a spatial/social mode that is of a particular milieu. If we consider maps as representations that chart known terrains, and always underpinned by certain discourses – namely power, territory, politics – then we might also conceive of remapping as a procedure that reconstructs the terrain as well as provides new symbols for charting it. This procedure critically investigates the discourses that are taken for granted, as a means of telling 'other stories' that may not feature in hegemonic systems.

Our choice of a map as extended metaphor allows alternative stories, marginalised voices and new perspectives on the subject of Athens. In short, the potential offered by this choice of metaphor allows for a multi-layered investigation into the urban landscape; it applies hybridity, openness, and complexity as central tenets to such a research project. Urban communities remap the urban fabric as they navigate through it, but their map remains constantly in motion, providing more of a liquid display than a fixed sense of Athens. This brings to mind de Certeau's analysis of the 'moving, intersecting writings' of everyday city residents 'shaped out of fragments of trajectories and alterations of space' (1988, p. 93). In a world where territories are always already invaded, transgressed and where borders become spaces of radical contingency there is an urgent need for remapping. To remap means to engage into a compelling negotiation of firstly space, in which the local and the global are combined in many different ways; secondly, to re-work stereotypes which critically reflect on identity markers normally reliant on hegemonic patterns of exoticizing the 'other'. Finally, there is the need to consider feelings of empathy, to engage with perspective taking, to develop the ability to experience from the point of view of others; and define practices such as inclusion, recognition, and openness.

In order to remap one must transcend personal boundaries and insecurities; if mapping the world starts by defining 'home', then remapping starts with the understanding that the old home needs to be left behind because it is locked into the frozen time of national and fixed imagination. Home is more of a symbolic space than a physical place. Remapping as a project attempts to leave behind closed traditions and engages with ideas of an open present, encourages mobility over stability; promotes difference as the stimulus of novelty; suggests that decision making should be participatory; and recognises that reason bows to no absolute truth. In essence it holds the promise of a new land, an imagined world where many worlds fit. It is a dynamic concept defined by the vigour for (and of) change.

If we consider maps as representations that chart known terrains, and always underpinned by certain discourses – namely power, territory, politics – then we might also conceive of the destruction of these maps as a process of remapping the terrain and providing new symbols for charting it. When we imagine the erosion of boundaries and the creation of new territories of dialogue, we should be able to remap our indigenous landscapes in order to include those who remained invisible and marginalised because they could not fit the cognitive, moral or aesthetic map of the dominant world.

Mapping this volume

The topics are clustered around 4 interrelated themes 'Spatial Politics', 'Untold Stories', 'If These Walls Could Talk', and 'The Revolution Will Not Be Analyzed'. The selected chapters were chosen for the breadth and specific insight each offered into the ways politics, the social and the urban intersect. Readers may prefer to dip into various sections, although as a whole, the volume provides multiple perspectives on its subject – the city of Athens.

Section 1 'Spatial Politics' considers urban spaces as sites of contestation, through acts of resistance, protests and spatialized manifestations of 'community'. Each chapter engages with mapping the concerns, ideologies and practices of a politics of the street. Thomas Maloutas provides a sense of the ways class and social mobility served to define the spatial distribution of people in Athens. Maloutas' research draws on detailed data exploring the ways the Olympic Games of 2004, for instance, remapped the city in relation to housing. As such, his chapter marks the terrain of investigation of sociospatial change. Vassilis Arapoglou's chapter on the urban uncanny in relation to homelessness policy is in two parts; the first outlines a set of theoretical concerns, while the second half offers a close reading of contemporary municipal policies and practices. In her chapter, Orsalia Dimitriou sketches four critical moments in the contemporary milieu that have come to characterise Athens as a series of spaces occupied by social movements. Yannis Kallianos further develops the sense of spatial politics by mapping a psychogeography of protests. His chapter suggests that we can understand changing urban spaces through exploring the markers of 'disorder'.

The second section 'Untold Stories' undercuts the grand narratives to focus on the everyday stories and acts of 'performing' revolution and responding to crisis. Contributors consider the 'transformative' effect of the crisis at a micro-level of social production; zooming in from the faceless multitude to encounters of intimate, local and specified concerns. Margarita Komninou & Hartwig Pautz' contribution presents empirical data on the rise of expropriation as acts of resistance. Their chapter invites readers to reconsider the ways such acts seek to remap the dominant working of consumption in light of the erosion of economic sphere. Georgios Karyotis & Dimitris Skleparis offer an elucidating chapter on the mass hunger strike conducted by 300 migrants in central Athens in 2010. This event placed the precarity of migrant bodies at the centre of the *polis*, and as such, served to render the political and ethical 'problem' of migration visible. The final chapter by Sappho Xenakis & Leonidas Cheliotis in this section considers the inter-relationship between austerity and crime.

The chapters in the next section 'If These Walls Could Talk' engage with a new street-level language that has twisted, innovated, and filled in the gaps of a culture's hegemonic discourse. In this section street art, slogans, and photographs of urban gaps appear as visual markers of the shifting, complex discourses of power struggles, marginality and counter-cultures that establish a new reality that must be seen and heard. Orestis Pangalos offers a close reading of the genealogies of the street art 'epidemic' in Athens, referring to the relationship between wall painting and social conditions. Pafsanias Karathanasis' chapter explores the extent of street art in Athens, placing the art form in a particular context. He draws on insider knowledge of user-generated content in order to map the cultural production of this urban art form. In his chapter, Konstantinos Avramidis characterizes the political street art scene in Athens by exploring intersections with highly politicized urban spaces. His work seeks to define political wall writing as a practice that invents a 'public' that runs counter to the dominant public sphere. The final chapter in this section is from art historian Konstantina Drakopoulou, and is accompanied by images from Bleeps.gr. The chapter examines the artist's work as a public expression of social phenomena.

The final section 'The Revolution Will Not Be Analyzed' critically reflects on the role of the media and the academy from within Greece and across international media platforms. Individual chapters focus on specific examples of media (and the supporting discourses) to wider implications of reporting on 'crisis' – since the associated panics are transnational in effect. In his chapter, Theofanis Exadaktylos tackles the rise of populism in Greece by giving account of the ways voter sentiment has corresponded to the shifts in power in recent years, with a focus on the double election of 2012. Marilena Zaroulia & Philip Hager unpack some of the difficulties of Greece's position in Europe. Their chapter offers a view of the dichotomies of 'sensible' and 'insensible', suggesting that Europhilia or Euroscepticism are relative approaches that become more marked in times of 'crisis'. In her chapter, Zacharoula Christopoulou gives an account of myth in relation to the on-going project of constructing and perpetuating a sense of 'national identity'. Myrto Tsilimpounidi's short contribution reflects the need for academic discourse to engage with unfolding notions such as 'crisis'. She argues that despite the difficulties of analysing emergent situations, there is a need for exploring *logos* in relation to *praxis* – suggesting that the role of the academy must be remapped in light of the need for multiple vocabularies of resistance to the erosion of logic and rationality seen in this socio-political milieu.

Collectively, the chapters in the volume bear witness to multiple manifestations of change in the urban metropolis of Athens. They focus on examples of creativity, solidarity, counter-cultures and resistance that have burgeoned in the era of austerity without glorifying singular models as 'solutions' to the crisis. Rather, the authors hope to draw attention to unfolding practices, tactics and strategies that are playing out in Athens, and elsewhere in the world, as the neoliberal world order is being challenged. The experiences explored in the book point towards wider issues of ethics and responsibility that this era of rapid political and social change seems to demand.

Part 1: Spatial Politics

Chapter 1

The Archaeology of the Decline of the City Center: Residential Location Choices of Affluent Groups

Thomas Maloutas

Dominant discourses about the center of Athens focus on degradation and decline. Interest in the city center developed mainly as the city was preparing for the Olympic Games of 2004 and big investments created hopes for its considerable upgrading. Before that period the city center had rarely been an issue on the social and political agenda. Planning in Greece has traditionally played only a small part in the development of cities that had been largely self-regulated; at the same time, the very rapid growth of Athens during the first post-war decades led to the gradual decline of the city center, especially since the 1970s. This decline is corroborated by changes in the social geography of Athens. The affluent groups greatly increased their specific weight in peripheral locations at the expense of the center, and particularly in the northern and southern coastal suburbs as well as in some parts of the more distant periphery. Housing prices have rapidly increased in those areas, in contrast to the broader central area where they became increasingly affordable.

The Olympic Games of 2004 triggered the production of important urban infrastructure that was lacking for several decades. In the preparation period there was investment in the city's organization, functionality and appearance. This accumulated investment had a positive impact, first of all, on the center which was rediscovered and gave the impression that it could have the same fate with other city centers which were successfully regenerated after long periods of decline. The Olympic

Games in Athens, however, were not related to a concrete and elaborate strategy of urban and regional development, apart from the general expectation that they would have a positive impact on the city's tourist industry and the quality of life of its inhabitants. In contrast to other and relatively successful cases –like Barcelona– the opportunity of the Games for Athens was entirely wasted on serving the pretentious image of a modern and powerful Greece, which was pursued at all costs. Organizing the Games in Athens was therefore, not a vehicle for accomplishing the city's strategic targets, but a target in itself. The city had to hastily improve its organization, functionality and image to become eligible for the Games rather than use the occasion for its long term and sustainable improvement. At the end of the Games the objective of the adequate organization of a major athletic event was met, but investment in the city and its center stopped abruptly.

The negative outcomes of the Games for Athens were reinforced by international events. September 11 increased greatly the cost for security and reduced returns following the fear of terrorist attacks that affected the number of visitors. On the other hand, the cost of the Games was already increased due to the option of building permanent infrastructures for circumstantial needs and to the internal inability to produce a coherent plan of Olympic venues from the beginning which resulted in indecision about the location of sites and extensive moving around until the last moment (Souliotis et al., forthcoming). The city center followed, to some extent, the fate of Olympic venues. No advantage was generated by the investment in expensive infrastructure that found no post-Olympic use, while maintenance became a financial burden.

The dominant discourse on the city center can be easily related to the disenchantment of certain social groups and organizations by the unfulfilled promises the Olympic Games had created about its upgrading. These groups and organizations have been using their *voice* to promote their vision about the center, where they would like to invest or had already invested. The discourse on the city center is obviously not formed by groups that the dominant discourse depicts as accountable or at least as part of the problem. The voice of these groups is usually weak and often mediated. Following Zukin (1995) the groups without voice rarely have a vision for broader urban issues or areas, like the fate of the city center. When they articulate a discourse about the city, it is usually restrained to the small scale of lived experience and addresses pressing issues of displacement threats and marginalization.

This chapter focuses on the content and causes of the decline of the city center in Athens and, in particular, on its relation to the devaluation produced by the changing options of upper and upper-middle social groups in terms of residential location. The gradual relocation of these groups to peripheral areas has not only affected the housing market and the city's social geography; it eventually reshaped in a centrifugal way the map of social and commercial services, as well as the map of employment.

Decline and regeneration of city centers: the international experience

Processes of decline and regeneration of city centers have mainly been identified in, and discussed for, cities of the Anglophone world that constitute the dominant contextual paradigm in the international literature of Urban Sociology and Geography. Industrial development rearranged activities and re-patterned social groups in the space of precapitalist cities. Industrial activities and warehousing of raw materials located around city centers attracting working class housing in a period when workers' distance from the workplace had to be small. The nuisance from industrial activities and the concentration of working class groups in areas that increasingly featured downgraded living conditions induced higher social groups to opt for suburban residence (Fishman, 1987). The modern decline of the city center refers, therefore, to the reversal of the social patterning of the precapitalist city, where higher functions, power structures and elites located at the center and other functions and social groups were found in the periphery at a distance from the center inversely proportional to their social importance. This reversed socioeconomic patterning of the city was initially described by the Chicago School as the model of modern cities (Knox & Pinch, 2006).

Problems of industrial city centers, during the era of their important growth, were not considered problems of the center, since the affected areas were much more extended with respect to the whole city. They were considered and dealt with as urban problems in general that differentiated cities from rural areas in a period of unprecedented urbanization led by industrial development (Lees, 1985). The city center became a problem under conditions created by the crisis of Fordism and Keynesian arrangements, by economic restructuring and de-industrialization in what used to be the advanced industrial countries and cities. The decline of the city center appears, therefore, as a problem of the post-industrial city; and this decline became an item on the social and political agenda not when the problems were growing, but when conditions and social agents appeared with alternative projects for city centers.

De-industrialization in post-industrial cities in the Anglophone world led to liberating space in central areas and, at the same time, drove part of the local working class to unemployment. On the other hand, capitalist globalization has induced cities in different parts of the world to compete increasingly for investment in order to make an opportunity out of the crisis, according to a neoliberal euphemism. In most industrial cities in crisis the activities that could replace declining industry were not obvious. The development of high-end producer services for multinational corporations of global reach has been the privilege of few cities, such as London, New York or Tokyo, which possessed the necessary requirements and were anyway less dependent on their local industries (Sassen, 1991). Most cities in the economically advanced part of the world during that transition period had to find either a very specific specialization –which could rarely be found outside their development path– or to follow the general model of turning to cultural industries and tourism.

The investment in cultural industries and tourism had the paradoxical impact of leading to homogenization the cities that tried to promote their specificity and authenticity. This happened because they ultimately offered a similar product to be consumed by the middle-class visitor in terms of content, with the differences between cities being limited to its packaging, i.e. to the cities' urban histories, layouts and architectural distinctiveness. The general strategy of investment in cultural industries and tourism is closely related to the city center, necessitates its regeneration and usually involves preserving elements of its industrial heritage as part of the city's new image.

The more the transition strategy to the post-industrial era is successful, the more the demand and pressure to regenerate the center is increased. Corporate activities demand more office space, while the attraction of highly skilled and highly paid jobs in high-end producer services increases the demand for quality housing in central areas. Those who belong to this corporate elite look for housing in central areas because they are usually young, very mobile, work long hours without regularity, and have no restraining family ties or other social ties with the city, since they usually come from outside. Their profile induces them, therefore, to go for the way of life of the city center rather than for the suburban way of life. The new economic functions in the regenerated city center and the demand for high quality housing have been very important parameters in attracting investment since sizable profits could be expected from increasing land values.

The processes that shaped the sociospatial profile of post-industrial cities have not been politically neutral. In the Anglophone world the political shape of the transition to the post-industrial city was greatly affected by the governments of Thatcher and Reagan and the growing dominance of neoliberal ideas and policies. The need to regenerate city centers was mainly considered under the prospects for profit that the new demand for central space could yield. The negative effects of deindustrialization were considered the price urban societies had to pay to restart their economies, so that the latter would provide the means to cover social needs in the future. This prosperous future of the liberal economic doctrine, however, always remains a prospect, while in the meantime part of the restructured urban societies are marginalized or literally expelled. Cities in the traditional industrial North of the US, like Detroit and Buffalo, have lost hundreds of thousands of people from their central areas, and a similar –even though less extreme– fate awaited Manchester or Liverpool in the UK. At the same time, the unleashed commodification of post-industrial city centers created important rearrangements in the sociospatial hierarchy of residential areas. The rapid transformation of former working class areas near the center to areas of interest for higher status groups has often led to the massive displacement of former residents and to their marginalization through the process of gentrification (Smith, 1996; Lees et al., 2008).

The decline of urban centers during the industrial era and their regeneration in the post-industrial period refer in fact to the particular historical path taken by the industrial city of the Anglophone world and to the political options that dominated their regulation and planned their future as they were deindustrialized. This model, which is often portrayed as ecumenical in the international literature, does not do justice to what happened in most other parts of the world. In continental Europe, as well as in many other places outside the Anglophone world, social elites have never abandoned city centers and managed instead to push industrial activities and working class housing to the urban periphery. In this sense, in most cities around the world there is no historical experience of a massive and radical depreciation of the center due to the fact that industrial activity was not omnipresent at their centers and its rapid decline did not create thus the broad margins for massive regeneration pursued under specific political orientation schemes. In most cases, space liberated by industrial activities was rather limited restraining the profit promises that the 'rent gap' (Smith, 1987) could sustain. Moreover, in many countries of Western and Northern Europe, political traditions and welfare structures did not allow the unleashed neoliberal regulation of social problems, like unemployment, or the negative impact of rearrangements in the urban tissue, like the displacement of former residents from regenerated areas. It is not, therefore, by chance that in these regions industrial cities did not lose their work force at comparable rates; it was rather the outcome of concerted efforts for social protection and reintegration to the labor market of what economic restructuring designated as redundant. Furthermore, the development of processes, like gentrification, has been less intense in the largest part of Europe due to specific measures and policies targeted against segregation. In East Asian cities processes of decline and regeneration of city centers were equally moderate. This was due, mainly, to the developmental state and the various egalitarian measures it brought to the labor market (Hill & Kim, 2000; Hill & Fujita, 2003; Fujita, 2012) that reduced the impact of deindustrialization, which was already less severe in most countries of that region.

Recent decline and prospects for regeneration: The residential location choices of the affluent groups and the center of Athens

The development of Greek cities – Athens in particular– has been closer to the model of continental Europe. Its center remained the locus of high status functions and power institutions, and it harbored the great majority of higher socio-professional categories. This situation started to change in the 1970s. Between 1971 and 1991 the center of gravity for these higher categories relocated gradually to the periphery: in the beginning of that period 62% of their members lived in the city's central municipality and in the end this percentage was reduced to 27% (table 1).

	Socioprofessional category			
	Upper / upper-middle		Working class	
Social profile of residential area [1]	1971	1991	1971	1991
High (new suburban)	**6,1**	**24,8**	5,3	7,1
High (traditional suburban)	3,9	5,4	0,3	0,2
Intermediate	15,2	19,4	13,8	14,3
Working class (traditional suburban)	11,1	19,8	47,6	44,1
Working class (new suburban)	1,4	3,1	11,4	15,8
Centre (Municipality of Athens)	**62,2**	**27,4**	21,6	18,5
Total	100,0	100,0	100,0	100,0

Table 1: **Percentage distribution of selected socio-professional categories by sociospatial type of residential area (1971 and 1991).** (Maloutas, 1997, p.3).

The decline of the center –in the sense of the decreasing number and percentage of upper-middle class members that choose the center for residence– does not make of Athens a belated example of urban decline following the industrial city model of the

Anglophone world. The main difference is that decline of the center in Athens has never been related to industrial activity; it was related, on the contrary, to the way the broader central city area was heavily built during the post-war decades. Intensive building during that period led to high densities in the central municipality and was not accompanied by the required infrastructure in terms of transportation and other amenities. This led to a precipitated deterioration of living conditions that became even worse following the rapid increase of private cars and the emergence of air pollution.

The declining attractiveness of the center can be observed, first of all, in the declining number of residents in the central municipality (Municipality of Athens). While the number of its residents increased steadily during the first decades of the post-war period, following the upward trend of the whole region (Attiki), it started shrinking in the 1980s and still follows the same declining trend. The declining number of residents is in fact much higher if we focus exclusively on the native Greek population. The decline in the population of the Municipality of Athens between 1981 and 2001 was about 130.000 persons, and a further decrease of 90.000 occurred between 2001 and 2011. Taking into account that the percentage of foreigners in the municipality was 20% in 2001 against only 2% in 1981, the decline in the native Greek population of the municipality during that period was about 265.000 persons.

It is clear that the center of Athens lost population during the last two decades of the previous century and, on the other hand, that this loss was especially important in terms of native Greeks; the loss was partly compensated by the important increase in the number of foreign citizens. Decline and immigrant presence are, therefore, somehow related. The relation, however, is not that of a 'white flight' as suggested by the dominant discourse and vividly expressed by the statement of Prime Minister Antonis Samaras, leader of the conservative party New Democracy, that 'we shall reconquer our cities' (statement in the intersecretarial convention of his party on March 29, 2012).

The move of the population towards the periphery[2] has not been socially homogeneous. Between 1971 and 1991, when immigrant presence was still insignificant, the retreat from the center was very unequal for different social groups (table 1). 'Retreat', in this case, covers both those who literally moved residence from the center to the suburbs or the outer periphery and the new households whose first residential location was in the periphery instead of the center, i.e. where they would normally settle following the traditional pattern of locating near the parental residence.

Table 1 shows that there has been an important rearrangement of the location patterns of major socioprofessional categories between 1971 and 1991, especially in terms of center and periphery. Focusing on the categories of managers and professionals in both the private and public sectors, on the one hand, and of salaried workers, on the other, the emerging changes in location patterns are quite different. The former moved mainly to new peripheral areas of high social profile where they multiplied their percentage distribution by four (from 6,1% to 24,8%) as well as their specific weight in respect to the rest of categories in those areas: their percentage distribution was almost identical to that of all categories in 1971 (6,1% against 6,2%) and had doubled in 1991 (24,8% against 13,7%). At the end of that period 30,2% of these high occupational categories resided in high social profile areas out of the center. At the same time, they had increased their presence in intermediate areas and even more so in working class areas[3] where, however, their specific weight remained relatively limited. But the most spectacular change in the residential pattern of these categories is certainly the decrease of their presence in the center where their percentage was more than halved (from 62,2% to 27,4%). In sum, the higher occupational categories rearranged their residential pattern in Athens between 1971 and 1991 by moving away from the center and settling mainly in suburban areas of high social profile.

At the other end of the social spectrum, the spatial rearrangement for salaried workers has been much less spectacular during the same period. The changes in their residential patterns have reduced their segregation since their presence was increased –even though to a limited degree– in areas of high and intermediate social profile and was reduced in traditional working class areas (see also Leontidou, 1990 where, however, the extent of this reduction is exaggerated). New working class areas were the exception where the percentage of salaried workers increased considerably. In the city center their percentage was reduced but only to a rather small extent.

Therefore, the spatial rearrangement of residential patterns towards the periphery in Athens is due much more to choices of the higher occupational categories that gradually turned to the suburbs since the 1970. The importance of this turn becomes greater if we take into account the growing specific weight of these categories: while they amounted to a fourth of the number of salaried workers (skilled and unskilled) in 1961, in 2001 their number was a bit higher than the number of workers.[4] Turning now to more recent developments in the decline of the city center, the following sections explore mobilities in relation to social profiles.

Table 2 shows, first of all, that the balance of arrivals and departures is negative for the two higher categories and positive for the two lower ones. Moreover, it appears that the positive balance for the lower categories is due mainly to arrivals from other countries, i.e. mainly to the growing immigrant population. The withdrawal of the upper and upper-intermediate occupational categories from the center and the stronger presence of lower ones remained, therefore, the dominant tendency during the second half of the 1990s. The size of the changes was,

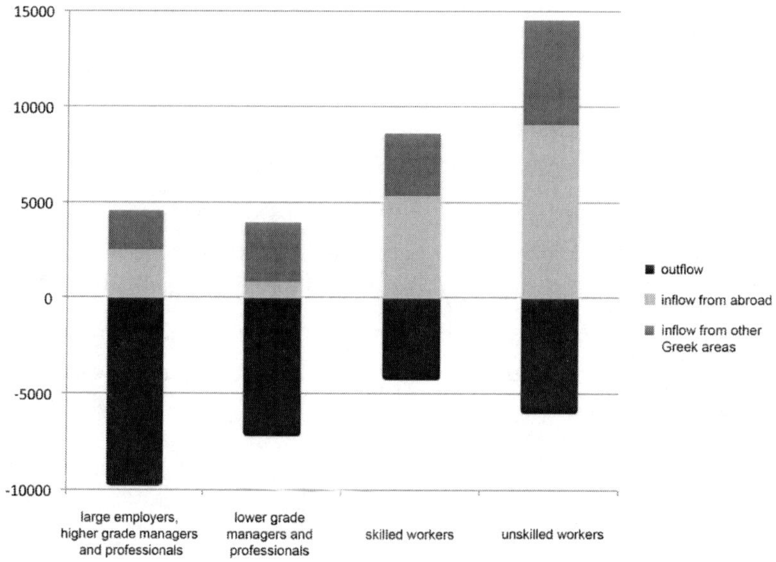

Table 2: **Number of residents that settled in the Municipality of Athens between 1995 and 2001 by occupational category* and geographical origin** and number of residents that moved away.**

* Four indicative broad categories

** Distinction between previous residence in Greece or abroad

Data source: EKKE-ESYE (2005).

however, relatively restricted and reduced the impact on the municipality's social structure. Pinpointing this tendency is perhaps more important in order to dispute the alleged opposite trend of a 'back to the city' movement since the late 1990s (Maloutas & Alexandri, forthcoming) than to corroborate the social content of the continuing suburbanization. The evidence presented here is limited to 2001; the Census of 2011 will reveal later developments, but my guess is that there were no radical changes in this respect.

Through the processes summarily described, the social profile of residential areas in Athens in 2001 (Image 1) depicts the city center –the Municipality of Athens at the center of the map– as being no longer a major pole of upper and upper-middle social categories, but rather an area of intense internal diversity. Noteworthy, in this respect, that all the census tracts in the category 'mixed and socially polarized' –i.e. tracts where opposite social categories coexist in relatively large proportions– belong to the central municipality. This coexistence is the social basis of the *vertical social differentiation*, observed around the center of Athens, that brings together households of relatively distant social position within the same apartment building, where they are spatially allocated following the hierarchy of floors (Maloutas & Karadimitriou, 2001).

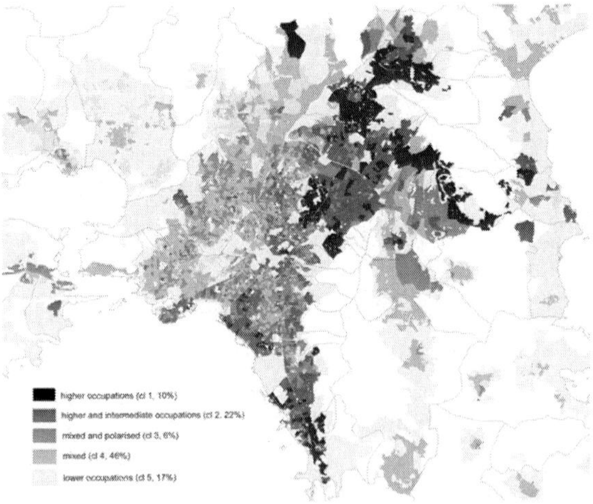

Image 1: **Social profile of residential areas in Athens[5] at census tract level (2001)** (Maloutas, 2007: 753).

Causes of decline and plans for regeneration

Summing-up, the decline of the center of Athens and its gradual abandonment by the higher social strata was not related to the concentration of industrial activities and/or working class groups –as in the classic model of declining inner city areas in industrial cities of the Anglophone world– but to different causes. The decline that started in the 1970s was mainly related to the aggregate result of the great number of condominium building operations, following the dominant and very popular housing production system of *antiparochi*,[6] as well as the rapid growth of the number of private cars that contributed to congestion and air pollution. The frenetic building activity through this system increased population density to a great extent, especially in the areas around the center. Only during the 1960s the population of the central municipality increased by 50% or a quarter of a million inhabitants (Maloutas, 2000: 29) and living conditions in the center deteriorated precipitously. At the end of that decade the rate of housebuilding increased further, following legislation enacted by the dictatorial regime (Law 395/1968) that gave a bonus of 20% building surface to landowners at no cost. The decline of the center was accelerated by the absence of the required infrastructure to support the new population and take care of the problems created by the large and increasing volume of private cars.

The decline of the center of Athens was the result of policies that never paid attention to the consequences that intense and relatively uncontrolled housebuilding created on the urban scale, since they were exclusively turned to short term reheating of the economy through building activity and to achieving political gains through facilitating the distribution of land rent to several social groups (Economou, 1988). This rent consisted of public capital (in the form of tax reliefs, tolerance of illegal – and therefore untaxed – housebuilding, and unhindered increase of building coefficients) and was primarily appropriated by affluent groups, since it was mainly landowners that were the beneficiaries; and rent increased according to the surface and value of land they possessed. However, due to the important segmentation of urban landed property, rent gains have also been distributed in a socially rather dispersed way. At the same time, the particularly large volume of new housing, produced through the system of *antiparochi*, provided affordable apartments to a wide social specter of housing demand. The impact of this system can be assumed by the fact that in Athens there were only about 1.000 apartment buildings with five floors or higher in the early 1950s compared to 35.000 in 1980 (Maloutas & Karadimitriou, 2001). This increase was almost entirely realized through *antiparochi*.

Therefore, the decline of the city center is due to the combination of policies that favored the housebuilding rash of the 1960s and 1970s without concern about its urban impact, and to the short term and shortsighted exploitation of the gains they offered to small private investors without concern for the aggregate and long term result. A substantial part of the city's affluent categories has profited from the *antiparochi* housebuilding process in direct or indirect ways. When its negative impact started to become noticeable, these strata started abandoning the center and relocated to the suburbs. The gradual population outflow has led at first to the disuse of a part of the large housing stock around the center; it was especially the small apartments on lower floors and basements, which were mostly hit by high building density and population increase since they were the ones that mainly became darker and noisier.

Some years later, the devalued housing stock found new users. Immigrants, whose presence became substantial since the early 1990s, were attracted by this disused stock since the *laissez-faire* policies on both immigration and housing did not provide any other sustainable solution for them. The existence of this devalued stock is one of the main reasons for the much greater concentration of immigrants in the city center rather than in the working class areas of the periphery, where the available and affordable housing for rent was, and remains, limited.

In this sense, the decline of the center of Athens started well before the important inflow of immigrants and the appearance of homeless people, drug users and other vulnerable groups who increasingly take the blame for the center's current condition.

These groups were, therefore, attracted by the center due to its former decline that made it affordable in terms of housing and symbolically within their reach.

During the preparation period for the Olympic Games of 2004 the center received important investment and showed potential for substantial regeneration. This investment, however, has not been related to a systematic and long-term strategy for the city and its center. Moreover, it stopped as soon as the Games were over. The large investment in transport infrastructure was left to work for landowners who happened to be located in locations that became privileged, without compensation for the public interest, in the same way the gains from the increase of building coefficients were appropriated by landowners a few decades earlier. At the same time, the sudden stop of investment in the city after the Games and the disillusionment about the impetus they would create for different economic sectors, like tourism, was accompanied by disappointment and neglect illustrated characteristically by the abandoned and decaying Olympic venues.

The discourse on the decline of the city center is therefore mainly related to this disappointment from the prospect of a regenerated, middle class friendly and money-making center, which seemed possible in the period before the Olympic Games. Immigrants have become the scapegoats of this frustration, which is increasingly coupled with and reinforced by the intense malaise produced by the economic crisis. The scapegoating of immigrants is further nurtured by short-sighted politicians throughout a large part of the political spectrum expecting to draw political gains from defending anti-immigrant positions.

On the other hand, the solution to the real and complex problems of the city center does not coincide, and could not coincide, with the aspirations and the vision of investors, many of whom are seeking a lucrative investment that would once more come at low cost following a large public investment. If, on the contrary, resolving the problems of the center is to be attempted in a spirit of social justice and cohesion, much more is needed than the couple of beautification and police control, which is usually enough for most investors in city centers.

In the current period of severe crisis, and taking into account the financial restraints and the dominant political orientations that reduce the redistributive potential of expected policies, the prospect of regenerating the center of Athens without leading to a violent redistribution of resources at the expense of the weakest groups, becomes particularly difficult.

Chapter 2

The Governance of the Urban Uncanny: The Neoliberal Crisis and the Political Incapacity for Social Reparation

Vassilis Arapoglou

From context to theory: governing uncanny spaces and homelessness

Often in scientific conferences, political or social debates on urban and social policies in Greece, the image that emerges is that of the ghetto. According to dominant representations, the ghetto is an inner city area, neglected by the state, invaded by illegal immigrants, deviants and criminals who threaten the security of an entrapped population, mainly middle class Greek families that increasingly face the risk of destitution and pauperization. This image, put forth largely by the media shortly after the Olympic Games in Athens in 2004, has gradually consolidated the agenda of inner city reforms.

In the early years of the 21st century my PhD research and activism was concerned with homelessness in Athens and attempted to challenge the official rhetoric concealing exclusions of non-deserving clients from shelters and 'clean-ups' of public spaces from illegal immigrants (Arapoglou 2004). My subsequent work has been associated to the studies of the National Center of Social Research (NCSR) documenting that spatial concentrations of the migrant population are not ghettos. Even in areas of escalating deprivation, the picture is far more complex than the one presented by the media (cf. Maloutas et al., 2012; Arapoglou & Maloutas, 2011; Arapoglou et al., 2009, Arapoglou & Sayas, 2009).

A summary of the NCSR studies can familiarize readers with

the Greek context. Urban restructuring in Athens was initiated by the Mega Project of hosting the Olympic Games in 2004. The Games became an emblem of urban development since the mid 1990s in complete accordance with economic policies and accession to the European Monetary Union. Spin-doctors shaped the image of 'powerful Greece', celebrated in the opening ceremony of the Games and EURO 2004. Yet, socio-spatial fragmentation has increased in spite of the generalized euphoria of the pre-Olympics period. Such development excessively relied on the building and tourist industry. Female employment, growth in low skill service occupations and casualization of migrant labor contributed to social polarization. Migrants from the Balkans gained access to basic services only after ex-post legalization measures whilst social policies were gradually contracting. Speculative real estate development and consumption was supported by the expansion of public and private credit, in favor of the banking system and large construction companies. Sprawling, suburbanization, and entertainment-led gentrification transformed areas adjacent to the newly constructed athletic, transport, or cultural facilities. In the post-Olympic city, these processes slowed down and private pressures on increasing public spending intensified. The financial crisis of 2008 and accumulated debt set a barrier on rolling out gentrification and urban sprawl. Moreover, migration waves further diversified to include asylum seekers from the Middle East and Asia, but ex-post legalization was halted in 2006, leaving the newcomers in absolute destitution and vulnerable to racist attitudes, authoritarian policing, and inter-migrant rivalry. Notably, migrant enclaves evolved within central city areas of middle class composition. Despite some middle class flight to the suburbs, central areas retained significant socio-ethnic mix, the main socio-demographic aspect becoming diversity rather than isolation.

Nonetheless, research evidence and policy suggestions of the

NCSR found no receptive audiences, whilst local politics and urban planning became saturated with xenophobic discourses and racial conflicts. It was particularly during the advent of the debt crisis that racist violence culminated. A sad period of racist mobilizations in inner city Athens was initiated in 2009 and growing support for extreme right parties found strong expression during the local elections in 2010 (Kandylis & Kavoulakos, 2011) and the national elections in 2012. As the bail out pact contributed to the deepening of the recession, unemployment in the metropolitan region of Athens escalated from 9,3% in the first quarter of 2009 to 23,2% in the first quarter of 2012. Visible poverty and homelessness attracted the attention of the media and policy makers during the end of 2011. It is rather clear, that after a decade of neglect, homelessness entered the agenda as only one element of concern, a signifier of pity in 'no-go' areas of disorder and criminality; the so-called ghettos of Athens. In January 2011, I was invited to participate as expert in an advisory committee on the 'Homelessness Action Program' drafted by the Ministry of Health. I wondered: was this the end of policy neglect, a sign of change?

This chapter sketches out a conceptual framework to capture the evolving picture of the neoliberal crisis and the management of its social consequences in urban settings. To do so, this chapter will attempt to bring together psychosocial theorizations of repressive political ideologies with a contextualized conception of neoliberal urban reforms. Combining the two perspectives can help us to understand the political and ideological shifts in neoliberal urban and social policies and their incapacity to promote social integration. Thus, the first part of the chapter is conceptual, whilst the second part unravels the story of my participation in the Ministry of Health advisory committee on the 'Homelessness Action Program'. Examples and empirical references in my story elucidate the context out of which my theorization of the neoliberal responses to the crisis evolves.

Planning of this program is still in progress and so the ideas presented here are only tentative.

Rather than accepting the prevalent discourse on the so-called 'ghettos' I alternatively suggest talking about the representations and feelings associated with policies and social dynamics that give shape to 'uncanny spaces'. I am trying to elucidate a process whereby the forfeiture of the possibility of symbolization leads to the dysfunction of communication and the creation of alienated subjects in urban settings.

Freud's text The Uncanny (*Das Unheimlich,* 2003) has been valued by critical social theory and by urban sociology. Amongst its most famous influences in social theory is in the study of anti-Semitism by Horkheimer and Adorno (2002) in *The Dialectic of Enlightenment* and the *The Location of Culture* by Homi Bhabha (1994). The uncanny is not a structural category of Freudian metapsychology; it is an aesthetic category referring to specific types of experience. Precisely because it is an aesthetic category, it becomes valuable, since it recognizes that feelings and the possibility of giving them meaning can be the heart of the analysis.

According to Freud the uncanny is an element of anguish, the discomfort and the feeling of fear when the representation of what was repressed later resurfaces. Therefore the uncanny is 'nothing new or alien, but something which is familiar and old-established in the mind and which has become alienated from it only through the process of repression' (Freud 2003, p. 240).

But let me slightly deviate from Freud's suggestion when he states 'it must be a matter of indifference' whether what is unhomely 'was itself originally frightening or whether it carried some other affect' (Freud 2003, p. 240). It can be argued that it is necessary to name and communicate this 'other affect' in order to discover if its particular qualities relate to different developmental positions in the history of the subject and types of relations with significant others.

Freud emphasizes that the experience of the uncanny is a feeling of discomfort that comes from the loss of control of the material reality, from the doubt of the real existence of a representation, as in the case of a double or a ghost. Freud clarifies that an uncanny effect 'is often and easily produced when the distinction between imagination and reality is effaced, as when something that we have hitherto regarded as imaginary appears before us in reality, or when a symbol takes over the full functions of the thing it symbolizes, and so on' (Freud 2003, p. 240).

As the feeling of discomfort dominates in everyday life, so urban scholars increasingly have to deal with uncanny experiences, such as those described by Freud. Freud's own emphasis on symbolizing difficulties opens up an analytical trail to understanding the uncanny in object relational terms. It also enables us to discern 'primitive' forms of thought that give rise to uncanny experiences in contemporary cities (Pile, 2005). Here, I wish to consider a wider range of communicative dysfunctions. My theoretical compass in reading the Freudian text is Segal's work on symbolism and Bion's work on the unconscious processes that inhibit learning and change (Segal, 1991; 2007).

According to Segal (1991; 2007) 'symbolic equation' and 'symbol formation' are two modes of symbolism, which pertain respectively to Klein's 'paranoid-schizoid' and 'depressive' position. In the symbolic equation, the symbol-substitute is confused with the original object. Symbolic equations involve splitting and projective identification to maintain ideal objects and to control persecutory ones. A gradual awareness of the difference between internal and external reality is maintained as subjects advance to acknowledge depressive anxieties. Symbols are used to overcome the loss of the object, which has been accepted, and to protect the object from one's aggressiveness. Moreover, Segal (1973) emphasizes the difference between two distinct mechanisms in coping with despair and guilt: manic defense and reparation. In early responses to depression, omnipotence serves to control bad objects and restore good ones. Moreover obsessive mechanisms are used in repetitive efforts to repair the object and to relieve the persisting feeling of guilt. Manic defenses are associated with feelings of control, triumph and content. Segal (1991) notes the possibility that symbols can revert to symbolic equations in the use of projective identification as a defense against depressive anxieties. This can also be the case when social realities become traumatic to subjects. Consequently, symbolic and communicative distortions of an uncanny quality may result from defenses to both paranoid-schizoid and to depressive anxieties, as I will in the following sections explain.

Segal (2007) related symbol equations with Bion's (1962) ideas about the incapacity of the caretaker to contain the infant's anxieties and respectively to assist subjects in building a thinking apparatus by which to process stressful conditions. I wish to expand her views further in arguing that concrete symbolic equations betray the incapacity of government to contain unconscious feelings associated with Bion's (1961) three types of 'basic assumptions'.

Bion (1961) identified three types of responses to insecurity in groups, which he termed 'basic assumptions': fight-flight, dependency, and pairing. The fight-flight assumption involves projecting hatred through violence against an enemy, or flight from a hated object. Paranoid-schizoid processes in moral panics and scapegoating indicate the dominance of fight-flight assumption. The dependency assumption gives expression to depression and guilt about the leader failing the group's expectations or about feelings of greed and aggression. The group is sustained by a leader who is believed to offer protection and magically solve its problems. Often the history of the group and dogma is used to protect group members from intrusive ideas or change. The pairing basic assumption involves projections concerning the birth of a messiah. Pairing, aims to produce a person or idea that will save the group from destructiveness and despair, but in order to do this hope must never be fulfilled. Pairing usually finds expression in ideas related to marriage, including disputes between mating partners, which can give an end to the misfortunes of the group. An aristocratic mentality attaches importance to breeding a leader capable of inspiring hope and, at the same time, confidence that the leader will be similar to the group members. When depressive feelings prevail, one of the parents hesitantly participates in mating and so the messiah is born out of wedlock.

Hopper (2003) suggested a fourth basic assumption: 'Incohesion: Aggregation/ Massification'. He argued that traumatized groups oscillate between 'aggregation' (i.e. minimal social interactions in accordance to free market capitalism) and 'massification' (i.e. submission to totalitarian rule). In the sections to follow I retain Bion's three basic assumptions to elaborate the interactions between paranoid-schizoid and depressive anxieties related to neoliberal experimentations. However, I also acknowledge the possibility that successive government failures may lead to massification and aggregation as suggested by Hopper.

Moments of Neoliberalization: the crisis and its management

Homelessness has been one of the most potent symbols of the social costs of neoliberalism in advanced capitalist cities and its treatment provides an empirical basis for understanding the management of the neoliberal crisis (DeVerteuil et al., 2009; May et al., 2005; Cloke et al., 2010). The punitive framing of homelessness (through street clearance and containment) has been mostly advanced through conservative governments whilst charity and caring (expanding shelter and day care provision from charities) has been an additional concern of welfare reforms. It has been convincingly argued (May et al., 2005; Cloke et al., 2010) that this combination of punitive and caring responses signifies a new mode of neoliberal governmentality. Although I am sympathetic to this approach, I also find that its Foucauldian orientation neglects that unconscious processes lie beneath the technologies of government aiming to shape the spaces of welfare provision.

Like May et al. 2005, I am going to elaborate a conceptual framework to highlight the contradictions of contemporary urban social policies, drawing on the work of Brenner, Peck, Theodore (2010a; 2010b) for the variations of *actually existing neoliberalism.* However, I also draw on psychosocial theories that focus on the unconscious dimensions that shape group mentality and deviance from democratic government. To do so I draw on a rich tradition of theory and research, which makes use of Bion's intuition of emotional life in groups and complex organizations (Hopper, 2003). In my attempt to find possible intersections between psychoanalytically informed research on group emotions and Foucauldian understandings of governmentality I acknowledge the different epistemological origin of the two traditions.

Brenner, Peck & Theodore (2010a, 2010b) coined the term 'actually existing neoliberalism' to conceptualize the contextually embedded dynamics of neoliberal policies and their contradictory effects. I give particular attention to two issues in their conceptualization, which can be further elaborated as interfaces to psychosocial theorizations. First, neoliberalization is an open-ended process and develops by bringing together destruction and reforms. Second, although the neoliberal doctrine is premised upon a one-size-fits-all model of policy implementation, the process of neoliberalization actually breeds extraordinary variations when reforms are imposed within specific local and institutional landscapes. Brenner, Peck & Theodore (2010a, 2010b) distinguish between two different processes through which neoliberal policies emerge. One is the process of deregulation and the *'rolling back'* of important state operations and the other is the process of re-regulations and the unfolding of new institutions seen as necessary to support the process of privatization in the gaps that are created from the withdrawal of the state. These processes are not necessarily created in distinct chronological phases, but can coexist and interact.

With the appearance, though, of a crisis in neoliberalism, matters begin to change and we see a tendency to experiment with short term solutions, trial and error governance, and opportunistic regulations that do not touch upon the true substance of market functioning– what Brenner, Peck & Theodore recently called 'zombie- neoliberalism' (Brenner, Peck & Theodore, 2010b; Peck, 2010). A series of monstrous and morbid phenomena may begin to appear within the bounds of 'death and resurrection' of zombie neoliberalism. Peck (2010) writes about the intensification of the oppression in the poor neighborhoods of the capitalistic metropolis, following the reasoning of Wacquant (2009) about the combined use of social welfare and penal policies as a response to rising social insecurity. It can further be argued that authoritarianism is but one of the ways to manage fear and insecurity and, of course, not everyone is going to consent with its use.

It is for this reason, that cohesion and criminal insecurity gain priority in urban and social policies. Indeed this priority is advanced by the converging ideologies of leading political parties and transforms the management of fear and social suffering by a historically unprecedented coupling of 'fight and flight' or 'depressive' expectations as explained later on. Nonetheless, there is a continuous feedback between the demands of the scared public and its leaders and so policy contradictions can be thought of as symptoms and not simply results of a vicious leadership.

During its consolidation, neoliberalism did not only undergo adjustments to its local institutional surroundings, but it articulated with the available discourses employed in the government of social conduct. That means that neoliberal policies are rarely pure. The actually existing form of neoliberalism could be nationalist, racist, sexist, or centered on the family, according to the local circumstances. The hegemonic project is wide open in the political game. During the crisis, it is expected that the articulation of discourses regulating spatial identities and practices will change. Nonetheless, such changes are initiated from above and, through processes of transnational policy transfer have distressing effects on receiving societies.

Consequently, the shaping of neoliberal technologies of government is subject to experimentation in local conditions. It is now widely understood, particularly through the British example, that the dispersion of governmental powers involves the multiplication of policy actors and non-statutory agencies usually responsible for welfare delivery. Thus, technologies of government apply to both controlling interagency relationships at various scales and to communication of all the agencies involved with the wider public and their clients. Communication techniques become a vital part of government technologies, and so the role of the media complements the role of policy experts. The media, think tanks, and spin-doctors are in search of ideas and discourses that will give shape to effective leadership. To use a potent metaphor, they are experimenting which kind of 'social milk' can feed subjective awareness, thinking, and relating. It is at this point possible that top-down attempts to transfer neoliberal ideas into local contexts are in conflict with older ideas, already internalized by subjects. But communication techniques may also use established emotional attachments, memories, or traumas to support neoliberal change. Hook (2005) stresses that technologies of this kind very much rely on the capitalization of pre-oedipal and pre-linguistic bonds. Hence, it can be further argued that their signifying power relies on giving name to dread and on using the emotional distress of the public for political gains. It should also be stressed that technologies of government are shaped by the defenses to unconscious anxieties, which they are supposed to manage (after Hopper, 2003). The risk of government failure is high, because, by inception, the object of government is uncanny: i.e. a set of relationships saturated with greed, envy, fear, helplessness, anger, and fragmentation. Extreme emotional instability is a reason for policy experimentation, as in the cases of the changing mentality of groups failing to perform their tasks that Bion (1961) insightfully detected.

Table 3 is a proposal to categorize the technologies of government according to the unconscious processes that they attempt to manage during times of crisis corresponding them to the specific ways that object relations are formed. The central idea is that the management of the crisis entails a 'destructive' moment, wherein *'technologies of deregulation'* primarily advance defenses to schizoid-paranoid unconscious processes, and a 'pseudo-creative' moment, wherein *'technologies* of *emergency reforms'*, mostly set in motion unconscious defenses to depressive processes. The *'destructive'* moment is associated with punitive discourses, fearful images, and prophecies of social collapse; on the other hand the *'pseudo-creative'* moment finds expression in images of omnipotence, spectacular reforms, and limited acknowledgement of social suffering though charity provisions. Thus conceived, a key problem of neoliberal government is that its object is negatively defined (in-security, in-cohesion) and so policy actors, leaders and followers tend to reproduce their stressful attachment to this negative object. This actually, reinforces an unrealistic engagement with combating common fears, and ghosts of the past, rather than cooperation towards learning and change.

Table 3 aims to highlight the deployment of communication and normative practices that reproduce the social divisions and defenses against distressing and painful experiences-maintaining the subjects in alienated and powerful relationships.

What is noteworthy in object relations approaches (e.g. Layton, 2006; Froggett, 2002; Hoggett, 2006; Hopper, 2003) is that the politics of solidarity are founded upon the recognition of vulnerability, compared to the way the neoliberal management relies on its repression, escape to prosperity and omnipotence and pseudo-solidarity. Table 3 is only a stylized representation of interconnected processes. The classification is tentative and can be modified according to local circumstances. For example, the distinction and the dynamics between paranoid-schizoid and depressive defenses require a subtle analysis in particular case studies. Table 3 is a grid, which currently has only two dimensions, but it can be expanded to include policy coalitions, 'twinning' or 'pairing' of leaders, as well as rebellion and hope for the democratic government. It is also a matter of concern that failure of policy experiments can further intensify despair and

Roll back neoliberalism **Destructive moment** *Technologies of deregulation*	**Roll out neoliberalism** **Pseudo-creative moment** *Technologies of emergency reforms*
Fiscal austerity on municipal government Elimination of public monopolies for municipal social services Dismantling publicly funded projects Retrenchment of local relays of national welfare systems	Fiscal responsibility Local entrepreneurialism Networked forms of local governance Community based and private approaches to social service provision
Governing the Urban Uncanny	
City Warfare (space as 'sword') Spaces of fight	City salvation (space as 'shield') Spaces of flight and salvation
Social & Territorial Splitting (prevalence of spatial denigration) Territorial stigma Street warfare Punitive discourses/ blaming assaults Deserving- non deserving poor Intensified Surveillance of public space Street-Cleansing Detention Camps	Social & Territorial Splitting (prevalence of spatial idealization) Fast track investments Gentrification Philanthropy & pity Emergency provisions & compulsive care Guilt and care for the deserving poor

Table 3: **The neoliberal government of the urban uncanny**

aggressiveness, and consequently give rise to totalitarian rule.

The first row in Table 3 highlights some important institutional changes during 'roll-back' and 'roll-out' neoliberalization. Brenner, Peck and Theodore (2009) write, in perhaps ironic tone, about reforms, which correspond to the Schumpeterian notion of 'creative destruction'. I suggest that 'roll-out' neoliberalization during a crisis can be better conceived as a 'pseudo-creative' process for two main reasons. First, the market rules remain intact. Second, the quality of reforms often relies on defenses against depressive anxieties rather than a capacity for real change (similar emphasis on the lack of authenticity and resistance to democratic change is given by Hopper, 2003). Consequently, I suggest that technologies of deregulation and technologies of emergency reform become the two prevalent paths of urban government.

The second row of the table in Table 3 aims to bring to the fore how technologies of government shape urban forms and experiences during the evolution of neoliberalism and its crisis. Uncanny spaces become objects of government by way of splitting between, on the one hand, 'denigrated', and, on the other, 'idealized' spaces. Accordingly, two distinctive norms of belonging and relating take shape, which give expression to feelings of helplessness and despair.

Technologies of deregulation destroy national systems of social protection and their local relays (Table 3). Of course, this can be the result of greed and envy, as a growing literature suggests for multinational corporations and corrupted governments. The corrosion of safety nets can be perceived by the public as a 'failed dependency' (Hopper, 2003), like losing a leader or the ideals of government, feeling betrayed or maltreated. This becomes evident in metaphors of the abandoned, looted, or neglected city. Eventually envy is directed towards the leaders, who are perceived as able but unwilling to help, as well as to the city newcomers, who are perceived as invaders. City warfare becomes the object of government (Table 3). The combination of symbolic and physical decay becomes the norm and space is used as 'sword': a way that safeguards belonging by satisfying feelings of envy, hostility and anger. Folk devils roam the city in prevalent media and planning representations (Cohen, 2011). Moreover, the media, conservative governments or racist organizations can be thought to be performing a negative symbolic function. They are apt to host unconscious fears and feelings emerging locally and then return it to the audience using spectacular images. They are in search of raw sensory impressions in the city realm, which are turned into indisputable 'facts'. They take up local dreads and translate them to, what Wacquant calls territorial stigma (Wacquant, 2008). The collapse of proper symbolism results in compulsive performance. It is not as if the city is annihilated but the city is becoming an object of annihilation.

On the other hand, 'technologies of emergency reform' advance promises for survival and change (Table 3). In describing the efforts to rescue neoliberalism, Peck used a very powerful metaphor about the 'frenzied attempts to reboot (and sometimes to rebrand) the rickety regime of market rule' (Peck, 2010). As with computer rebooting, destruction and desire for survival are so closely linked; in fact 'shutting down' and 'restarting' the system is performed with a single operation in an almost compulsive and manic act, an attempt to get rid of despair. Fiscal responsibility, local entrepreneurialism, local networks, community based and private approaches to social service provision can be thought of as attempts to rebut urban government.

Significantly, emergency reforms rely on the idealization of the city's nostalgic past, or of its promising neoliberal future. The salvation of the city becomes the object of government (Table 3). In their struggle for a new hegemony, political leaderships promise to take care of war casualties, protect the vulnerable from retaliating enemies, and lead the people away from battlefield to the safe haven of consumption. Space can be used as a 'shield' protecting the idealized city and the attachments of urban citizens to it. Thus, idealization is a way of keeping the city pure and safe and of protecting neighborhoods from the abuse of corrupted leaders or city newcomers. This is why policing and caring are so closely interlinked. Idealization can also be a means of regaining loss of control, a source of omnipotence for scared subjects who uncritically identify with leaders and aspire to their reforms. The process of idealization becomes evident in gentrification plans, often involving a dual transformation of space. Landscapes of consumption and security are built via fast track investments in the leisure industry and real estate. At the same time, landscapes of compassion are reserved for the victims of neoliberalism. The logic of emergency in such cases dictates that care must have immediate outcomes and its recipients should be rehabilitated in a speedy manner to the norms of independent living and employability. Loyalty to values and respect of the dogma are vital for achieving cohesion. Policies promote a false sense of individuality according to bureaucratic and scientific norms. Similarly, social solidarity can be pretentious and ritualistic. Humble norms of social conduct apply to both leaders, who give up some of their power to the ultimate goal of city transformation, and to potential followers who wish to belong to the city. For both the leisure industry and the care industry, territorial control is vital, as is the demarcation of socio-spatial boundaries. A territorial boundary, as symbolic-equation, has to be rigidly enforced to expel in a safe distance fears and aggression that can spoil local identities. Usually, the end-result is a series of adjacent areas of wealth and destitution.

A chronicle of the crisis: Ghettos and Homelessness in the collapsing city

Let my story begin in January 2011 and end in May 2012. This period will suffice to describe the deployment of both technologies of deregulation and emergency reforms, punishing and caring responses to the crisis. It also offers a good length of time to reveal the interplay of political actors, vested economic interests, charities and the media in attempts to shape the urban future.

January 2011 was a rather special month. It coincided with the appointment in office of the new Mayor of Athens. Yiorgos Kaminis, Greek Ombudsman and professor of constitutional law, resigned from his position, to run in the local elections which he ultimately won in autumn 2010 with the support of the small Party of the Democratic Left and the PASOK. The coalition's program ('Right to Athens') was a typical example of 'roll-out' neoliberalism. The humble spirit and commitment to the cause of reforms was soon to be evident, so too his professional commitment to justice. Unlike his predecessors, the Mayor attended the New Years Dinner for the homeless without extensive media coverage. The Mayor denounced the role of the charismatic or the populist leader. On the contrary, he appeared to be an exception among untrustworthy politicians who failed to keep their promises. He insisted that his plans could succeed if citizens undertake their responsibilities. The rhetoric of the past seemed inverted. The people do not depend on their leader. The leader depends on its public. This type of leadership is also consensual, leaving aside futile political antagonisms. I am arguing however, that the 'Messiah' should not be confused with the charismatic or populist leader. Bion (1961) reminds us of unconscious processes in groups: the 'Messiah' can be born out of wedlock, despite his/her aristocratic crib is notably a being like the rest of us, and, can be easily replaced as groups strive to recreate hope.

It is worth examining the first TV appearance of the Mayor in the MEGA Channel footage 'Investigation' by the journalist Pavlos Tsimas on January 6, 2011. January 6th, in the Christian orthodox calendar, is the day of 'Theophany', the baptism of Jesus by John in Jordan and the receipt of the Spirit of God. Kaminis' political baptism was not held in water, with all its purifying qualities. The footage was set in the parking space of waste collection vehicles, adjacent to the garbage dump of Fyli. Let us consider the significance of the journalist's call and his encounter with Kaminis in such strange surroundings. The 'city-garbage dump' becomes the object of government. The footage is titled: 'Mayor this is your city: Can you change it?' In the opening scene the journalist declares Athens is a 'collapsing capital'. Fear of annihilation and symbols of death surmount the footage. The journalist 'guides' the Major to his own city. Indeed, the guidance of politicians by journalists in decaying areas of Athens has become a popular communication technique during the crisis. Biblical images unravel through the guidance to the 'wounds of Athens': criminality, prostitution, drug trafficking, and homelessness. Significantly, televised images do not disclose their biblical connotations, but claim a kind of uncontestable realism. This iconography of the 'real' deprives communication from its symbolic functions. An uncanny feeling results from the difficulty to distinguish between image and reality, symbol and 'thing'. The city *is* a garbage dump and so the best response is to evacuate, literally, its polluting contents, including politicians at the top and marginalized groups at the bottom of the social hierarchy.

Subsequently, the management of unconscious splitting involves both denigration and idealization. Denigration refers to a generalized condition of despair encompassing the city and its wounds. Nevertheless, through the dialogues of the journalist and the Mayor, envy is directed towards the corrupted administration of the conservative party and populism in general. Indeed, blaming the conservatives was part of the successful tactic of the Kaminis' coalition for wining the elections. Moreover, 'garbage' signifies broken promises by populist discourses (including the two leading parties interchanging in power for 30 years).

Let us also pay attention to this humble profile, which can shape idealization of the leader and identifications with him. The technocratic/ aristocratic profile of Kaminis was conceived out of wedlock, PASOK was hesitant to the political wedding with the reformers of the Democratic Left. However, the flirtation of the 'center-left' was more attractive to the public than the fighting between PASOK and New Democracy. In all its humility, the technocratic discourse silences the consequences of neoliberal doctrine or grossly underestimates them. Austerity is not a factor that reproduces the crisis but a trial to reach a new era. The armory of technologies of emergency reforms is fully deployed to reach the end of destitution. Tidying up the municipal budget, public/private partnerships for regeneration, charity and private initiatives can address the humanitarian crisis.

If we return to images in the mountainsides hosting the garbage of Fyli we can recall that *theophanies* in the Old Testament have a strong association with mountains. Does the city provide the theatre for theological hope? Greeks then, like the Israelites in their Exodus from Egypt, must go through a trial. A pessimist view would have it that humble dependence to the servants of neoliberal dogma is the way out of the crisis. An optimistic view would be to reconsider vulnerability and ask which new institutions can enhance democratic processes.

January 2011 was also significant because it initiated the re-organization of government technologies. Plans for regenerating the center of Athens were associated with its security. A ministerial committee on the 'Historical and Commercial center of Athens' was set and held its first meeting on January 5th. Press releases and interviews of various ministers became the main sources for the Daily and the Electronic Press. Significantly, the committee allocated the role of policing to Ministry of 'Citizen's Protection' (a euphemism for the Ministry of Public Order). The discourse on city warfare and aggression found new targets mainly recruited from undocumented migrants. Clean- ups of 'abandoned houses', plans for removing immigrants to boats, establishing detention camps, and the building of a fence along the Greek borders with Turkey were the means to 'de-ghettoize' the center in consecutive months. The Mayor of Athens and the Head of Region were said to be the 'allies' of the Government in the plan to Rescue the Center (NEA 7/2/2011). Gradually, alongside criminality, the risk of exploding a 'hygienic bomb' was added to the repertoire of justifications for cleansing the inner city from migrant shelters, drug addicts and prostitutes.

May 2011 was a difficult month for the government negotiating its midterm fiscal plan with the Troika against the background of protesting 'indignant citizens' in city piazzas and Syntagma square (Leontidou 2012). Incidentally, theft and murder of a Greek citizen by two foreign nationals initiated racial vigilance by neofascist groups. Mayor Kaminis attempted to distance himself from racist claims and policing failure. He also announced his own proposals for the regeneration of the center, arguing for the need to regulate and contain protests. Articles in '*Kathimerini*' ('Daily Press') and '*Ta Nea*' ('The News') reproduced the ghettoization discourse, while many backed up the Mayor's proposals. Political protest in city streets lasted for over two months until 30 July. A fragile majority in the Greek parliament voted for the Midterm fiscal pact whilst a massive operation by riot police was used to crush the protesters. The following days, the police in response to the Mayor's claims, evacuated Syntagma Square of any remaining tents and equipment. It is worth commenting that Kaminis' humble spirit and caring for the city went in hand with the excessive aggression of the government to protesters.

With growing popular discontent, George Papandreou failed to convince both his party and the European leaders to hold a referendum on the debt deal. In November of 2011 Lucas

Papadimos, professor of economics and former vice president of the European Central Bank accepted the mandate to lead an interim coalition government. The administration of Papadimos had to approve the controversial bailout program, secure the tranche of emergency aid, and reach agreement with private bondholders to finalize the bailout pack. To return to the metaphor, both Papadimos and Kaminis were born out of wedlock. The technocratic profile was attractive to middle class strata but the political support of the coalition government was weak.

During the following months the Greek government in collaboration with the European Commission attempted to speed up the process of public administration reforms. 'Technical assistance' was offered to Greece for the delivery of the EU/IMF adjustment program and the absorption of EU funds. Reforming Greek public administration in a neoliberal manner has been seen as key to success. Although the European Commission came to recognize the detrimental social impact of the crisis, its roots were said to lie in corruption, bureaucracy and bad government. Like Janus, the European Commission had two faces: one was moralizing to justify deregulation and corrosion of the system of social protection, the other was humanitarian to assist those on trial. The Greek political elites did not hasten to inhabit the Commission's split.

In February President Barroso met with Prime Minister Lucas Papadimos to consider how the Commission could help the Greek government to address the social consequences of the crisis. Poverty, homelessness, and the humanitarian situation faced by migrants and asylum seekers were emphasized in subsequent EU reports. The Greek Government was advised to give priority to the most vulnerable groups and urban regeneration as to make effective use of EU structural funds.

Before New Years' Eve the Prime Minister held a meeting with his ministers, the Mayor of Athens and the Archbishop of the

Church of Greece on 'Actions of social protection, employment and solidarity'. After completion of the meeting, the Prime Minister declared:

> Our country now gives two *battles*: One is fiscal consolidation and economic restructuring that will put the economy back on a growth trajectory and to *defend our position in the euro*. The other is the *battle of our society* to address the consequences of the crisis, combating unemployment and protecting social cohesion. The government, in cooperation with local government and the Church, decided to strengthen and coordinate our actions to support employment and social solidarity' (Prime minister's press office 28/12/2011).

In January 2012 Prime Minister Papadimos and Mayor Kaminis jointly attended the New Years Eve Dinner for the homeless. In ritualistic exhibition of solidarity and humanitarian concern, the two leaders avoided TV coverage but press releases were widely distributed. January was a cold month – harsh for the increasing number of those living on the streets. Press coverage reached an unprecedented volume and frequency compared to the prior ten years.

In February 2012 an Advisory Committee to the Ministry of Health was set to assist the administration in drafting a *'Homelessness Action Program'*. I accepted the invitation to become member of it. The committee included 19 members with a wide representation of ministries, the Greek Ombudsman, umbrella NGOs, the city of Athens, and the Church of Greece. An administrative group of four members, including 2 of ministerial advisors and 2 civil servants, was also formed to assist the committee in its daily tasks. A senior civil servant in the Ministry of Health and Social Solidarity headed the committee. During the first meetings there was hope, in recognition of the fact that first time such an inclusive board was set up and acknowledgment of the significance in the rise of homelessness was made. A pressing matter was to offer an operational definition of homelessness, so that homeless people could be recognized as a 'vulnerable group' and accordingly EU funds could be drawn for their relief.

To many members of the Advisory Committee, particularly from NGOs, the deadline for producing new legislation was extremely tight and scepticism was expressed for adopting this kind of 'emergency planning'. It was as if the Government prioritized absorbing EU money, and had hypocritically declared its solidarity to the increasing risks of homelessness. It was particularly representatives of the public administration who supported the urgent need for drafting new legislation and policy measures. On the 29th of February 2012, Law 4052 was passed describing the new competencies of the Ministry of Health and the Ministry of Labor for the application of the EU/IMF finance agreement. The Minister of Health, Andreas Loverdos, explained to the parliament that it was necessary to pass the law overnight because the next morning the Government should have presented to the Eurogroup a legislative framework for the adjustment program (Proceedings of the Parliament 29/2/2012).

PASOK MP former minister of Health John Kremastinos aptly conveyed the warlike atmosphere of policy making.

> So then Mr. Minister, I recognize all your hard efforts, and in my opinion is necessary to form a caring state. That is, just like in real wars, when there are dead, the equivalence here is the existence of the hungry, the homeless, and the malnourished. As with the wounded and the amputees of war, here we have the equivalent of the homeless and the pensioners in poor health. These are the invalids of the war today... You must set up a caring state, which will essentially give priority to humans. It should be stressed to our partners in the European Union that Greece cannot be converted to a cemetery of people. This is tragic (Proceedings of Parliament 29/2/2012).

After only two weeks of preparation Article 29 of the Law set out a definition of the homeless, for the first time in a Greek legislative document.

> 1. The homeless are recognized as vulnerable social group to which social protection is provided. Homeless persons are defined as: All persons legally residing in the country, who lack access to safe and adequate accommodation, owned, rented or freely released, and which would meet the technical requirements and basic amenities for water and electricity. 2. The homeless include particularly those living in the streets or shelters and those who are hosted, out of need, in institutions or other closed forms of care (Law 4052).

This definition, with a notable modification, was agreed during the meetings of the Advisory Committee, which ultimately decided to rely on the homelessness classification of FEANTSA (the European Federation of Organizations working with the homeless). The initial agreement was a relief for homeless rights advocates and was viewed as breaking away from a narrow definition serving the containment of the visible homeless. Nonetheless, it was to the surprise of the members of the Advisory Committee that a single phrase was added to the proposed definition during the passing of the law. The phrase that was added overnight was 'legally residing'. So homeless could be only those legally residing in the country, i.e. excluding undocumented migrants or people in the early phases of applying for asylum. The change was made under the request of the right wing party of LAOS as documented in the following intervention of its spokesman:

> Sir (Minister), you come here and give a definition that says that as homeless are defined all persons living in the country. So, is an illegal immigrant who has just entered the borders

> automatically a homeless person who wants protection? Why don't you clarify the definition of 'all persons who reside legally in the country?' If he is a legal resident, then he should have the need for some protection. But anyone who has problems in his country and comes here, he automatically wants protection from the Greek state? (LAOS MP E. Polatides in the Proceedings of Parliament 29/2/2012).

The proposal of LAOS was adopted without discussion by the government.

The Advisory Committee had discussed in advance the entitlements of migrants and acknowledged that different provisions should be made to different categories of migrants and asylum seekers. But it also considered that basic human rights for dignity and shelter apply to all residents in the country, even if they are to be found in detention camps, prisons or hospitals. It was also a matter of concern of organizations working with people in the early stages of applying for asylum or even supporting the repatriation of undocumented migrants that minimal provisions should be offered to their clients. The assistance of severely destitute populations through street work and outreach was complicated by the legal amendment put forward by LAOS. In addition to humanitarian concerns the amendment undermined the documentation of homelessness because it becomes extremely difficult in any count to verify who has legal documents and who does not. In effect, the amendment replicates a split between the deserving and undeserving poor. For the deserving (Greeks, approximating the profile of the 'new homeless') emergency plans for caring were made. The undeserving (aliens), forming the dangerous classes, had to experience a series of policing attacks, violence and public shaming operations just before the national elections in April and May 2012. The Ministers of Health and 'Citizen's Protection' attracted the criticism of international Human rights organizations when in May 2012, during policing operations and forced hygiene inspections, the police prosecuted HIV positive sex workers, posted the women's photographs on the Internet and used the media to alert possible clients to proceed with HIV tests.

In an attempt to relieve of the middle classes from the morbid atmosphere, which the government itself was creating Mayor Kaminis and Minister of Development Anna Diamantopoulou, jointly presented a strategic agreement for a 'New National Plan to Restart Athens, Create Jobs and Support Social Cohesion' in mid April 2012. As a typical case of regeneration the plan includes the promotion of entrepreneurship, sustainability, and cohesion. The title of the plan betrays a policy compulsion, a manic attempt to 'Restart Athens'. Despite the ambitions of official rhetoric it is a way of drawing EU funds to run more or less standard municipal activities, which are currently under-resourced. During the presentation of the program to the press Minister Diamantopoulou confirmed her agreement with Minister Chrisohoides to establish Detention Camps for the deportation of illegal immigrants and supported Kaminis' proposal for the containment of demonstrations in the city center. Thus, through her speech, she vividly illustrated how both sides of splitting combine in neoliberal policies.

Within this context the Committee on the 'Homelessness Action Program' struggled to continue its work from March to June 2012 and overcome a series of rising obstacles. I will summarize the most important ones.

In the very same law (4052) that provided the legal definition of homelessness, the department leading the Advisory Committee on homelessness was transferred to the Ministry of Labor. Other than cost containment concerns, this move is also part of a strategy for merging government departments and exercising centralized control following the advice of experts from the European Commission. It also signifies priority to employability over social protection objectives. The confusing result has been that the Ministry of Labor proceeded to draft and implement its own 'Action Plan for a Network of Immediate Social Interventions' to address the psychosocial needs of the poor and the homeless. Eventually two distinct ministries engaged in disagreement about their competencies. It seems that attempts for centralized control to implement a cost-containment agenda neglect on-going working operations, increase insecurity within the administration, and multiply the sources of conflict.

Fatigue, disappointment and confusion were gradually emerging within the Advisory Committee. Sarcasm and black humor was a response of the members of the group on the announcement of bad news about dismantling services, which were vital for planning. Numerous examples include the closing down of social housing organizations, legislative changes to facilitate forced evictions, introduction of fees for health services and accommodation in psychiatric shelters, reduction to benefits and pensions for the mentally ill and the disabled, wage cuts and the freezing of payments to social service workers. The list could continue.

At the same time a technocratic discourse of euphemisms was escalating in planning procedures and documents. Is the title 'Action Plan for a Network of Immediate Social Interventions' not a notorious invention? 'Social interventions' in place of corroding public institutions, 'immediate' to avoid speaking of 'emergency', 'network' to connote private-public partnerships. As a member of the Committee I found it extremely difficult to explain to civil servants how the ideology of individual responsibility permeated many of their suggestions or how tight bureaucratic regulations for shelter provisions neglected the needs of the homeless themselves. It was as if the ideological milk of a false individualization and technocratic solutions, poured to the administration via EU jargon for more than two decades, was soaked together with financial flows.

Epilogue

In this chapter, I have tried to link a widespread feeling of the uncanny in Athens, with the psychosocial consequences of the neoliberal crisis and its management. Governing an uncanny city primarily relies on defenses against splitting processes and runs through communicative dysfunctions like contagion of fear, hate and violence, on the one hand; hesitant participation, pseudo morale, technocratic and messianic discourses, on the other.

However, the desire for equality and justice could initiate a process of democratic change. I am thinking of the commitment of the members of the Advisory Committee as a sign of hope and realism. Long hours were spent in meetings, often, after office hours, which many members attended at the end of an exhausting day with their fragile clients, without any remuneration, sitting in a cold room as heating in the premises of Ministry was turned off for cost containment. There must have been something more profound that held the group together than a sense of expertise or professional interest. There must have been some glue stronger than despair.

I recall the voices of demonstrating health professionals against cuts in mental health services outside the library room where we met. I remember a number of colleagues to be sharing their time between the occupation of the first floor of the Ministry and the meetings of the Advisory Committee on the second floor.

I feel I have been used as an alibi for legitimating versions of neoliberal reforms. I am afraid that initiatives like day-centers for the homeless, street work, soup kitchens, socially run medical centers that sprung spontaneously as acts of solidarity are now falsely replicated in the jargon of reforms. I know it is this mimicry of planning that we should contest, and so I regret I have not spent more time with the protesters outside the building of the Ministry.

Chapter 3

Four Acts in/for Syntagma

Orsalia Dimitriou

In the last few years the city center of Athens has been the arena of an increasing number of clashes, demonstrations, insurrections and movements that caused abrupt social and political transformations. The public spaces of the city - that are the material constructions of social, cultural, economic and political realities - are mirrors of those changes. Using the example of Syntagma square which is the main statutory public space, and a number of events that took place there – events ranging from protesters burning of the Christmas tree during the urban insurrection of December 2008 to the violent police attack during the 'indignants' movement in 2011 – I would like to investigate the idea of the emergence of a new public. This novelty is created by the rejection of the existing participatory framework of democratic political procedures set by the State, as the new public is forced to actively redefine itself through the very quest for and implementation of the new models of the participatory framework.

Using a number of theorists who are working on contrasting notions of democracy defined by different ways of political participation, and attributing the notion of incumbent democracy to the official state discourse and the notion of critical democracy to the emerging public and its movements, I will attempt to provide a framework for examining the aims and claims of each side regarding the definition of democracy. Moreover I will draw on the importance of maintaining the expression and visibility of different political claims and projects in public space, even if they are conflicting and violent, as an essential characteristic of democratization. Finally, the framework of conflicting political notions will be used to provide a new perspective on the new spatio-political movements, debating that the lack of stability, efficiency and representative agency that are characterizing them, are in fact intrinsic and desirable characteristics that aim to empower and critically redefine the notion of the public.

Syntagma Square

Syntagma is the main statutory space of Athens and one of the oldest ones. Its creation coincides with that of the Modern Greek state in 1834. The spatial characteristic of the square, its design and its position in the city - as depicted in the first urban plans of Athens and as the plans were gradually modified and implemented from 1933 and throughout the 19th century - were expressing both the socio-political characteristics of the era and the aspirations of the new governing class (Bastéa, 2000). The presence of the King's palace and later of the parliament at the east side of the square emphasized the political character of the space. The building, since it was built, was visually imposed over the open space and was a direct reference point of the citizens' political claims. Accordingly, the open space of the square was always modified in reference to the palace-parliament complex. The uses of the square depended both on the urban habits of the era and the permitted borders set by each period's legislation.

Since its origin, the square has functioned as the stage where the different acts between sovereignty and people have been performed both emphasizing the hegemony of the governmental mode, as for instance in military parades or official ceremonies and as expression of political opposition and disagreement to governmental decisions. The name of the square which in Greek means constitution is indicative of this relationship - it was named after the bloodless revolution that took place on the 3rd of September 1834, when rioters demanding a constitution gathered in the square under King's Otto window and forced him to yield to their demands.

Throughout the turbulent political history of Greece (absolute monarchy, constitutional monarchy, dictatorships, democracy and reconstitution of democracy) numerous political actions and counteractions have taken place in the square: rallies, riots, revolutions, demonstrations, ceremonies. In addition to this, Syntagma square was also for more than one hundred years the location of unofficial politics discussed in the cafes that surrounded the square. This characteristic of the square as the space of everyday politics and debates was gradually disappearing for a number of spatial, social and political reasons. Some of them are the construction of the monument of unknown soldier in 1929 that disturbed the direct connection of the parliament with the square[1], the post-war planning regulations that increased the traffic and cut out the surface of the square from the surrounding functions, the demolition of many of the meeting places after the 60s, the military junta of 1967 that inevitably turned the few remaining cafés to tourist spots rather than places of political fermentation, the construction of the metro station and the spatial modifications before and during the Olympic Games in 2004 that further fragmented the space. The spatial segregation and fragmentation of the space coupled with the widespread de-politicization of public spaces that took place during the 90s and 00s and turned most of them to places of leisure and consumption and, thus, converted Syntagma square from a vivid lived and experienced political space to a meeting point, a space to cross rather than a space to familiarize and a space to which to get attached.[2] This tendency did not reduce the political function of the space since it was, and still is, used as the stage of dissent, because of its extremely charged symbolic and representational value, but it rather transposed the character of political expression. Many times before and since 2011, the political acts were expressed sporadically and ephemerally in the stage of Syntagma square – for example most of the demonstrations are starting from the square but do not remain there -

without requiring a continuous and everyday presence of the public in the space.

The lack of everyday political activities in the city's public spaces could be indicative either of a climate of perceived political stability[3] or of political indifference and cynicism. Nothing lasts forever though, since everyday life is not unchangeable but continuously shifting and dependent on historical circumstances (Lefebvre, 2008). During and after the events of December 2008 and the unprecedented changes the events caused to the Greek society coupled with the start of the global economic crisis, had led to the political re-charging of the space.

Act I: The tree goes

In December 2008 the center of Athens became the arena of a violent urban insurgency that followed the death of a sixteen-year-old student who was murdered by the police. On the first level the murder of the young boy fuelled all of the frustration against alleged police incompetence and brutality. On a deeper level it condensed into a single act all dominant measures, politics and ideologies which imprisoned youth in a pre-determined future of antagonisms and disappointments (Stavridis, 2011). The initial demonstrations and violent protests against the police soon broadened to encompass protests against youth unemployment, social inequality, corruption, state inadequacy, higher education reforms among other perceived grievances (Economides & Monastiriotis, 2009). The emergence of the global recession at the same period intensified the urgency of the claims.

In the middle of the burned, looted and rioting city and in the middle of the main statutory square, the tall fake Christmas tree of the municipality, 'the tallest of Europe' as the municipality declared proudly, was standing as a symbol of the happy festive and consequently consumerist period. Not for long though, as inevitably the presence of such a symbol in a rioting city was deemed 'unsuitable' and a group of rioters set it ablaze. Pictures of the burning tree with the parliament in the background made it to the headlines around the world[4] and caused the fury of the mayor of Athens.

Act II: The tree stays

In a desperate act to restore 'normality' in the center, and while the riots were still on, the mayor ordered and installed a new Christmas tree. During the opening ceremony on December 16th, that culminated with the illumination of the new Christmas tree, the mayor of Athens declared: 'In spite of all those who do not love this city we insist on decorating it and celebrating, because the kids of the city deserve all the festive moments of which we deprived them in the previous days'[5] and urged all citizens to continue visiting the commercial center of the city and continue with their shopping, so that the Christmas celebrations could go on undisturbed. In doing so, he completely ignored the reasons that mobilized the riots and the deepening crisis that prevented many citizens to shop and be festive as usual, as well as the fact that murdered Grigoropoulos was also an Athenian kid. Furthermore, his statements implied that there was a 'proper' and 'objectively correct' use of the city during the Christmas period and this was obviously neither rioting nor protesting.

On 20th of December 2012 a group of young people, outraged by the mayor's gesture to spend public funds on a large plastic tree in a post-apocalyptic city center, encouraged the public call to decorating the new Christmas tree with household waste. And while the event of garbage decoration was still on and the participants responded in absolute synergy with the festive spirit by decorating the tree with what they consider as appropriate garlands, the mayor ordered the police to intervene. This act resulted in another powerful image, which is counter-balancing the one depicting the tree ablaze: three lines of riot police in full gear surrounding and protecting the Christmas tree.[6] The absurdity of a police-protected fake tree amidst a smashed city was further intensified by the fact that during the previous summer the state machinery was accused by the public and environmentalists of not protecting adequately 2,700 square kilometers of forests that were burned during massive forest fires.

Act III: The movement stays

Not everyone could have guessed that what appeared to be the peak of the crisis in 2008 was in fact just the beginning. As the Greek crisis was deepening, dissatisfaction with the existing political system was growing, regarding politicians, political parties, and the current democratic process that was leaving very few opportunities for public participation in the making of decisions that were affecting the citizens' welfare.

On May 2011 following a call for protest against the government's austerity measurements that was organized by social media and inspired by the square occupations in Spain, thousands of people flooded Syntagma square and the surrounding streets. This first gathering marked the beginning of a movement named as the 'Greek Indignant Citizens Movement'[7] or simply 'Movement of Indignants', a name drawing parallels to the Spanish movement of 'Indignados'. This movement portrayed substantially different qualitative and quantitative characteristics to any previous political actions. Apart from the large public participation and long duration, its novelty was also based on the fact that the movement was absolutely peaceful, it had no official organizers and representatives, it was not party-affiliated, and it included people from all social strata, political beliefs and ages, even traditionally[8] conflicting ones like anarchists and nationalists, communists and priests.

While the movement lasted Syntagma square had acquired a

different spatiality; it was organized in upper and lower parts that the participants characteristically called the Dionysian (corporal) and the Apollonian (intellectual). This distinction marked the space of two different but interconnected ways of expressing political opposition. The first one, the Dionysian, was the part closest to the parliament where the dissent was expressed in spontaneous bodily gestures, movements, songs, cries and chants. The second one represented metaphorically the mind within the body, hosting people's assembly and the movement's camp (infirmary, translation center, radio station, sleeping tents, etc.). The main aim of the movement was to shape a common public sphere, where everyone would meet and everyone could articulate an opinion, a place of direct and unmediated participation according to the model of the archetypical agora. Panourgia (2011) writes that 'young people who had never before bothered themselves with politics - either in its ancient Greek sense of caring for commons (common spaces, common governance, common jurisdiction, common rights, common responsibilities) or in the modern sense of partisanship - caused (again) the emergence of a polis'. The indignant movement rejected the existing participatory framework of democratic political procedures set by the State and was actively implementing new models generated by the participation of the public in the movement. Its long duration that affected the everyday life of the participants for a period of time and the function of the assembly turned the square not only into the usual stage of dissent but also into the actual place of political fermentation.

ACT IV: The movement goes

On July 28 2011 and during a forty-eight- hour general strike a small number of protesters clashed with the police in front of the Greek parliament and other areas of central Athens. Using this isolated incident as an excuse, the police attempted to evacuate

Syntagma Square of protesters, as well as other key protest spots in Athens employing an excessive, disproportionate and indiscriminate use of force criticized by foreign media[9] and *Amnesty International.*[10] Video footage[11] shows the police throwing tear gas at citizens trapped inside the underground metro stations, throwing stones, beating brutally defenseless and elderly people, driving through the crowds on motorbikes, destroying the tents and sending hundreds of people to the hospital, some of which were seriously injured, permanently blinded or deafened. The unprecedented - during democratic times - violence continued throughout the night and on 29 June, the day when a new package of largely unpopular austerity measures was passed. Despite the violent police attack the protesters returned to the square, used human chains to wash off the surface of the square from chemicals and tear gas and reset the movement camp.

The extent of brutality used by the police, as well as the number of mobilized officers, clearly denoted that the target was not a small group of violent protesters but the movement on the square. For various MPs, mostly from the governing party, the movement was undemocratic and therefore should not have taken place in front of the parliament. Even before the outbreak of violence, on 29th of May the vice-president of the Greek government declared that 'movements without ideology and organization, that is to say movements based on anger, can only lead to either an ineffective release, which at the end of the day is of no interest to the political world, or pave the way for an undemocratic change of regime by organized groups'.[12] In the same manner the deputy Minister of Foreign Affairs commented on 31 of May: 'I can accept tougher questioning and criticism, but not the leveling of our political system. Democracy can give a solution. The flattening of our democracy can only lead to a slippery road. The majority of the Greek people can be angry, but not under these circumstances'.[13]

Divergent acts

The notion of the public includes much more than a bodily spatial presence, without diminishing to the least the importance of this presence. It is a political notion – since it is dependent on the notion of the citizen and the notion of public sphere. As such, it differs significantly according to the definition given by each political system, but even within the frame of the same system it is unstable and highly conflicting. As Mitchell (2003) argues the definition of the 'public' is a constant struggle between top-down policies and bottom-up claims for the public.

Judging from the answer of the State to the different described actions in Syntagma via its regulatory apparatus - the police - but also from the accompanying official discourse -political statements and mainstream media - it is quite obvious that there is a discrepancy between what the state perceives as participation in public and what the public perceives as their right. Both parts are operating in what they recognize as a democratic framework but each one is attributed different characteristics and sets different borders to it.

The reason I chose to mention those specific public acts that are completely heterogeneous in their performing characteristics, number of participants, duration, social impact etc. is twofold. Firstly, because when coupled in acts and counter-acts, they clearly illustrate the increasing schism between the state authority and public, with the acts of December 2008 functioning as harbingers of that rupture. Secondly, their spatial manifestation is condensed in symbolic meaning – for example the burning of a tree has different gravity if it takes place in a backyard after Christmas than if it is in front of the parliament while rioting and before the holidays start. In that sense the term 'to act'[14] is selected to describe actions, accomplishments and processes of doing, but also to denote successive parts of a 'play' staged in Syntagma square, in which the actors are possibly reading from different scripts.

The contrasting definitions of democracy and political participation

> Trying to understand democracy is like reaching into a black plastic bag. You can feel a large object, but accurate description is difficult because the shape is extremely complex [...] the object concealed within the plastic bag is thus strangely elongated, for it has two bulbous and tangible lobes (Blaug, 2002, p. 104).

There is historically a fundamental dichotomy in how we perceive democracy and participation in democratic procedures. It is possible that democracy is not one continuous project that reaches up to the state and down to the grassroots and the public, but it might entail reciprocally exclusive political projects. Fagence (1977) writes that democracy and participation fit the common mold of the social and political sciences with their clutter of discrepancies between theory and practice, and between aspiration and implementation. Such discrepancies seem to pervade not only the theoretical body of literature (Blaug 2002) but also the institutionalized expressions of democracy, whether 'the liberal variety of the 'free world' or of the socialist expression of communistic republics, or of the strange hybrids characteristic for the developing nations in the 'third world'' (Fagence, 1977, p. 20). Democracy in contemporary liberal conception follows schismatic definitions. Schumpeter (2010), whose theory of 'competitive democracy' or 'democratic elitism', is for many an accurate description of what passes for democracy in contemporary western nations (Blaug & Schwarzmantel, 2001), defines it as an institutional arrangement for arriving at political decisions in which individuals acquire the power to decide by means of a competitive struggle for the people's vote. His focus on democracy as a decision-making method and his emphasis on 'democratic self-control' offer great autonomy to leaders. The claim suggests that once they (the voters) have elected an individual, the political action is his/her business and not theirs. Blaug and Schwarzmantel call Shumpeter's theory 'a far cry from the ideas of popular sovereignty and active citizenship' (2001, p.4).

In opposition to Schumpeter's elitist approach is Habermas' notion of 'deliberative democracy' based on an expanded public sphere as the space where the ongoing constitution of democratic culture occurs through rational-critical debate between equal citizens (Habermas, 1992). Habermas' core elements of democratic theory are: a developed public sphere, which is produced and maintained in a civil society by means of a discursively constituted consensus; constitutionally grounded legal procedures; and finally, an established democratic culture, based on widely known and accepted norms (Segre, 2011). The public in this ideal democracy is created to respond to moments of crisis or abuses of political offices and gather in order to revise and 'reinvent' political power and authority (Loehwing & Motter, 2009). Based on the democratic definition of Habermas, Loehwing and Motter (2009) approach the question of democracy in terms of how it can result from civic rhetorical action, rather than how a democratic institutional arrangement can better accommodate the demands of more individual and group interests and they distinguish between a problem solving model of democracy and a democracy as culture-generating paradigm.

Chantal Mouffe (2000) uses the concept of 'agonistic pluralism' to present a new way to think about democracy that is different both from liberal consociational and deliberative theories of democracy. For Mouffe liberalism's main principle is an availability of a universal consensus based on reason. Accordingly, the typical liberal understanding of pluralism dictates that the many perspectives and values, when put together, constitute a harmonious and non-conflicting ensemble (Mouffe, 2005b). What democratic theories based on rational consensus fail to acknowledge is the hegemonic nature and the ineradicability of antagonism.[15] To think politically according to Mouffe 'it is necessary to abandon the dream of final reconciliation and to discard the idea of the public as a space oriented towards consensus' (2005b, p. 809). The perspective of 'agonistic pluralism' reveals the illusion that a fully achieved democracy could ever be instantiated, and it keeps the democratic contestation alive. Consequently the democratic process should always allow for the possibility that conflict may appear and to provide an arena where differences can be confronted (Laclau & Mouffe, 1998). This arena is a commonly shared symbolic space where the conflicting parts are mutually recognized as legitimate adversaries and not enemies. Based on democratic politics of pluralistic agonism the 'res publica' is envisaged as a multiplicity of public spaces of agonistic confrontation (Mouffe, 2005b).

Jane Mansbridge (1980) also defines two distinct types of democracy, the unitary and the adversary. Unitary democracy is based on the assumption of common interests between its participants. Founded on the norms of friendship, unitary democracies understand equality in terms of 'equal status' or 'equal respect'. The decisions are negotiated in a face-to-face interaction and the decision rule is consensus. On the contrary, adversary democracy is more suitable to accommodate conflicting interests. It is based on the assumption of equal protection of interests and the decision rule is the majority rule counted in secret ballot. Though the two types of democracy are defined by contrasting characteristics, Mansbridge concludes that unitary democracy is 'more suitable to small-size and relatively homogeneous communities' (1980, p. 282) and that unitary and adversary democratic values can coexist and be used in defining methods of polity in different sized communities; a citizen can therefore participate in a polity by voting anonymously, and in another one by participating in face-to-face negotiations and discussions. Regarding democratic participation, Mansbridge observes that different views of how participation should be institutionalized clearly emerge when one considers the kinds of problems faced by grassroots associations in their efforts to be democratic. Such associations must empower their participants, and at the same time provide for good and quick decision-making.

A different side than Mansbridge's distinct but possibly symbiotic relationship of unitary and adversary democracy is expressed by Richard Blaug (2002), who distinguishes two diverse and mutually incompatible political projects that he calls 'incumbent' democracy and 'critical' democracy. Examining why the efforts of deepening democracy - in order to expand from the state and reach the local, the civic and the grassroots - is failing, Blaug has concluded that the reason lies in the critical difference of the definition and therefore of the aims of democracy that each side is referring to and tries to achieve, and the lack of communication between the parts. Those two competing discourses lie in distinct social and political locations and are differently located within the structures of power. Incumbent democracy is a view of democracy coming from the center of such structures and critical democracy from the periphery; in the first case democracy appears as a set of institutions to be respected, protected and improved, and in the second, democracy becomes a method of challenging those institutions (Blaug, 2002).

Equivalently, the principles of participation in incumbent and critical political projects, according to Blaug's definitions, vary greatly. Participation in incumbent democracy is largely characterized by voting, by normalized interaction within structured groups and by orderly civic involvement. The strength of incumbent democracy lies in its effectiveness, which is achieved through institutions. Critical democracy, on the contrary, seeks to empower politically excluded voices and challenge existing institutions without necessarily seeking to occupy the sovereign position. Participation is direct, unmediated and horizontally structured with minimal institutional arrangements and decision-making preceded by open argumentation and debate. Blaug writes that 'with participation seen as good in itself, democracy becomes an experience' (2002, p.106).

The emergence of a new public

Trying to situate the acts of Syntagma Square within a democratic framework, one faces a similar feeling of bewilderment like searching into Blaug's black plastic bag, as both the public and the state define the bulbous and complex object of democracy differently.

For the public that assembles in the square or burns the Christmas tree the existing democratic system is close to Schumpeter's ideal, an elitist[16] approach to democracy that leaves great autonomy - to the extent of unaccountability - to the elected leaders and reserves political action for the parliament and not for the public. Based on Habermas' notion of democracy the public in Syntagma square is indeed formed in order to respond to moments of crisis and alleged abuses of political office by the authority. Furthermore, the daily assemblies based on deliberation between equal members and civic rhetoric action had extended the public sphere and set a culture-generating paradigm of democracy. But the deviation from this ideal Habermasian democratic prototype comes from the fact that there are not constitutionally grounded legal procedures to acknowledge a public that refuses the accepted norms and asks for a reconstitution of democratic culture. Such a possibility is rejected as not related to the political word and the deliberation between the state and such public is denied. Moreover, this rejection does not take place in the frame of an agonistic relationship, such as described by Mouffe's democratic model, where the conflicting parts recognize each other as legitimate adversaries. On the contrary, the parts are perceived as illegitimate and undemocratic opponents that constitute a highly antagonistic and violent relationship. It is also quite clear that

Syntagma acts cannot be described by Mansbridge's differentiation of unitary and adversary democracy, since none of those two models can describe the indignant movement: a large-size, non homogeneous polity that was further resisting any institutionalization of political participation.

It is then possible that the described acts in Syntagma square express two antagonistic definitions of democracy strategically opposed and possibly incompatible: incumbent and critical democracy. Indeed, they are simultaneously in operation, sharing the same space and the same time. The public space of the square becomes the common ground where those clashing claims are visualizing. What becomes crucial is primarily to understand that making the conflict visible is not an impediment but an essential part of democratization. Staeheli has demonstrated that 'the unruliness and the struggles between those who seek to maintain particular kinds of order and those who would disrupt it are at the heart of democratization, or of the enactment of democracy' (2009, p.74). She believes that those struggles may be most powerful when they involve spatial transgressions that differ from spaces of formal, institutionalized power and cause a relocation of the public sphere. Staeheli has argued that disorder can be a powerful tool in fostering democracy because it highlights the conflicts that are inherent in democratic politics. While disorder can undermine the process of democratization by making participation in public life and governing impossible, the suppression of disorder and the eradication of the disorderly public is a greater threat to democracy (Staeheli, 2009). Consequently, maintaining the possibility of divergent acts to take place in Syntagma Square is essential for democratic politics. Those who decorated the Christmas tree in December 2008 with garbage garlands were neither the public who hated their city nor the personifications of democratic enemies, but rather a public who challenged the set social norms thus indicating the urgency of a political change.

Understanding the acts of Syntagma square as indications of inherently different political projects also sets a different base for evaluating their political and social importance. Quite often the critique of the described Syntagma acts[17] is based on notions of success, result and progress that are connected to efficiency, institutionalization and hierarchical organization, which are characteristics and assumptions deeply rooted in the idea of incumbent democracy. On the contrary, the vagueness, the slow decision making, the temporality and the impracticality of some aims could be considered negative for the engineers of one type of democracy and positive assets for the other. A participant in the Spanish square movement illustrates the abovementioned differences: 'in the square, the discussion itself is more important than its conclusion. The responsibility is to defend and extend this [...] it is very difficult to think about tomorrow when you are wrapped up in the events of today. It is even more difficult because the rhetoric of the political class has always held forth on 'tomorrow'. In this movement, tomorrow is unthinkable for the moment. There is only now' (Kaejane, 2011).

The strength of critical acts, viewed through the lens of critical democracy is to voice to diverse opinions and demands, to empower and to further extend the public's imaginary in directions that are not within the existing social and political norms since those are dictated and constituted by rules and values based on incumbent democracy. Visualizing, but more importantly, experiencing the claims for a different democratic participatory framework is producing - slowly but progressively – a different kind of public.

Chapter 4

To 'Lose One's Way' in a City in Crisis: Techniques of Navigating and Walking in Spaces of Disorder

Yannis Kallianos

> Not to find one's way around a city does not mean much. But to lose one's way in a city, as one loses one's way in a forest, requires some schooling. Street names must speak to the urban wanderer like the snapping of dry twigs, and little streets in the heart of the city must reflect the times of day, for him, as clearly as a mountain valley (Benjamin, 2006, p. 1).

What has intrigued me in this passage by Walter Benjamin in his reminiscences, 'Berlin Childhood around 1900', is the idea that there are spaces in the city which, no matter how controlled, surveilled, quantified, measured, delineated and mapped, still retain a certain degree of ambiguity. These are everyday sites that hold valuable knowledge about the city itself as well as the social and political practices of its people. However, their ambiguity is rendered by the fact that even though the above categories mentioned do not cease to apply when explored from a different point of view they can reveal signs, practices and connotations that were not visible before, but, in fact, were never really absent.

My argument is that, in the period of 'crisis' in Athens the ambiguity of these sites, the fact that their everydayness is constituted on antithetical and oppositional elements and practices, is transparent for all to see. That is because the set of everyday relations that constitute crisis which, have been arranged around continual social change, personal and public uncertainty, and rapid political transformations, force people to engage with the

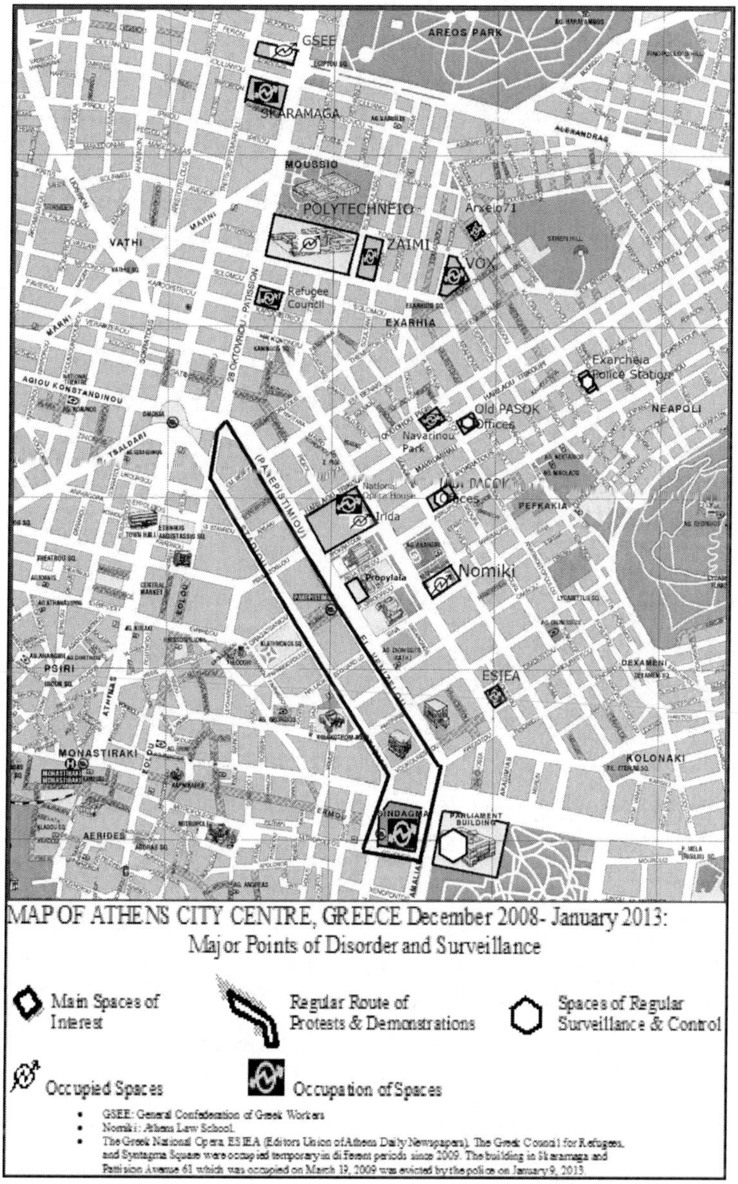

Image 2: Major Points of Disorder and Surveillance. Map: adapted by author.

city in a totally different manner. In a sense, the way people experience public space has changed. It is under this perspective that this chapter has been conceptualized and written. My objective here is to portray a city in transformation. What are the visible and non-visible sites of these transformations in the city center of Athens? In which ways do people engage with these sites and what social and political practices have contributed in their production?

What I aim to do here is to offer a variety of ways of navigation and walking in the city center of Athens that exposes the ambiguity of these sites. I wish to do this from the point of view of 'disorder'. I draw my understanding of the term 'disorder' from Richard Sennet (2004) who considers it as the main element to create diverse, even 'anarchic' urban communities where different classes, ethnicities and cultural practices can mutually coexist. In opposition to the idea of homogeneity and control the idea of disorder will be used to mean a process of diverse, non-authoritative and collective interaction in and with the public spaces of the city.

Opposing the usage of public spaces as centers of commerce, consumption and privatization, spatial practices that produce disorder inscribe on the body of the city, meanings, signs, marks, cracks and symbolic patterns that encourage a different understanding of these spaces. Demonstrations, riots as well as squatting and graffiti are amongst these practices that create situations where people can engage with each other in a different manner in public spaces as well as interact with public spaces in other ways. In certain contexts these practices can be conceptualized as oppositional to existing hegemonic frameworks in times of crisis and will be introduced here as a practical guideline of how to lose one's way in Athens. In a constantly changing setting, disorder will become the methodological constant of walking the metropolitan center in order to identify sites that reflect multiple and even contradictory connotations, according to who acts upon them and how.

My intention is to explore this continuous struggle of diverse and opposing interpretations that gradually developed in Athens since 2008 based on the ways it has been inscribed on public space. Our navigation in the city center of Athens has as its primary objective to bring to light these transformations and the effects they have had on the politics of public space of the city. Walls, streets, alleys, pavements and buildings all will be explored here as the main sites of this change. What is at issue is that these sites reflect different ways of how people position themselves in the social field. To lose one's way in the city then becomes all the more important because it also requires a process of re-inventing one's position in the city and thus, one's place in the community.

Navigating the city, Athens in disorder

According to Nikolaidou (1993) Athens city center is divided into two major districts. Syntagma (Constitution) Square is in the East side. This is where the Parliament sits, surrounded by civic services and private offices, commercial enterprises, and it is also the banking nexus. This space has always been used by the upper and middle upper class. On the other hand, the West side and around Omonoia (which can be translated as amity or solidarity) Square is the space of retail trade and all sorts of peddlers (Nikolaidou, 1993, p. 129). This is now the place where refugees and immigrants have built their lives and homes. The area between three main Squares, Syntagma, Omonoia and Monistiraki, creates a triangle known as the commercial triangle.

The city center of Athens is also notorious for being the main site of demonstrations, riots, squatting and other kind of anti-systemic political activity. These actions reflect a contestation over the uses of public space. Since 2008 actions that promote a non-homogenous, non-segregated, anti-hierarchical usage of public space have strengthened and multiplied opposing order, control and normality as features that constitute institutional space as such. To navigate then in a city in disorder means to be able to recognize the sites where the contest over the use of space is taking place. This is essential in our study of social change that is intrinsic to the situation of 'crisis' in Athens.

In his suggested theory of navigation, Alfred Gell (1985) takes into account three distinct factors:

a The territory, which is the real world, the physical space and the location.
b The map of the territory, what he calls 'compendia of non token indexical spatial beliefs' (1985, p. 280).
c And the images of the territory, that is 'the perceptually based beliefs about what is where in relation to a percipient subject, i.e. token-indexical spatial beliefs' (1985, p. 280).

To navigate in a spatial and social setting an everyday practical mastery and familiarity with the social practices that produce space and location is required which is not presupposed in the geographical mapping of the territory. This is because even though the 'Cartesian space', meaning the map as the 'models of all possible routes,' (Gell, 1985, p. 273) remain the same, the practical space, can modify or change according to the 'the activities, perceptions and bodily attitude of the subject' (Gell, 1985, p. 273).

For example Mavromichali Street appears in the map as the narrow street that connects Alexandras Avenue with Acadimias Street and the city center. However, it is much more than a connection line between two main points of the city. It can be argued that this street works as an invisible line that separates Kolonaki district, the bourgeois capitalistic space of Athens center, from Exarcheia, the space of radical groups, students, and bohemian youth culture. To navigate on Mavromichali Street means to navigate through the signs and marks that produce the arbitrariness of this line.

At the junction of Isavron and Mavromichali Street the two sides of an old building have been used as a scrapbook where free verses, pieces of newspapers, notes, poems and self-improvised rhymes of a political essence have been inscribed. Even though almost all walls in Mavromichali Street are marked with slogans or graffiti the signs on this building, which have been there for more than a year now, are refreshed and new ones are added, demonstrating patience and discipline. As this line extends towards the city center we find the Exarcheia Police station as another pole of these sites of contestation. Situated in the junction with Kallidromiou Street this police station is part of a zoning of control around Exarcheia and has been attacked with petrol bombs in several occasions during the last decade.

As a matter of fact, the entire city center can be navigated merely based on these sites of police control and blockade. Since the revolt in December 2008 the control zone around Exarcheia and the city center has radically changed, thus, forcing political practices to change and re-locate. Particularly Mavromichali is even more integrated in this zoning since the main offices of PASOK[1] moved from Charilaou Trikoupi to Ippokratous in 2009. For several years riot police that used to guard the old offices of PASOK were the target of attacks with stones and petrol bombs by youths and radical groups. The former offices of PASOK in Charilaou Trikoupi are just a few meters away from the place where Alexis Grigoropoulos was murdered by police on December 6, 2008. Across from these offices on March 2009 a parking lot was occupied by the people of Exarcheia and turned into the 'Self-organized Park of Navarinou and Zoodochou Pigis'.[2] After the main offices of PASOK moved in Ippokratous Street riot police increased in numbers and their zone of control expanded. They now guard the new offices but also, control Mavromichali Street junction with Navarinou Street.

To reach then Acadimias Street from Mavromichali Street one has to also pass through armed police in riot gear. Having said this, on days of national strike or other main political events that take place in the city center, the zoning of surveillance and control becomes even denser spreading out all around the city center.

Mavromichali Street ends when it meets Acadimias Street where the building of the Greek National Opera is situated. In January 2009 and only a few weeks after the December 2008 revolt it was temporarily occupied. The university building Irida, in the same street, was also temporary occupied during the last days of December 2008. For Gell, ''navigation' consists of a cyclic process whereby images generated from maps are matched up against perceptual information, and perceptual images are identified with the equivalent coordinates on a map' (1985, p. 280). In this kind of navigation though, the images of the past are also juxtaposed with the representation of the present, creating an obscure negative image that bears political connotations. The images of the 2008 December revolt are constitutive of spatial practices of disorder in times of 'crisis'.

When we reach Panepistimiou Street this collage of past images converges with present marks of burned buildings, broken pavements and ruptured marble staircases. Only this time they have been enshrouded behind construction sites or merely aluminum plates. Banks branches, the Starbucks coffee shop in Korai Street, the metro station staircase, bus stops, advertisement panels and telephone boxes bear upon them these marks. All the way through Panepistimiou there is evidence of this contestation over space.

Especially, Syntagma Square has been one of the most prominent spaces of this contest since 2010. Almost, every demonstration, sit-in or march has the objective to stay outside Parliament. This was even more evident during the three months occupation of Syntagma Square in May-July 2011 by thousands of people. Those who took to the streets occupied Amalias Street, the main street outside Parliament, and engaged with the public space of Syntagma Square in a unique innovative way. They stopped traffic, created assemblies, re-organized the space outside Parliament and contested the institutionalized framework of public space. In their effort to defend this space from riot police pavements where broken and used for ammunition, trash bins were lit to lessen the effects of tear gas, and several public or private materials were used as barricades or destroyed.

Since 2008 this pattern of disruption and destruction is repeatedly appearing in the city center of Athens. In the 2008 December revolt and the May-July 2011 Syntagma Square occupation, as well as other events of national strike, traffic had stopped and people walked in the middle of the streets or sat down and rambled around. The qualities of the public space changed from a space of transportation and commerce to a space of meetings and social interactions. Most importantly there was a significant change of the materiality of public space in Athens. If we see the attacks against specific material targets in public space as actions that transformed the urban motif, a pattern is revealed. According to Lefebvre (1991, p. 39) social space reflects a certain kind of political ideology. The attack then on traffic lights, pavements, numerous commercial billboards, bus stations and telephone boxes reflects a discontent with the existing reality as it is imprinted on public space (control, commerce, bureaucracy, etc.). These destructions, apart from a practical scope, which is to defend and to organize attacks or counter-attacks, are also an attempt to disrupt normality. The material world of the city center is being attacked because it works as its structural backbone and because it is a spatial representation of order and normality. However, this ferocious attack on the materiality of the city center of Athens does not emanate from a strategic assessment. It resembles a 'blow by blow' operation that, as Michel de Certeau argues, attempts to 'seize the possibilities that a moment offers' (1980, p. 6) and to use space in a tactical way inside the 'practiced place' (de Certeau, 1980) of the state.

Ways of walking in spaces of disorder

Athens has always been the site of protests, demonstrations, and riots. However, the last few years and especially since the December 2008 revolt, events of disorder have transformed. The rising number of people in the streets, the heterogeneity of participation and collective action and their political and social background, the spatial expansion and spontaneity of these events as well as the high level of violence are some of the most important differentiations from the 'pre-crisis' era. As a result, this change on the materiality of the city never really stopped. Even more, the everyday life of the city has been essentially marked by these events since the way people interact with the city has been essentially affected. Disorder has left its marks on the city center like in no other place in Athens. The spatial practices that constitute these acts of disorder make up another city in the city and create spaces (even temporarily) that challenge 'the univocity or stability of a 'proper'' (de Certeau, 1988, p. 117).

According to de Certeau 'to walk is to lack a place. It is the indefinite process of being absent and in search of a proper' (1988, p. 103). Likewise, crisis forces people to regularly re-position in the social field. The qualities however, of the 'indefinite process of being absent' are subject to change according to context. On a day-to-day basis, different people require different operational skills to navigate in the city. Consider this question: Which places represent what for whom? The walk of an immigrant street vendor in Ermou Street, for example, differentiates from that of a consumer. Ermou Street, the most commercial street in the heart of the city center, is constantly under the surveillance of different police units. In the same place street vendors demonstrate their merchandise by laying it on big sheets on the street. This is a collective work. Most importantly it requires constant mobility. In Ermou Street, in particular, the street vendors are constantly on the alert. Their sheets are laid down in such a way so that they can easily and quickly wrap it up with all the merchandise in a bundle and run off the nearby alleys to avoid police. A timid, tentative walk is then exercised by immigrants, which requires different rhythms of walking, stopping and running if necessary. In the same place different spatial practices are used in order to walk through it. For de Certeau the pedestrian movement is a specific pattern of specialized practice that makes up the city. Here we can add that this is a combination of heterogeneous practices that depend on situations. Characteristics such as race, class, and ethnicity make up the habitual patterns of walking in the city.

From above, the practice of walking may well resemble a swarming homogenous act. This is deceptive. The multitude, which swarms the city, is constituted upon a set of diverse spatial practices that converge. This coming together is a non-canonical pattern of diverse ways of walking the city. What is of issue is the political nature of this differentiation. In events of mass protest gathering in the city center of Athens the way that different people and groups create their path and inscribe their traces on space is indicative of the kind of politics that is being exercised. Walking in the city does not merely mean to move in predetermined pathways but to be able to make your own path (Ingold & Vergunst, 2008). The most common gathering points of a demonstration in Athens are the National Archaeological Museum, the Polytechnic School, Omonoia, Propylaia or Syntagma Square. In retrospect, these five points create a continuous line from Patision Street all the way up to Syntagma Square. In the city center police lines are set around to create a non-traffic zone and shops have closed. In fact, because of the frequency of protests and riots in Athens most of the major retail shops in the city center have set up roller shutters in their shop fronts. As the crowd slowly gathers at the starting point of the demonstration, police forces which, in this case have a critical role in determining and controlling the walking path and pattern of the multitude, have already organized their positions in relation to the 'designated' space of protest. Riot police are strategically positioned in relation to the collective walking pathway of the demonstration. Since 2011 in events of protests and demonstrations a metallic police barrier is also being set up in the beginning of Vassilisis Sofias Avenue to prevent protestors from reaching the main entrance of Parliament. In addition, police helicopters surveil the territory from above.

From that point of view, it can be argued that the city center is a demarcated and over controlled protest zone. It acquires the qualities of a protest space only within a certain timeframe. However, since 2008, there have been several examples when unrest inside this area was 'out of control' or even, when it expanded outside this area. Antonis Vradis calls this the 'termination of the spatial contract' (2011, p. 214). According to this idea public space can be contested as long as the practice of contestation is temporary. This secures that two main features will be indispensable for every protest: a) the protest can take place within a specific territory (read city center), and b) its temporality. Since 2008 both of these characteristics has been challenged by the multitude.

It can therefore, be argued that in Athens the characteristics of permanence and spatial expansion beyond the borderlines of the city center have altogether transformed protest events but also, the way people engage with the city on an everyday basis. What is at issue is that protest/unrest events and everyday life, which, prior to 2008 were relatively distinct, now seem to gradually converge. Even though in demonstrations walking differentiates from everyday pedestrian movement I argue that through sites, traces and situations of subversion and inversion the way we walk in the city has been ultimately affected by one another. What relates the two is that walking can potentially transform into a collective exercise.

In demonstrations the walking path is not limited to sidewalks and pedestrian crossings since traffic has stopped. Footsteps may follow similar directions but can choose alternative ways of walking towards the destination. In their singularity they connect with each other creating a set of arrangement that interrelates. Walking becomes both an individual practice and a collective operation. Footsteps collide, intersect, and separate; the same pattern is repeated over and over again.

Throughout the years people in protest events have learned to apply different spatial practices in order to make their own pathways. Inside protest block footsteps are defined by human chains that act as protectors from the police. There is a ritualistic tone in their walk, a lot of stopping and waiting involved depending on the circumstances and, as if in a procession, the rhythm is set by the slogans shouted from the megaphone. This is more evident in student militant left groups. The front lines of the main block hold a huge banner while the person with the megaphone walks a few meters ahead. When the demonstration begins, the megaphone sets the rhythm of walking. Then in coordination those in the front line start to parade. The slogan keeps the rhythm of walking and the block temporarily continues in this formation. Depending on the situation a block can have tight guard lines on each side of the body of the march. If there is no megaphone then the rhythm is set by the spontaneous slogans.

In demonstrations a variety of potential movement takes place. Tentative at times, definite and assertive in others, experimental or formalized, patient as well as impatient, all these movements are defined by the situation in which they occur. During the last few years this potentiality of movement in Athens has taken new forms and has acquired new patterns. While old ways of walking are still exercised, new ones have appeared that are constituted mostly around what can be called a tactical walking. I draw on the meaning of the word tactic here from de Certeau (1988). While strategies are organized structural projects that seek to colonize a visible, specific space, tactics, are by contrast, dispersed, concealed and transient. They are improvised practices 'in response to the concrete demands of the situation at hand' (Gardiner, 2001, p. 172).

> Lacking its own place, lacking a view of the whole, limited by the blindness (which may lead to perspicacity) resulting from combat at close quarters, limited by the possibilities of the moment, a tactic is determined by the absence of power just as a strategy is organized by the postulation of power (de Certeau, 1988, p. 38).

This pattern of walking during events of unrest in the city that defined the political practices of December 2008 revolt is increasingly becoming a dominant form of spatial practice. In the events of December 2008 it was small groups of people that followed the main body of the demonstration and organized on-the-spot collective practices. This spontaneity is defined by the situation and gives tactical walking the benefit of remaining uncategorized, unreadable, and un-symbolized by official power. In a discussion on spontaneity of collective action in Athens Dimitris Dalakoglou (2012) argues that recent spontaneous events, such as the Syntagma Square occupation movement, had such enormous social dynamics precisely because 'people in a sense were preparing for it and because it was in direct communication with some of the existing repertoires of resistance' (2012, p. 540). In the everyday life one way that 'knowledge' of spontaneous action is disseminated has to do with tactical action that does not entail an array of structural functions. For the small groups of people that continually re-assemble in different spaces spontaneous spatial practice is inscribed on various spaces in Athens as a set of traces.

These traces may become permanent either, as memories of symbolic action or, by having an actual effect on the organization of daily life. This way of walking challenges, altogether the experience of a demarcated, controlled, consumerist and surveilled city because it is constituted on a framework of acceptance of difference of practice and objectives.

In spaces of arbitrarily and antithetical activity walking becomes a method of training 'to deal with the daily challenge of alien and alienating territory' (Jacks, 2006, p. 69). To paraphrase Benjamin, walking in Athens in times of crisis requires a certain degree of schooling.

Lines of Disorder

There is something in common between walking in a demonstration, riots, a spontaneous march, the occupation of public spaces and navigating signs of disorder; if we understand all these as interconnected spatial practices of positioning and acting in public space then a pattern of interweaving lines appears. Such lines can be the product of different purposes and tactics as well as they can have a beginning and an end or they can be ongoing. In addition, they can be purely figurative/symbolic, as in lines that connect points and sites within the city. For example the regular route of demonstrations in the city center can be one of these lines. Most demonstrations begin in Propulaia Square, walk Panepistimiou Street all the way to Omonoia and then take the route of Stadiou Street towards Syntagma Square. Usually, this route ends where it begins, in Propulaia Square. A representation of this route will be a line that actually creates a closed circuit, with the same beginning and end (see image 2 above).

In another example, events of social unrest in the city center can be represented as an interconnected assembly of lines that have different directions and length. Such lines are the organic synthesis of heterogeneous practices. They are symbolic threads.

In the previous example the city center is the main site of inter-working movement that extend to line-threads as shoots grow from rhizomes. By contrast, lines can converge coming from different directions creating an active knot. In December 2008 when students took to the street they created small demonstrations in their neighborhoods. These small gatherings marched all the way from the peripheral districts to the city center and in particular, outside Parliament. Since 2010 several local assemblies have assimilated this spatial practice. In events of major protests and national strikes, neighborhood collectives/assemblies create small gatherings in their districts and collectively 'walk' towards the city center. Symbolically, these lines connect the city center with each district in the peripheries of Athens, thus, creating a common space where these local assemblies can meet and act together.

In this view, the Syntagma Square occupation in 2011 was a prime example of such political knots. The diversity of walking paths converged in the public space of Syntagma with the intention not merely to explore by walking the space but to insert new social and political modalities by 'not moving'. It was an assertive action to change the old lines and create another pathway to political practices. For me these kinds of lines resemble the 'lines of a meshwork' in the sense that Tim Ingold is using the term, as 'the trails along which life is lived' (2007, p. 81). Ingold borrowed the term meshwork from Lefebvre (1991) who talks of archi-texture rather than architecture in order to emphasize the importance of treating each site in its context, surrounding and associated networks (Lefebvre 1991, p. 118). Lines can also be actual traces on the body of the metropolis. Ingold (2007, p. 43) recognizes two main kinds of traces:

a Additive: when you create a line by adding a material
b and, reductive: when you create a line by redacting material from a surface.

In events of unrest and mass gatherings both kinds appear. Flyers, graffiti, writing slogans on walls, and throwing rocks are some of the ways to add a material on the surface of the metropolitan space. Reductive traces would be the practice of breaking pavements and staircases that create traces of violent rupture of public space.

In addition, there is the practice of reassembling or rearranging materials that are already set up in an ordered and established manner in the public space. During the course of events of social unrest, public space is marked by a number of different practices. Material damage, burning, and barricading are some of the practices that reconfigure public spaces and leave traces. These traces challenge the rearranged set of geometrical and social spatial practices in the everyday. What does it mean then to escape these categorical paths that are made up for us to walk and create other lines, other ways of walking and interacting with public space and the city? Can we actually escape them and what kind of walking would that imply? The city is made of everyday paths that people walk invent, describe, name, and imagine. These paths are lines that make up a map of social practices of being in the city. If events of unrest then represent a social and political situation of 'crisis' in the city, then the lines they create reflect the way people engage and react within this situation.

If we follow these lines closely we will see that not only they interact and intersect, but that they do so more in certain sites than in other. In specific places people's pathways meet more often and in some cases they converge, maybe for a while. But there is something more about paths and walking that create lines, which makes this inquiry interesting. These lines also transgress certain territories, they trespass, appropriate and leave traces in places where they 'should not', and by that, I mean that in Athens 'writing' on the path is a practice of reminding to the passenger the symbolic nature of this walk. As de Certeau puts it, in the everyday 'the language of power is in itself 'urbanizing,' but the city is left prey to contradictory movements that counterbalance and combine themselves outside the reach of panoptic power' (1988, p.95)

These walks inscribe memories on public spaces that challenge official interpretation of events. Official power requires the monopolization of public space in order to dominate memories. The interpretation of historical events by the state is critical in defining the meaning of the past in the stakes of the present. It has been argued that the way memory is constructed and used is closely related to the production of public space, since 'popular and official memories codefine (sic) each other, often in shifting relations, but the state controls public spaces critical to the reproduction of a dominant memory while marginalizing (sic) the counter-histories of peasants, women, working classes, and others' (Low & Zuniga, 2003, p. 22).

Casey makes a significant distinction between the terms collective and social memory and that of public memory in that the latter always occurs in a specific place (2004, p. 32). According to Casey this place not only lends itself to the remembering and facilitates it, but it also, 'in certain cases embodies the memory itself' (2004, p. 32). According to the same author this is because public memory 'is radically bivalent in its temporality, for it is both attached to the past (typically, an originating or traumatic event of some sort) and attempts to secure of further remembering of that same event' (Casey, 2007, p. 69). Casey asserts that it comprises two characteristics: 'it signals a major event in time that is a turning point for a given point of people, and it bears on particular places in which that event occurred and is remembered' (2007, p. 74).

The public memories, which have been ascribed to places in Athens, have defined the features of political activity. Public memory has a distinctive function in that it reaffirms a sense of collectiveness when different people ascribe similar values and meaning to a place. This means that a memory becomes public when a community or a group shares it - a process that requires active participation, and thus, no spectators.

Go vs. Chess: Positioning in Athens

What I tried to do in this short study of walking, movement, and lines, within the context of crisis in Athens, is to shed some light to a certain extent to the spatial practices of disorder. My primary goal was to give an understanding of change during this era as this is inscribed on the body of the metropolis. What is of issue is that the continuous events of mass gathering and unrest have an effect on the everyday experience of the city. This study then is about different ways of positioning in and interacting with the city.

To make my argument about positioning more explicit I draw on the oppositional qualities of the games Chess and Go as developed by Deleuze and Guattari in their book *Capitalism and Schizophrenia: A Thousand Plateaus* (2005). Chess, they say, organizes its properties around the codification of Chess pieces that 'have an internal nature and intrinsic properties from which their movements, situations, and confrontations derive' (2005, p. 352). Go pieces in contrast 'are elements of a nonsubjectified machine assemblage with no intrinsic properties, only situational ones' (2005, p. 352). This means that the qualities of each piece define its action in the field. While chess pieces function in a structural way, Go pieces apply tactics that emerge within a situation. Most importantly, both games reflect a totally different perception of space:

> in chess, it is a question of arranging a closed space for oneself, thus of going from one point to another, of occupying the maximum number of squares with the minimum number of pieces. In Go, it is a question of arraying oneself in an open space, of holding space, of maintaining the possibility of

> springing up at any point: the movement is not from one point to another, but becomes perpetual, without aim or destination, without departure or arrival. The 'smooth' space of Go, as against the 'striated' space of chess (Deleuze & Guattari 2005, p. 353).

By placing side by side, the 'smooth' space of Go and the 'striated' space of chess, 'the nomos of Go against the State of chess, nomos against polis' (2005, p. 353) we can now discern the features that make up these conflicting spatial practices. If Chess 'codes and decodes space', Go territorializes or deterritorializes it reflecting 'another justice, another movement, another space-time' (Deleuze & Guattari, 2005, p. 353).

The city is the setting of this battlefield of movements. In an era of crisis the establishment and conceptualization of public spaces as commercial, under surveillance, controlled and demarcated is constantly challenged by spatial practices of disorder. Power structures can no longer impose one line for all to walk, or an official navigation structure to validate one way of positioning in the social field. The lines of dissent express a daily conflict between different experiences and knowledge that shapes public space.

Part 2: Untold Stories

Chapter 5

Reactions to the Crisis: Collective Expropriation of Supermarkets

Margarita Komninou and Hartwig Pautz

Image 3: Expropriation of Supermarkets

Collective Expropriation of Supermarkets

It's Wednesday morning. Twenty-five people enter a supermarket. They take several goods (without paying) and then rush to a nearby street market where they distribute those goods for free. Why? (Tick the appropriate box)

a) Obviously, they are part of a marketing campaign.
b) They are simply tramps and thieves.
c) They believe that they are 'Robin Hoods' and will spend all

their life feeding the poor.

d) Because *we* decided to take back some of what belongs to all of us. To take back from those who steal our lives on a daily basis. Our aim is not to fill a few shopping baskets with goods. Rather we want to show how all of us can assert and manage the goods for which we are working as slaves so as to cover at least our basic needs. It's them, the big corporations, who are the 'thieves' in this story... (Communiqué, 2009).

Introduction

The financial, economic and political crisis, which began in 2008 and has affected countries in Europe and beyond, has created fertile ground for a variety of forms of grassroots politics and everyday political struggles to emerge. This chapter focuses on one such form: collective expropriation of food products from supermarkets in Greece and in particular in Athens.

A short excursus on where we locate our discussion of this phenomenon within the academic discourse is in place. For some time now, the concept of 'consumption' has generated debate. Here we contribute to this debate, as we argue that the sphere of consumption provides a point where the 'personal' meets the 'public' – a point where the numbers on bank statements become real problems in the struggle of individual everyday survival. In this chapter we are not going to talk about 'consumer power' – a term born out of market ideology and employed to strengthen capitalist exchange relations. Should readers want to know more about this view on consumption and consumers they do not need to go far; the latest trends in academic thinking embrace such views. There is a growing body of literature on 'political consumerism' and 'ethical consumption' that discusses and sometimes promotes the notion that a consumer has 'power'. Such perspectives understand our purchasing power as empowering; consumption is viewed as a new form of political participation (Stolle et al., 2005) and even as an alternative to voting (Shaw et al., 2006). Nonetheless, academia and marketing almost exclusively focus on issues of *choice* between products, and emphasize the role of 'morality' and 'ethics' in consumption (Clarke et al., 2007) by providing explanations, for example, as to why we (should) buy goods adorned with 'fair-trade' and 'organic' labels.

Instead, here we are interested in people who – as 'activists' rather than as 'consumers' – exercise their power in the sphere of consumption not through established mechanisms within the rules of the market such as boycotting or 'buycotting' (Friedman, 1996), but through market disobedience and in particular through acts of 'expropriation'. In our contribution we want to give space to one untold story of which many have been unfolding in the streets of Athens since the start of the crisis. An untold story of people entering supermarkets, grabbing basic food products and distributing them, for free, to whoever wants them. This chapter is based on secondary data (including activists' statements, published mass media outputs and documents sourced from Indymedia).

Consumption as a field for 'doing politics'

The collective expropriation we are discussing here is not a new form of rejecting and transcending 'normal politics' with their elections, political parties, parliaments, pressure groups and trade unions. In Europe, collective acts of appropriation as a form of practiced solidarity and self-help can be traced back at least to 1970's Italy, with the development of the *'autoriduzione'*, *'spesa proletaria'* and autonomist movements (Balestrini & Moroni, 1988). More recently, in 2002, the Catalan YoMango movement organized a day event of collective expropriation of goods in order to 'take to the extreme the free circulation of goods' (quoted in Andrews, 2005). In 2004, French electricity workers helped poor families to free power. In the mid 2000s, German activists claimed geographical mobility as a social right and denied the legitimacy of transport fares. At the same time, the 'Superheroes' (playfully masked activists) raided shops and supermarkets in the context of the Euro MayDays 2004 and 2005 (Pautz & Kominou, 2012; Hauer, 2005). Some activists see this form of political praxis as having the potential to bridge the divide between 'activists' and 'ordinary people' by addressing real needs while at the same time stimulating thinking about power and property.

The specific context in which such political activities have taken place can be described as 'state transformation' (Leibfried & Zürn, 2005). State transformation is a process in which the roles of the state are fundamentally challenged and changed; these changes affect economic, welfare and labor market regulations but also the overall legitimacy, as seen by its citizens, of the nation state due to the internationalization of state power and the loss of parliamentary control over politics. Some of the consequences of the transformation of the state consist of rising inequality, the crumbling of welfare state provisions, the increasing scepticism of citizens vis-à-vis their political institutions and the growing power of 'the market'. The current crisis, certainly in Greece, has accelerated some of these processes. The near-implosion of the political party system was illustrated in the elections of May 2012, where the two formerly dominant parties of the center-right (Nea Demokratia) and center-left (PASOK) received their worst election results since 1981. Only a combined 40% of the Greek electorate trusted these two parties, whereas even in 2009 they still held about 77% of the total vote (European Election Database, 2012).

We are examining a particular example of resistance to Greek state transformation and 'austerity politics' of which we think that it may have a transformative impact on Greek grassroots activism even beyond the crisis. To be more precise, we are looking at 'social crime'– to use Eric Hobsbawm's term (2001) by which he analyzed the meaning of social banditry in proto-capitalist societies undergoing drastic social change. The 'social bandits' who are the protagonist of this chapter are anarchist activists in Greece, active particularly in its urban centers and first and foremost in Athens. Between 2008 and 2012, they carried out over fifty 'expropriation acts': in groups of twenty or so, masked activists enter supermarkets, collect mostly basic groceries and distribute them among passers-by or leave them in the middle of a busy street market in socially deprived urban districts nearby.

These acts – which combine symbolic and practical solidarity with those suffering from the crisis with an open rejection of the notion of property – have remained limited to anarchist groups. This is despite finding widespread support, if opinion polls and anecdotal reports of spontaneous applause from the 'crime scene' are to be trusted. However, as we discuss in more detail later, these acts are part of, and have contributed to other forms of collective grassroots activity and solidarity in the 'sphere of consumption' in Greece.

In the following, we will focus on the Greek supermarket expropriators, place them into context with further moments of resistance in the sphere of consumption and tentatively discuss whether the ideas behind appropriation and price reduction praxis may have reached the Greek middle classes to develop a wider transformative impact on Greek politics.

'Taking what's ours anyway': supermarket expropriations since 2008

Between June 2008 and March 2012, over fifty acts of collective expropriation, all of them in branches of large supermarket chains, took place across Greece. The expropriations occurred in several Greek cities; while most were recorded in Athens, others also occurred in Thessalonica, Kavala, Xanthi, Larissa, Patra and Volos. In all instances, the expropriators appeared to be from local backgrounds and carried out carefully planned actions following a similar pattern.

The first of these collective expropriation acts occurred in June 2008, well before the 'December Riots' of the same year. Twenty unarmed persons entered a supermarket in the Athens neighborhood of Exarcheia – a poorer area with an anarchist political history – and left with trolleys full of basic foodstuffs. Immediately afterwards, the goods were distributed to random passers-by in a street market nearby, together with a leaflet addressing the issue of rising food prices. Exarcheia was chosen because it was familiar urban terrain for the expropriators. As one of the activists said:

> Our actions always take place in the working class and immigrant quarters, for example in Exarcheia, Agios Panteleimonas, Peristeri, Neos Kosmos. And always on days when there is a so-called people's market beside the supermarket and when streets are busy (Savra, 2008).

Indeed, street markets in Greece present opportunities to the expropriators to communicate with people on median and lower incomes, since 'the mood there is also a barometer for the mood in the population' (Savra, 2008). This first act of expropriation happened at a time of growing dissatisfaction with the center-right government of Kostas Karamanlis whose administration had been involved in a number of financial scandals since its re-election in 2007. It was also the time when economic recession started affecting Greece and worries over inflation and the rising cost of living were growing. After all, inflation reached 4.6% – its highest in a decade (Inflation EU, 2012) – and in particular food prices increased by up to 20%. This goes towards explaining why the reactions of witnesses to the expropriation and redistribution acts were usually 'positive and inspiring; in a few minutes the shopping trolleys are empty', as Savra (2008) narrated.

A further act followed in early September 2008 in Thessalonica. Again, about thirty people wearing black hoods expropriated a shop, part of the Masoutis supermarket chain. They took basic products such as pasta, rice and milk, and distributed them on a street market. Calling themselves 'Initiative Against Rising Prices', they presented their protest as resistance to 'the consumerist mechanism that places profits ahead of survival' (Communiqué, 2008b).

Then came the December unrests after the shooting of Alexandros Grigoropoulos on 6th December by Athenian police. For three weeks, between the 6th and 27th December, in a number of cities across Greece, disaffected protestors had running battles with the police. Government buildings, shops and banks were targeted with arson attacks. During the first three days of the riots, Reuters reported that already over 130 shops had been destroyed (Flynn & Kyriakidou, 2008). While the unrest was triggered by the shooting, it arguably expressed more than simply outrage over the deed; 60% of Greeks did not see the riots as perpetrated by 'thugs' but understood them as part of a wider 'social uprising', as a poll indicated (Eleftherotypia, 2008). Up until the riots, twelve incidents of collective expropriations of supermarkets had occurred. However, while shoplifting and looting of stores was a fairly common practice during the riots, only one incident of collective supermarket expropriation – i.e. an organized collective act with a specific political purpose – was reported during the riots. This occurred in Thessalonica on 17th December.

Acts of collective expropriation continued throughout 2009 and 2010 in the context of demonstrations, strikes and turbulent electoral politics that saw a PASOK government under Georgios Papandreou come to power in October 2009. With the crisis far from abating under the new government, expropriations continued. On 9th March 2010, a group calling itself 'Desperate Housewives' raided a branch of Sklavenitis, a supermarket in the

Athens suburb of Kaisariani as a reaction to the announcement of new harsh austerity measures imposed by the government. As a newspaper reported, there had been eighteen such acts in Athens and ten in the rest of Greece until that point (Vradelis, 2010). Four months later, on 7th June 2010, 'The 40 Thieves Without Ali Baba' entered a My Market branch at Egaleo, Athens and distributed their goods at a street market. Again, a few days later, in Thessalonica a group calling itself 'The Thieves' Thieves' (Communiqué, 2010a) took basic foods and destroyed the shops' surveillance system. Upon leaving they set fire to money from the tills and posted video footage on Indymedia Athens (The Thieves' Thieves, 2010). This is what the activists can be heard shouting on the video:

> We are anarchists. We might be covering up our faces but we are not going to harm anyone. We are just going to take some essential stuff and we'll leave. We want to do a symbolic act. We will take the money and we'll burn it outside (The Thieves' Thieves, 2010).

While these actions were non-violent, at least one involved the setting on fire of a supermarket in May 2010. A note, left by the activists, said: 'whatever cannot be expropriated will surrender itself to destruction' (Communiqué, 2010c).

It seems that the police was rather helpless in the face of the appropriations in urban territories that are often not easy to police; this was the case in particular when the expropriators made precautions by using 'garbage bins to close down some streets' and 'made sure that we knew of the police's moves before and during' their action (Communiqué, 2010a). Police spokespersons tried to play down the acts, at least initially: 'They have never stolen money or hurt anyone. They ask people to remain calm but use ambush tactics, jumping over cash desks. [...] When they attack without hoods, people are surprised to see that they are mostly women', as a police officer told the media (Reuters, 2008). The special Athens police squad formed in October 2008 to guard supermarkets has not been successful in preventing or interfering with expropriations. Until today, only in the city of Larissa arrests were made; a court trial against four activists was to begin in summer 2012.

The expropriations of 2011 culminated in five raids on Athens supermarkets between 19th and 31st December. Two of those incidents explicitly related to the supposed festive atmosphere of Christmas and New Year. When activists entered the Extra supermarket in Neos Kosmos in Athens on 19th December, they not only took basic products but also champagne, whisky, Christmas biscuits (*melomakarona*) and gift boxes. Similarly, on New Year's Eve, approximately eighty people – the highest number of activists ever to take part in a single action – raided a supermarket in Exarcheia and distributed the goods at a local Christmas market. The expropriation of luxury goods was, according to the distributed communiqué, an attempt to redress the inequalities experienced during the festivities by those without the means to participate:

> Within the framework of solidarity amongst the oppressed, and against the consumerist compulsions of our days, we expropriated goods from the supermarket Veropoulos […]. Our purpose is the redistribution of goods amongst our fellow people, in an attempt to break the climate of depression suffered by those who feel disadvantaged during these 'bright-holy' days, and who are not even able to buy the commodities needed to survive. […] We welcome 2012 with rage and class-consciousness, and we hope for individual and collective expropriations everywhere (Communiqué, 2011c).

With Greece entering the fifth year of crisis, most indicators show a continual worsening of the situation for the large majority of the population. Unemployment has reached an all-time high (2011: 18%; July 2012: 25%). In particular young people struggle in the labor market, as unemployment among 15 to 24 year olds has reached 55% in July 2012 (2011: 40%). Some are even talking about a 'lost generation' (Smith, 2011; Papachristou, 2012; Malkoutzis, 2011, Eurostat, 2012a). The costs of living have risen dramatically (Eurostat, 2012b) and images of people – not exclusively recruited from Athens' growing army of 20.000 homeless – looking for food in rubbish bins are ubiquitous reality in particular within urban environments. Lastly, suicide rates have increased sharply by 40% between January and May 2011 compared to the same period in 2010. Public health experts link this development to the crisis and compare it to similar observations in other countries (EuroHealthNet, 2011; BBC, 2012; Smith, 2011; Ethnos News, 2012).[1]

With the welfare state incapable of addressing the growing number of people who cannot cover even their basic food needs, civil society initiatives committed to the collection and distribution of free food and clothes to Greece's destitute and disadvantaged population have flourished across the country. In an attempt to regulate these initiatives, in 2012 the government announced plans to allow only official bodies including the Church, governmental institutions and certain NGOs to operate charity initiatives, such as the 'Together We Can' campaign.[2] No doubt, the expropriation activists understood this as a further reason to continue the practice of expropriation. After all, now solidarity acts were to be limited to a few institutions with a seal of 'approved' by the state so that, by implication, all other initiatives would be illegal.

On 10th of March, following the familiar pattern, activists raided a 'Veropoulos' supermarket branch in Ano Liosia, an Athens neighborhood. With the goods, activists distributed a leaflet entitled 'Charity: The Alibi of Barbarism' (Communiqué, 2012). Here, the activists addressed a concrete political issue that had so far not been explicitly part of the agenda of the expropriators' discourse:

> Living conditions have never improved due to charity and philanthropy of those in power. We only have to look at the so-called third world. The squalid living conditions co-exist with 'UNICEF', 'Doctors of the World' and dozens other charities. We believe instead that the only way out of the crisis is the struggle against all the oppressors of our lives and the struggle against the 'human-devouring' capitalist system. Faced with the hypocrisy of charity, we suggest self-action. One aspect of it is collective expropriation and the sharing of supermarket products at nearby street-markets. We, the ones at the 'bottom', for those of us at the 'bottom' (Communiqué, 2012).

As illustrated in the above communiqué extract, emancipation and self-praxis of those at the bottom layers of the society is – according to these activists – the only way forward. Under the motto 'Taking what's ours anyway', collective expropriation continues nowadays to be one more tactic in the pallet of protest tools for the Greek anarchist movement. In the section to follow, we discuss in more detail the political discourse underling these acts of expropriation as it unfolded through time and in relation to the framing imposed by the mass media.

The political discourse of the expropriators and their framing in the mass media

The supermarket expropriations in Athens and elsewhere in Greece are explicit acts of resistance against a political, economic and social system that the activists identified as dysfunctional. The crisis and the government's answer in the form of 'austerity politics' provided an opportunity framework for anarchist groups to spread the practice of expropriations. Equally important, the crisis has created the momentum to question anew the notion of property and to place resistance in the sphere of consumption besides the resistance in the sphere of production; in a time when the latter, through strikes and other trade union activity, has become increasingly difficult or even impossible given the growing precarity of employment in private, public and third sectors and the resultant lack of trade union power. The communiqués accompanying most appropriation acts and two more extensive pamphlets offer an insight into this political discourse of the expropriators. We decided to quote from these communiqués at some length for this section.

Activists consistently criticize the capitalist system as a failed system, responsible for the social inequalities and hardships faced by the underprivileged in Greece. Moreover, they criticize calls for obedience and dismiss hopes that a 'solution' can be achieved top-down:

> Today they tell us to share our poverty, to happily accept the ever-increasing intensity of exploitation, to be silent when facing mass redundancy, decreasing wages [...], to be patient because the legitimate economists and technocrats will find the solution (Pamphlet, 2011, p. 4).

The expropriators view their actions as a legitimate and emancipatory response, a grass-roots approach to the immediate problem of rising cost of living, public service cuts and growing unemployment. It is the surplus value of the goods stashed on supermarket shelves that legitimates expropriation. Ownership and property relations are contested, along with the monetary-exchange mechanism, which dictates consumption:

> The expropriations of supermarkets constitute the appropriation of products that we [should] own anyway by revoking in practice the money-exchange relationships, thus producing

> self-praxis and class solidarity (Pamphlet, 2011, p. 4).

Expropriation is viewed as one more tactic, a market-oriented act of resistance in the pallet of direct action. Activists call for this form of action to complement the social struggle that is performed through everyday life activities:

> Around us, a big chunk of the world lives in poverty, unemployment and brutality. [...] We are youth. Foreign. Locals. Students. Unemployed. Pensioners. Workers. We are those who live under oppression in every field of life. [...] It is time to wake up, to look around us, to act and to talk for ourselves and not through our masters. To define our needs. With equality, in solidarity, everywhere. With daily militant struggles everywhere. Squares, neighborhoods, associations, workplaces, schools, universities (Pamphlet, 2012, p. 8).

The political discourse of the expropriators has been, not surprisingly, distorted or ignored in much of Greece's mass media. Initially, as an activist said in 2008, media were reluctant to give the expropriators much coverage in particular after the 'president of the supermarket association threatened to sue TV stations should they report about the 'Robin Hoods'' (Savra, 2008). Despite this reluctance and the alleged intimidation of the media, it is remarkable that supermarket expropriators have not been vilified. In fact, within a discourse of 'justified grievances' the appropriators have benefited from relatively benign media reporting: 'They might hide their face behind hoodies [...]. However, they show a social face that moves the customers of the street markets', as a journalist reported (Ritzaelou, 2009). No doubt, journalists knew that as the crisis was hitting ever harder their readers would, to some degree and on some level, sympathize with such action directed against faceless supermarket corporations and their pricing policies. The distortion, as perceived by the activists, happened through the media's usage of the Robin Hood frame. The notion that they were 'noble robbers', doing for others what they cannot do for themselves, has been extensively deployed by the mass media to the potential effect that readers and viewers could sit back and expect the 'noble thieves' to take charge in the resistance against austerity politics. Naturally, activists see this frame as problematic and as a threat to their cause. The Robin Hood imagery was used only once by the activists themselves when they signed as 'Robin Hood, Zorro, Hulk and Others' (Communiqué, 2010b). Most communiqués bore the hallmarks of anarchist iconography, signatures reading 'The Raging Consumers' or more creative names such as '40 Thieves Without Ali Baba' and 'Desperate Housewives'. The majority of activists rejected this metaphor as it contradicted the meaning behind their direct action: the promotion of self-help and autonomous, leaderless collective action. The idea that they were committing 'theft', or that they were simply trying to restore an old and 'just' order, as implied in the Robin Hood metaphor, was also rejected. After all, the appropriators 'want everything for everyone' and their actions were to 'take back what always belonged to us' (Communiqué, 2011a; Communiqué, 2011b; Communiqué, 2008a).

In an attempt to highlight the misleading media framing, the 'Thieves' Thieves' – after an expropriation in Thessalonica where goods were kept by the activists rather than distributed – commented:

> From the beginning we had decided that the expropriated goods would be shared amongst the participating comrades and not distributed. With this choice we wanted to make clear that [...] the aim is not for some saviors of society to emerge. We want society itself to act and not to wait for a philanthropist 'revolutionary'. [...] When you are distributing goods

> it is not possible to know if the receiver is indeed in solidarity – even without acting it out– or just a hypocrite that cares for him/herself only and possibly will be the first one to give details to the cops in other instances. Of course we applaud similar actions from comrades that distribute the goods, since as we already mentioned above, the aims are the same. [...]. As for the term 'Robin of the Supermarkets': we perceive it constitutes one more classic attempt from the mass media to erase the original and ascribe a new meaning to these actions by portraying our comrades as an elite that steels for the poor, resulting in the distribution of the goods being presented in such a way that can lead to the narcosis and passivity of 'someone will think/act/care for us' (Communiqué, 2010a).

Despite the problems it generated, the framing of expropriation acts in the 'Robin Hood' terminology served as a catalyst for the development of the collective action itself. Activists felt misrepresented and therefore compelled to re-define and re-articulate the nature and meaning of their actions. Ultimately, this led to the development of a more concrete political consciousness of the specific act. This is particularly evident in the second pamphlet published in February 2012. Here activists reflect on past actions and on the specific media frame. They set out to produce an ideological backing of expropriation acts and tried to connect them with the sphere of every-day politics: 'we realize the meaning of such types of action, a fact that urges us to publicize and defend them in political terms' (Pamphlet, 2012, p. 2).

Is market disobedience a growing practice? Conclusion and outlook

By May 2012, fifty-three supermarkets had been expropriated. Of those, thirty-six were in Athens. In addition, one supermarket in Athens was set on fire in May 2010. Arguably, the praxis of supermarket expropriation represents one of the most radical moments of resistance to 'austerity politics' in Greece. But disobedience in the sphere of consumption has spread beyond the anarchist movement. One particular new movement is '*Den Plirono*' (translated as 'I Am Not Paying'). It started as action against road tolls in 2009. More recently, it took the lead in organizing local groups to oppose the cutting-off of electricity to people refusing to pay a new property-related tax that is paid through the electricity bill. Its resistance went beyond mere protesting as *Den Plirono* has taken direct action by re-connecting people to the electricity grid and by sharing DIY-information on re-connecting. *Den Plirono* also staged interventions directed at public transport providers by occupying metro stations and letting passengers use public transport for free. Lastly, supporters of this movement tried once to reduce supermarket prices through negotiations, albeit unsuccessfully. The movement's initiatives inspired the creation of a similar movement in Spain, the '*Yo No Pago*' movement, which campaigned against rising transportation costs in Madrid, Barcelona, Valencia, Seville and Bilbao in January 2012 (Alex B., 2012).

February 2012 also saw the appearance of the 'Potato Movement' (Henley, 2012). Set up by the local Consumer Union in the northern municipality of Pieria, the idea behind it rapidly spread across Greece. The Potato Movement urges consumers to collectively place large orders straight to producers in an attempt to abolish the middlemen and thus to reduce prices. To date, the initiative – greeted as well as criticized, for example by the Greek Communist Party – has successfully reduced prices by a third and consumers now arrange deals for oil, rice and meat products (Skai News, 2012b).

Another new development, demonstrating the anger and increasing despair of Greek citizens, involved German supermarket chain Lidl. In May 2012, residents of Xyrokampos in Volos besieged the local branch of the supermarket to claim free food for poor people. A residents' group named 'Open Meeting of Magnesia', whose members led their struggle under the slogan 'Free food for everyone', organized the action. To a local newspaper, one activist explained:

> It is inconceivable that the shops are filled with food, while hungry people are looking for food in bins and our children faint due to malnutrition! We require basic things to meet the needs of our impoverished fellow citizens who are suffering from the ongoing 'salvation package' imposed on us against our will (Thessalia News, 2012).

In this chapter we told the story of how a new form of everyday resistance emerged and developed. It seems that the crisis has already had a transformative effect on Greece's citizens who, in the wake of the near collapse of established political structures and living through the 'age of austerity', have lost faith in their country's future. After all, while expropriation of supermarkets certainly remained a new praxis of resistance limited to the Greek anarchist movement, other forms of market disobedience have been embraced by people and groups who neither share the same ideological platform and objectives as anarchists nor would have been politically active before the crisis; we briefly discussed the '*Den Plirono*' group to this effect.

Has collective expropriation become a successful political praxis against austerity politics in Greece? Expropriation (and distribution) expresses the rejection of particular social, economic and political conditions. Such 'social crime' (Hobsbawm, 2001) has the potential of becoming a culture of everyday resistance. Many in Greece's anarchist circles consider expropriation to be an appropriate praxis to bridge the divide between 'activists' and 'ordinary' people, in particular at a historical juncture with a government in meltdown, a retrenching welfare state, a catastrophic labor market situation and elites defending their privileges through an ever more delegitimized state. Thanks to the crisis and to the political action of expropriators, more people have started questioning the concept of property, existing power relations and the overall status quo. The resentment felt by many against public spending cuts, redundancies in the private and public sectors, transport fare rises, privatization of once public goods and services, the resentment against a discourse which preaches austerity to the majority of the population whilst remaining silent in the face of an ever-increasing gap between rich and poor, has further transformed into a thinking that goes beyond conventional 'reform ideas'. The '*Den Plirono*' movement and other attempts by local groups, constituted of formerly passive citizens and members of the middle classes, indicate such change. Maybe Greece indeed presents us with a scenario in which collective expropriation is successful as a method to forge links between existing 'resentment against state-imposed regulations and micro-political, often individual covert acts of appropriation based on anti-capitalist sentiment' (Kanngieser, 2008).

Chapter 6

Migrant Mobilization During the Economic Crisis: Identity Formation and Dilemmas

Georgios Karyotis and Dimitris Skleparis

Introduction

From the demonstrations and riots in Athens to the multiple nationwide general strikes, protest in Greece has captured worldwide attention, amidst the worst economic crisis of the country's modern history. Behind the headlines of austerity, however, another crisis, less visible but more persistent is also taking place, twenty years after Greece became unexpectedly host to large, mostly undocumented, migrant communities. A political crisis about the state's inability to develop a comprehensive immigration policy with a long-term view (Triandafyllidou, 2009; Karyotis, 2012). A societal crisis, with Greek public attitudes towards immigration remaining amongst the most hostile in Europe, according to Eurobarometer surveys (Karyotis & Patrikios, 2010). A humanitarian crisis, with international organizations like the United Nations High Commissioner for Refugees and civil society groups sounding the alarm over migrant rights and living conditions (UNHCR, 2010; Fundamental Rights Agency, 2011).

The Greek debt crisis that started to unfold in 2010 has further exacerbated these tensions and altered the dynamic between state, citizens and migrants. The result of the June 2012 Parliamentary election underlines the urgency to explore questions relevant to migrant activism and the migrant experience as a whole. Immigration, perhaps unexpectedly, featured as one of the hottest issues in the pre-electoral campaign. Parties of the interim governing coalition, PASOK and

New Democracy, who have taken turns to govern Greece since 1974, adopted a strong stance on immigration in an attempt to shift focus and minimize electoral retribution for their austerity policies. In the end, it was the newly-founded far-right 'Independent Greeks' party and the extreme-right 'Golden Dawn' who benefited the most from this polarization, with the latter entering Parliament for the first time with a shocking 7% share, up from just 0.29% in 2009.

These developments are hardly surprising: times of economic downturn breed intolerance and reactivate nationalist reflexes. With terms like 'ethnic purity' and 'racial unity' re-entering the public sphere, social tensions between citizens and migrants, as well as migrant activism, are a hidden reality of the economic crisis that is on the rise and hard to shake off. Examples of such racial tensions include the 2001 Bradford riots in Britain, the 2005 civil unrest in France, and the 2010 riots in Rosarno, Southern Italy. In the latter case, hundreds of mostly African immigrants clashed with police during a demonstration, blaming racism and their atrocious living conditions for the violence and carrying placards which read 'We are not animals' (Karyotis, 2011: 22).

Against this backdrop, about 300 immigrants originating mostly from the Maghreb countries and residing illegally in Crete, travelled to Athens and Thessaloniki in January 2011 and commenced a hunger strike, which lasted for 44 days. Supported by solidarity groups and Non-Governmental Organizations (NGOs), the hunger strikers put their lives at risk but achieved some concessions from the state with regards to their legal status. Their number, 300, is reminiscent of a heroic episode in ancient Greek history, where Leonidas and the Spartans willingly stood to their inevitable death against the mass Persian army in pursuit of higher objectives (Walsh & Tsilimpounidi, 2012). The difference, however, is that while the Spartans' sacrifice is glorified and celebrated, the migrants' battle soon faded into obscurity, after a short period of visibility.

The aim of this chapter is to analyze the migrant protest movement and particularly its attempt to create a collective identity through which it could maximize its pursuit of strategic objectives and increase its mobilization potential. Forming a collective identity is a crucial element in any protest movement, as it can facilitate its recognition by both prospective participants and outsiders. Identities are of course never fixed or tangible but they are rather themselves a product of social construction (Brubaker & Cooper, 2000). As Benedict Anderson (1991, p. 6) notes, identity is not something that is inherent in social groups and communities, but is constructed and transformed within and in relation to how it is represented. Therefore, protest movements and communities 'are to be distinguished, not by their falsity/genuineness, but by the style in which they are imagined'.

Framing is a key mediating factor in social construction processes, a notion that Wittgenstein (2001) succinctly captures, noting that language sets the limits of our world. When it comes to protest movements, imagining collective identities comes with risks and costs that have to be offset against any potential gains. How should demands be framed? What tactics are to be used to achieve objectives? What social networks and powerful allies may be brought on board to strengthen the movement and at what cost? To what extent do individual participants fit with the projected image of the movement's collective identity? These are some of the key questions that are central to understanding any protest movement and which are also very relevant to the migrant mobilization in Greece.

This chapter utilizes discourse analysis and a set of face-to-face interviews with migrant protesters and organizers of the hunger strike to analyze migrant activism in Greece during the economic crisis. It starts with a broad theoretical overview of framing, linking it to identity and the two dominant, competing frames that apply to immigration policy, the restrictive, realist one and the liberal frame. The following section provides a narrative of the hunger strike and draws on primary interview data to map the ethnic and ideological profile of participants and assess their migrant experience and evaluations of the protest action. The chapter proceeds to explore the framing of the protest movement by analyzing its official press releases during and after the action, as well the discourse of supporters and opponents, which, in different ways, challenged or supplemented elements of the projected collective identity. The overall analysis thus offers a comprehensive account of the protest movement, identifies tensions and dilemmas relevant to its attempt to construct a collective identity, and allows for the migrants' suppressed voices and untold stories to be heard.

Framing Effects, Migration and Identity

The framing literature offers a useful angle for studying the development of the migrant protest movement in Greece and for assessing competing discourses about its implications. In broad terms, framing involves making some aspects of a perceived reality more salient in discourse 'in such a way as to promote a particular problem definition, causal interpretation, moral evaluation, and/or treatment recommendation' (Entman, 1993, p. 52). Frames set the parameters and the points of reference for audiences to interpret, categorize and evaluate complex or ambiguous events, such as the migrant hunger strike (Benford & Snow, 2000). This may be achieved through subtle differences in the presentation of an issue or more direct attempts to draw attention to certain considerations, while ignoring others (Nelson, Clawson & Oxley, 1997). In that sense, frames can function like lenses that have the potential to shape the opinions of individuals regarding an issue (Iyengar, 1991).

In the political and social spheres, actors with vested interests are constantly engaged in framing conflicts about the correct or standard way to define an issue, each promoting a particular set of values and policy recommendations (Scheufele, 1999;

Lavenex, 2001). This implies that frames do not operate within a vacuum but are typically in direct competition with each other, while also constrained by 'pre-existing meaning structures or schemas' (Scheufele 1999, p. 105). Frames that are able to relate more closely to the specific socio-political and historical context and which are easily retrieved from memory are more likely to become dominant (Nelson, Clawson & Oxley, 1997). Successful framing 'occurs when in the course of describing a campaign, issue, problem, or event, a speaker's emphasis on a subset of potentially relevant considerations causes individuals to focus on those considerations when constructing their opinions' (Druckman, 2001, p. 1042).

In the area of migration there are two main frames competing for dominance (Lavenex, 2001). The 'realist policy frame' contains a prevailing interpretation of migration as a security problem. Rooted in a state-centric philosophy, the realist frame underlines 'the need to secure borders, restrict migration and homogenize all categories of migrants into a single policing-repression scheme' (Karyotis, 2011, p. 13-14). Irregular migration, in particular, is seen as a direct challenge to the legitimacy of the state, as it undermines the myth of control of its borders and many of its vital institutions, such as the army, police and the government (Anderson, 1991; Karyotis, 2012). When it comes to migrant protest movements, the only appropriate response from this perspective is, thus, to adopt a hard stance to suppress it, with the emphasis placed on the illegal status of participants, when this involves irregular migrants.

In contrast, the liberal frame shifts the focus from the state to the individual. Human rights considerations are at the heart of this approach, which is critical of the effects of restrictive policies on migrants' living conditions (Lavenex, 2001). Rather than seeing migrants as inferior or threatening, the liberal frame views them as potentially beneficial to the economy and deserving of respect, regardless of their legal status. In turn, migrant protest is understood as a symptom of an ailing political and social system, rather than as a problem in itself that has to be tackled with by any means. In an attempt to construct a collective identity, the participants and supporters of the migrant protest movement in Greece developed a discourse aspects of which relate to the liberal migration frame, as the subsequent analysis in this chapter will demonstrate.

The process of constructing a collective identity in social movement is, however, filled with dilemmas, tensions and the need for strategic decision-making. To begin with, for the protest movement to increase its external recognition, it has to appear homogenous and as speaking with one voice. Yet, fixing the identity of the movement in unambiguous terms endangers the possibility that some participants may not fit as neatly to the projected collective image and may thus be stripped from their individuality (Hekman, 2000). The question of how broadly or narrowly and in what ways to frame the scope and aims of the movement poses additional challenges. A movement with an all-encompassing and open identity maximizes its potential to mobilize new members, but risks losing its character and ability to differentiate (Jasper, 2004). Similarly, forming strategic partnerships with powerful allies, such as political parties or trade unions, to promote the objectives of the protest movement, strengthens the movement but may leave it exposed and vulnerable, should they decide to withdraw their support or attempt to exercise control over it for their own purposes (Gitlin, 1980; Chimienti and Solomos, 2011, p. 353).

To analyze these dilemmas and competing frames of the migrant hunger strike in Greece, this chapter utilizes survey research and discourse analysis. 52 face-to-face interviews with participants in the hunger strike were conducted in July 2012, using a structured questionnaire that included both open and closed questions. This was supplemented with a further set of semi-structured interviews with representatives of the social networks that supported the strike action. In addition, an extensive discourse analysis of all press statements released by the hunger strikers through their spokespersons was conducted, to explore their collective framing of the protest, in pursuit of set strategic objectives. Findings about the projected collective identity of the movement are contrasted to individual level data of participants, as well as to alternative discourses of opponents and supporters of the hunger strike.

Remapping the Profile of Migrant Protesters

Before assessing the profile of the migrant protesters through the analysis of scarcely available survey data, a detailed chronological narrative of the main events that led to the hunger strike and determined its course is required. Contrary to popular and media accounts of the hunger strike, it was not a spontaneous act but a carefully planned one, as revealed in interviews with protest organizers. It all started in Chania, Crete approximately 4 months prior to the commencement of the strike. Drawing on the experience of previous sporadic and fragmented migrant marches, and motivated by the worsening socio-economic conditions, a migrant movement with a more coherent basis started to emerge.

Social networks and NGOs were instrumental in the organization of the protest movement and in the construction of its projected collective identity. Members of the 'Migrants' Forum in Crete', a local NGO, conceptualized and penciled the hunger strike for November 2010 (Papagiannis, 2011), at a time when a new restrictive immigration law was being pushed through Parliament. A small core of volunteers initiated a campaign to recruit participants on a door-to-door basis. Concurrently, other volunteers went to Athens, Thessaloniki and Volos to mobilize further support, explore options and assess the feasibility of the planned action. After holding regular assemblies, a decision was reached to host the hunger strike simultaneously in the two major cities, Athens and Thessaloniki.

However, insurmountable obstacles at the planning stage forced organizers to postpone the action by two months. Eventually, on 21 January 2011, members of the solidarity movement prepared the ground for the imminent commencement of the strike, occupying and installing mattresses in an unused, newly refurbished building of the Athens Law School, a building which has a deeply symbolic meaning (Walsh & Tsilimpounidi, 2012). Other members travelled to Chania to accompany the migrants to the venues, on rented busses, where required. On 23 January, the migrants reached their destination, with the hunger strike beginning two days later, on the 25th. In total, 287 people took part, following a few last-minute withdrawals, 237 of them in Athens and a further 50 in the Labor Center in Thessaloniki.

Inevitably, the hunger strike, an unusual tactic which falls outside the normal 'protest repertoires' (Tilly, 1995, p. 26) and 'collective action frames' (Tarrow, 1992) in Greece, as well as in Western Europe, attracted significant national and international media attention and fuelled emotions of sympathy or condemnation. Support came from migrant groups and networks, NGOs, antiracist and university student bodies, labor associations, neighborhood initiatives, anarchist collectives, and political parties, particularly those to the left of the ideological spectrum. Some of these joined forces to create the 'Initiative for Solidarity', which, among others, organized demonstrations in support of the hunger strikers. The protesters themselves formed their own collective body, the 'Assembly of Migrant Hunger Strikers' (AMHS). They each held daily meetings separately but also communicated with each other and across the two cities through webcams.

Under immense pressure from state authorities, on 28 January, the hunger strikers were forced to evacuate the Athens Law School and escorted by police and members of the solidarity movement to the nearby privately owned building, 'Ypatia'. Removed from the public sphere (Mantanika & Kouki, 2011), the protesters complained that 'Ypatia' was unsuitable to host them due to space limitations, which meant that many of them had to sleep in outside tents. Meanwhile, in Thessaloniki, the action continued uninterrupted. In parallel to these, participants via their spokespersons and supporters tried to publicize their grievances through press conferences, interviews, distribution of brochures and the organization of concerts and marches, among others.

At all times, the solidarity movement's medical team monitored the deteriorating health of the hunger strikers. Seven protestors were eliminated from the protest on medical grounds on the 17th day and many others were hospitalized during the 44 days of its duration. Despite the realistic prospect of human lives being lost, which would damage the government's legitimacy and reputation (Dingley & Mollica, 2007), state representatives refused to meet with the protesters' representatives, until the later stages of the hunger strike. Eventually, on 9 March 2011, a deal was brokered to end the protest, in return for some changes to the participants' legal status. Their demand for full regularization was rejected but they were instead granted a biannually renewable status of 'indefinite tolerance', allowed to visit their home countries and promised to receive work permits that had still to be issued two years later. In addition, the government agreed to regularize all migrants across the country who could prove their continuous residence in Greece for at least ten years, knowing well that irregular migrants, in particular, would be unlikely to be able to provide the required supporting documents for this to be implemented, as past experience had proven (Fakiolas, 2003). Finally, the offer included the reduction of the necessary pension credits for the renewal of residence permits of all migrants from 200 to 120 per year, and the reduction of the essential credits for the issue of health insurance booklets from

100 to 60.

Our face-to-face interviews allow us to have a closer look at the composition and profile of the hunger strikers. Of the 287 participants, 100-120 had permanently left Greece and a further 40-50 were on holiday at the time the interviews were held in Crete, in July 2012. About 20 individuals refused the invitation to give interviews. In total, 52 interviews were conducted, each lasting approximately 30 minutes. The research was funded by the Carnegie Trust, whose support is gratefully acknowledged, and carried out in accordance with the standard code of practice for research including human beings; no individuals can be identified from the data collected.

All of our respondents were nationals of Maghreb countries, 48 of them from Morocco, 2 from Algeria and 2 from Tunisia. Most of the interviewees were in their mid-to- late 20s and single (92%). In terms of their employment status, 40% were working full-time at the time of the survey, 37% part-time, and 19% were unemployed. The majority of them found employment opportunities in the construction sector, as well as in the tourist industry

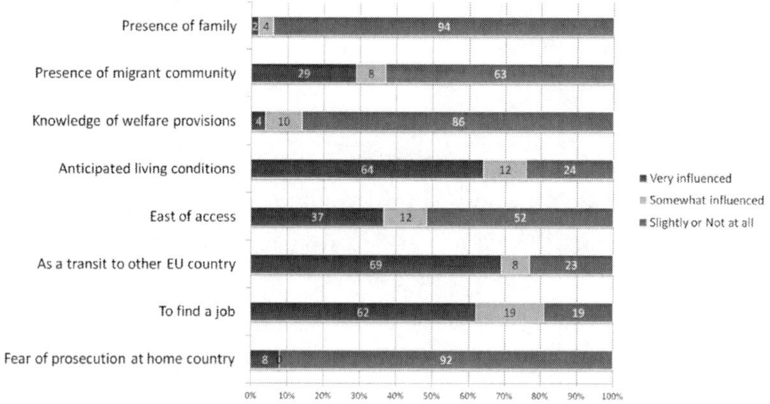

Table 4: Push and Pull Factors of Migration

Own data, collected July 2012. Question wording: 'To what extent did any of the following influence your decision to come to Greece (in %)?'

and agriculture. As was also the case with citizens, the impact of the economic crisis had been uniformly detrimental to their living conditions, with 90% noting that their life is worse (62% much worse) compared to before the crisis. Almost all respondents cited the reduction of employment opportunities as the main problem. The increase of racism and the prevalence of anti-immigration discourses in the political sphere was also an important cause of concern. Of those interviewed, a large minority, 46% had been a victim of either physical or verbal abuse, which is perhaps rather lower than expected, given their decision to participate in a radical form of protest.

Our data also allows us to see a snapshot of migration pathways and evaluate the participants' overall migrant experience in Greece. The majority of respondents, 73%, had been residing in Greece for more than 5 years. Only a small percentage, 9%, came to Greece regularly with a student or tourist visa. The remaining 91% entered the country irregularly via Turkey, through Samos (33%), Patmos (20%), other islands (18%) or the land borders in Northern Greece (21%). Table 4 plots responses about the drivers of their decision to emigrate. The most important motivation was to use Greece as a transit destination to another EU member state (69%). Pursuit of better living conditions (64%) and employment (62%) were also important drivers but not fear of prosecution in their home countries (8%). Findings also debunk some of the myths about other pull factors, such as the knowledge of welfare provisions and the presence of existing large migrant communities, which do not apply in this case. Overall, 40% expressed a desire to settle permanently in Greece, while the rest would seek to move elsewhere in the EU or return to their home country.

Table 5 plots the attitudes of protesters with regards to the main actors involved directly or indirectly to the hunger strike. Unsurprisingly, the solidarity groups (92%) and the strike organizers (67%) received the most positive evaluations. By

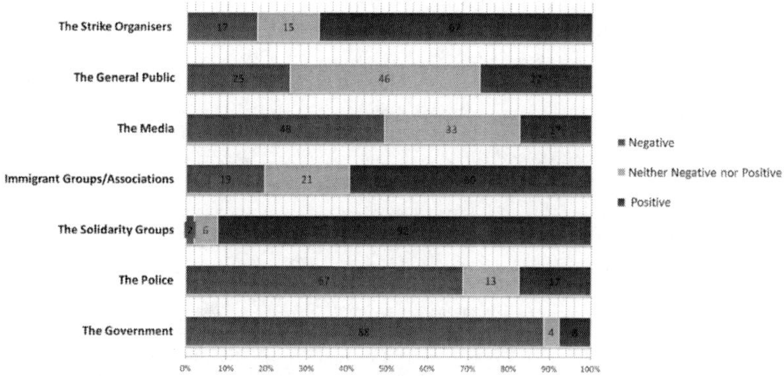

Table 5: Evaluations of Key Actors Involved in the Hunger strike

Own data, collected July 2012. Question wording: 'How positive or negative would you say the involvement of each of the following actors was in the strike action? (in %)'

contrast, only a small minority considered the government (8%) and the police (17%) as playing a positive role in the protest. Overall, the limited concessions offered by the state and its broken promises for further liberalization of immigration policy evidently left a sour taste in the mouth of migrant protesters. On a 0-10 scale, where 0 means 'not at all', and 10 means 'absolutely', the mean average of respondents' who retrospectively believed that the goals of the hunger strike were achieved was just 3.1, testament to their disappointment about its outcomes.

Framing the Migrant Protest

The economic crisis and the draconian measures introduced fuelled mass anti-austerity protest in Greece of unprecedented proportions. According to Rudig and Karyotis (forthcoming), 29% of the Greek adult population participated in either strikes or demonstrations in opposition to the measures in 2010, a level of protest that is only comparable to France of 1968 (Converse & Pierce, 1986). It is plausible that at such times of general mobilization and given the presence of a historically strong protest culture in Greece, particularly since the restoration of democracy in 1974 (Andronikidou & Kovras, 2012), migrant activists may have found the option of expressing their grievances through organized collective action an attractive one. The process of forming a protest movement, however, is inherently filled with dilemmas and challenges that directly or indirectly relate to its endeavor to project a collective identity. This section explores the framing of the migrant hunger strike, by systematically analyzing the main elements of the discourse of protesters, supporters and opponents of the protest.

During the hunger strike, the 'Assembly of Migrant Hunger Strikers' (AMHS) through their spokespersons issued fifteen public statements, which are the best source of information about the projected identity of the movement in an effort to attract support and legitimacy. In their first public statement on 23 January 2011, the protesters introduce themselves to the public as 'migrant men and women, refugees from all over Greece [...] [who] came here to escape poverty, unemployment, wars and dictatorships' (AMHS, 2011a). As the survey results in the previous section revealed, the hunger strikers were in fact only male migrants residing in Crete, not women, or refugees or pushed from their home country due to fear of prosecution. Participants were exclusively from Maghreb countries and predominantly from one state alone, Morocco. They already had an established identity and strong social ties after many years of residing in Chania, which, however, had to be re-imagined and reconstructed for the migrant protest movement to increase its appeal. The purpose of their opening statement is thus for the migrant movement to adopt an all-encompassing identity that should be inviting to the more than a million migrants and refuges across Greece.

Accordingly, the protesters underline that they are not driven by individualistic motives but act on behalf of and in the interest of all migrant groups in the country. In many cases, hunger strikes are associated with demands that relate to self, rather than others, or are an indication of underlying psychological conditions (Simeant, 1998; Silove et al. 2000; Fazel & Silove, 2006; McGregor, 2011). None of these apply in this case. The main aim of the collective action, as framed, is the regularization of all undocumented migrants in Greece (AMHS, 2011a). Furthermore, the protesters clarify that participation in the strike is a conscious decision: '[W]e are not mentally disordered. We started a fight through our own conscious processes. Our morale is very high and we don't need any kind of psychological support' (AMHS, 2011e).

The protesters opt for this radical form of activism fully aware of the risks they are taking. They repeatedly and emphatically state that '[w]e risk our lives because, either way, there is no dignity in our living conditions (…)' and '[w]e would rather die here than allow our children to suffer what we have been through' (AMHS, 2011a). Conviction that their struggle is a just one is omnipresent in their discourse and a source of commitment, self-legitimacy and even pride. The hunger strike is seen as their last resort in their pursuit of justice and a better life: '[w]e do not have any other way to make our voices heard, to raise awareness of our rights' (AMHS, 2011a). At the same time, the choice of this form of protest is aiming to exert more pressure on the government to address their grievances. In deliberately dramatic tones, the hunger strikers express their determination to 'exit this building either as winners or dead' (Dama, 2011).

Their emphasis in their framing of their collective identity as being first and foremost workers, irrespective of their ethnicity or legal status, is also strategic. They underline that their struggle seeks to 'send a message to every Greek and foreign worker to rise up […] This strike belongs to all of us' (AMHS, 2011d). On the contrary, their illegal status, which is a central aspect of their opponents' realist framing, is not hidden but attention is shifted away from it. They note that '[w]hether by regular or irregular entry, we came to Greece and are working to support ourselves and our families. We live without dignity, in the dark shadow of illegalness' (AMHS, 2011a). Projecting an image of them as being suffering workers, who do their best to provide for their families, is also meant to humanize their struggle and generate empathy among Greek citizens, who were experiencing relatable economic hardship at the time.

Furthermore, both the hunger strike as a form of protest (Simeant, 1994) and social performance (Walsh & Tsilimpounidi, 2012), as well as its framing as a labor movement are designed to appeal to left-wing audiences in particular. The protesters talk about 'the West', the 'multinational companies and their political servants', as being responsible for the economic crisis, echoing the discourse of left-wing parties (AMHS, 2011a). They reject the scapegoating of migrants for the economic problems and criticize the increasingly restrictive migration policies that only aim 'to resist attempts by working-class communities in peripheral countries to spatially reorganize their base of social reproduction in the global landscape' (Rodriguez 1996, p. 2). They recognize that their vulnerable position as illegal migrants enables employers and state agencies to benefit from the 'harsh exploitation' of their labor. Yet, they are keen to note that this applies to migrants and citizens alike and thus make a plea to 'our Greek fellow workers, everyone suffering exploitation, to stand with us' (AMHS, 2011a).

Finally, despite the role of various social networks in the organization of the protest, discussed in the previous section, the hunger strikers defend the independence of their actions against criticism that they are used by others to promote hidden agendas. They note that '[w]e take our decisions by ourselves during the assemblies we hold, and we do not get influenced by external factors' (AMHS, 2011b), reiterating in their follow-up statement that '[w]e, 300, took the initiative for that kind of struggle, without the intervention of political parties, organizations and individuals' (AMHS, 2011c). Along the same lines, they reject the notion that they are pawns in a bigger political game. They underline that they are not victims and they should not be portrayed as such: '[w]e are not those piteous, destitute migrants, deprived of housing, work and clothes that the media are describing'. Instead, they portray themselves as active political agents who 'came to fight, for as long as our bodies will allow us, for our rights and for a life with dignity' (AMHS, 2011b). The individual level data in our survey offer some support for this claim, as the majority of respondents were found to be interested in politics and holding post-materialist values with a left-wing orientation.

The discourse of the supporters of the hunger strikers is generally in alignment with that of the protesters, and particularly with the framing of the movement as a labor one. The Initiative for Solidarity refers to it as 'a struggle in the name of all workers' (Solidarity, 2011b), noting that '[i]t's on everyone's common interest (natives' and migrants') to get out of the grey zone. It's the only way to fight against undeclared employment («black work») [sic], exclusion and every form of exploitation' (Solidarity, 2011a). Similarly, the Union of Salaried Technicians (2011), expresses a view shared among most supporting groups that 'the migrants' struggle is interrelated with our own struggle for the cancelation of the policy that takes away the rights from workers and grants profits to the capital. It is a struggle against exploitation and oppression'. The exploitation of the working class is what unites citizens and migrants to a common cause. The scapegoating of migrants is seen as a direct assault to the rights of all workers, which serves the purpose of turning 'native workers against migrant workers, in order to create a division and instill fear among us, so that [the government] can continue unopposed to strip us of our lives' (Solidarity, 2011c). Supporters thus reject the 'us' versus 'them' dichotomy, arguing that '[t]he destitution of one segment of society signals the upcoming destitution of the rest' (Solidarity, 2011b).

The supporters also stress the political agency and independence of the migrant protesters, who decided to take this action 'on their own initiative and *without intermediaries*' (ibid, emphasis in the original). Similarly, Kokkino (2011), a component of the radical left party SYRIZA, emphasizes the political independence of the protesters and claims that 'a victory in their struggle will be a victory for the whole working class and youth'. Evidently, for the migrant protest movement, a consequence of inviting many actors, including political parties, to offer their support, is that they left themselves exposed to criticism that they are not autonomous, which both protesters and supporters are anxious to discredit.

Apart from these, the humanitarian element, a key aspect of the liberal framing of migration (Ellermann, 2010), is quite prevalent in the discourse of supporters. Many of them discuss the degrading conditions of social exclusion, prosecution and rising racism, which the migrants face in Greece (Oikologoi Prasinoi, 2011; Lathra, 2011). To generate empathy and relate to the socio-historical context, the Migratory Alliance (2011) also reminds the general public of the similarities between the migrants' circumstances and the suffering experienced by Greeks, 'in the not so distant past', when they were forced to emigrate 'in search for a better future, leaving behind their loved ones'. On the whole, Synaspismos (2011), the main component of SYRIZA, concludes that the hunger strike is a 'cry of desperation', with the Initiative for Solidarity (2011c) referring to it as 'a cry for dignity and humanity'.

Nevertheless, this humanitarian element is rather understated in the protesters' own framing of the hunger strike. A likely explanation for this is offered by the Migrants' Forum in Crete (2011), an NGO that was central in the organization of the hunger strike, as discussed in the previous section. In line with the protesters discourse, the Migrants' Forum sees the hunger strike as 'neither desperate, nor dead-end, nor hopeless' and the hunger strikers as 'pioneers of the migration movement', who constitute 'by far its most progressive part'. Strategically framing the hunger strike as a political act, rather than an act of desperation is a key aspect of the migrant movement's collective identity, which will allow it to project a stronger sense of political agency, longevity and sense of purpose, beyond the hunger strike itself. There were, of course, many who were critical of and even angered by the migrant hunger strike. Unsurprisingly, their discourse emphasizes a different set of considerations than those discussed above, ones that are informed by the realist, restrictive frame of migration. A key focus of these is on the migrants' illegal status, as well as the illegality of their occupation of the Law School and the Labor Center, which is described by an MP for center-right New Democracy as an 'invasion' (Antzoletos, 2011). Taking it a step further, the extreme-right, xenophobic party Golden Dawn (2011) cynically claims that these buildings have become 'a hotel for illegal migrants', and that if 'the 'antiracists' really believe in what they preach, they should take the foreigners in their homes'!

Another common theme in the opponents discourse is the representation of the hunger strikers as powerless victims, who are being exploited by some of their supporters to serve ulterior political interests and who are themselves incapable of any political agency. This is a view expressed not only by the socialist PASOK government and right-wing parties but also by parties of the left, such as the Greek Communist Party (KKE, 2011) and the Democratic Left (DIMAR, 2011). Indicatively, the Minister of Education, Anna Diamantopoulou argues that these 'unfortunate people that are in the Law School, did not find themselves there by chance. They were led and guided there'. She continues that the fact 'that political forces provocatively exploit human agony, in order to serve party interests, while abolishing university freedoms, is frustrating. The transformation of the Law School into a migrant camp is beyond the limits of tolerance' (Ministry of Education, 2011). Such claims seek to undermine the legitimacy of the protest movement. Furthermore, from the perspective of the government, diffusing blame is necessary in order to pre-empt and prevent a general outcry in the event of the death of any of the hunger strikers. Characteristically, the socialist Minister of Labor, Giannis Ragousis notes that the hunger strike 'is unfolding with the responsibility of the political guides, who are to blame for whatever is happening' (Star, 2011).

Finally, the realist framing of the migrant protest emphasizes the threats it poses to the security of the state and society. The hunger strike is framed as a threat to public order, with the Minister of Citizen Protection, Christos Papoutsis noting that such mobilizations can only create more social tensions and 'must be avoided by any means' (Enet, 2011). It is also seen as a threat to public health, with Andreas Loverdos, Minister of Health describing the protesters as a 'bomb of infections' (To Vima, 2011). Part of what makes them dangerous and inferior is their difference, a dominant frame in the securitization of migration (Huysmans, 2000; Karyotis, 2012). For instance, Anna Dalara, deputy Minister of Labor, states that 'these people [the protesters] do not have culture, they are different' (Flash, 2011). For others, it suffices to claim in vague terms that irregular migration 'undermines the security of our country' (Antzoletos, 2011), which in turn means that any support or sympathy for their struggle is unjustified.

Conclusion

The analysis in this chapter has illustrated the importance of framing battles that surround a protest action, such as the one undertaken by the 300 migrants in Greece in early 2011. For the protesters, the challenge was to project a collective identity with the greatest possible appeal, re-interpreting their existing identity as a predominantly ethnic community residing in Crete. Their decision to underplay humanitarian considerations in their discourse and instead present themselves as part of a labor movement was successfully designed to attract support and sympathy from other sections of society, particularly those in the left of the ideological spectrum. In their discourse, they thus strategically emphasized their commonalities with native workers, who are equally exploited by the government and capitalist elites, and who are also suffering by the austerity measures during the economic crisis. A similar finding is reported by Iskander (2007), who notes that the undocumented migrant protest in France in the late 1990s was also at its base a labor protest movement.

A side effect of this framing, however, was that the migrant protesters left themselves exposed to criticisms about their sincerity and autonomy of action, an issue that was underlined in the opponents' framing of the hunger strike. In the end, the migrants' protest may have reached the hearts and minds of many in Greece (Walsh & Tsilimpounidi, 2012) but did not result in a significant change in the state's immigration policy, as hoped. What it did achieve, however, was to plant the seed for the development of a stronger migrant movement, which may in the future be able to build on the measured success of the hunger strike and collectively work to advance the rights of all migrants. The formation of a new centralized migrant body in November 2012, which represents twenty different ethnic and migrant communities in Greece is a step in this direction (see TVXS, 2012).

Chapter 7

Crime and Politics in the Greek Crisis: Corruption, Common Crime, and Organized Political Violence

Sappho Xenakis and Leonidas Cheliotis

A number of studies in Britain and the United States have shown that adverse economic conditions, from unemployment and poverty to income inequality and a sense of relative deprivation, are linked to a growth in crime, especially in property and violent offences. There exist various and often tangled explanations as to how economic factors impact upon levels and patterns of crime. Unemployment, for example, is thought to strengthen the temptation to commit offences, but also to enhance the emergence of other instigators of crime such as lack of education and housing. It might thus be reasonable to assume that the 'credit crunch' of the late 2000s has fuelled a significant rise in property and violent crime on either side of the Atlantic. Available empirical evidence, however, suggests that the long-term trend of falling crime rates in the cases of Britain and the US has not undergone a reversal.

The relationship between economic recession, on the one hand, and levels and patterns of crime, on the other hand, has yet to receive sufficient criminological attention in the context of non-Anglophone jurisdictions, even though a broader international comparative analysis would seem necessary in order to better test this relationship. This brief essay focuses on Greece, a country that has in recent years found itself in the midst of a deep economic crisis. The Greek experience reveals that the economic downturn may be associated, in varying degrees, with a wider range of criminal behaviors than is typically acknowledged. It also illustrates that, just as politics has shaped the financial crisis itself, so too it has infused perceptions of the connection between the crisis and crime.

Financial crisis in Greece

In 2009, the OECD reported that Greece had proved to be better insulated than many of its fellow OECD member-states from the global financial crisis that had been triggered by the US sub-prime mortgage crisis of 2007. Within the space of a few short months, however, the revelation of Greece's own domestic financial crisis saw the country newly assessed as a major risk to the financial health of both its European counterparts and the broader international environment. Whilst all European economies were suffering from the reduction in liquidity caused by the global downturn, the emerging sovereign debt crisis of Eurozone member-states was proving to be most severely experienced in Greece. In response to Greece's admission in November 2009 that it was facing unmanageable levels of public debt, a succession of bailout packages were engineered by the Troika –the European Commission, the European Central Bank and the International Monetary Fund– each of which provided loans to Greece with the condition that the country implement a wide array of austerity measures, from spending cuts and public sector lay-offs to tax rises and the privatization of public assets. Whilst subsequent assessments of the effectiveness of the Greek state in imposing such measures and thereby lowering the deficit have been mixed, there has been little sign of equivocation in judgments of the social impact of the measures.

Even before the crisis, Greece had persistently manifested one of the highest levels of income inequality and poverty in Europe. With the imposition of austerity came surging levels of unemployment, which rose from 6.6% in May 2008 to over 21% by March 2012, with one in every two young people under 25 years of age being without a job. Living standards dropped, falling particularly sharply from late 2010 onwards (as evident, for example, from surveys of gross disposable household income and material deprivation). If income losses have been larger for wealthier proportions of the population in absolute terms, poorer groups have still suffered disproportionately from a significant drop of income. Relatedly, then, there has been a dramatic rise in negative health outcomes (including elevated rates of suicide) caused by cuts to health and welfare spending and the intensification of a gamut of socio-economic pressures on families and individuals (see, e.g., Kentikelenis et al., 2011).

Despite the commonplace inclination of political, media and scholarly commentators to reflect on the relationship between this litany of harmful developments and the 'problem of crime' through the narrow prism of property and violent interpersonal offences, we suggest that the relationship between crime and financial maelstrom in contemporary Greece is more clearly and accurately addressed from a broader perspective that additionally includes consideration of corruption and organized political violence.

Corruption

As the vast majority of domestic and international observers of the Greek crisis have reported, corruption has been a key factor contributing to the emergence of the country's financial crisis, organically related to over-expenditure and mismanagement of public funds. Successive scandals have illustrated, for example, the major role played by clientelist logics in determining the awarding of state contracts to civil and defense projects that are often of questionable merit (defense contracts being particularly significant for a country that has consistently spent one of the highest proportions of its GDP amongst NATO allies on defense). Clientelist forms of corruption have also lain behind the repeated provision of ad hoc exemptions and post hoc legalization to unfair and illegal practices (such as the regular pre-election wave of legalizations granted to illegally renovated and constructed properties), and the routine support for unnecessary and under-qualified public sector appointments.

The two political parties that alternately dominated government over the past thirty years (PASOK, on the center-left, and New Democracy, on the center-right) have readily resorted to the argument that all levels of society are to blame for the crisis, although emphasizing the responsibility of civil servants and the general public for colluding in practices of patronage and petty corruption. This argument has done little to mollify public frustration with patterns of grand corruption in which political, media and business elites have incessantly been implicated. Such frustrations have long stood at a very high level by European comparison, but they saw intensification following the onset of the crisis, and have increasingly turned to anger. Indeed, in combination with vocal criticism from foreign observers, the exasperation of the domestic public has placed significant pressure on Greek politicians to put a halt to treating elite corruption with impunity. Unfortunately, this has been pressure which they have proved overwhelmingly able to resist; notwithstanding the indictment of a former Minister of Defense in 2012, members of parliament displayed remarkable audacity when in 2011 they absolved themselves of any responsibility for the two largest cases of corruption to rock Greek political life in recent years: the Vatopedi and Siemens scandals. Both of these implicated members of PASOK and New Democracy, and concerned, respectively, a monastery land-swap arrangement, and security systems and telecommunications contracts (see further Xenakis, 2011).

To understand just why it is that mainstream politicians in Greece have remained so willing to maintain impunity towards elite corruption, given not only its role in generating the current crisis, but also the fact that public animosity has grown to such levels that politicians from PASOK and New Democracy have become unable to appear in public without risk of assault, it is necessary to acknowledge the way in which elite corruption has long functioned as a prerequisite to the maintenance of elite consent to the political status quo in the country. Moreover, an appreciation of the significance of elite corruption within Greek public life today is key to recognizing the political imperatives of shifting public attention instead to the risks of property and violent crime.

Property and violent crime

In the wake of the recent and ongoing financial crisis in Greece, public fears about property and violent crime appear to have risen dramatically, often in association with heightened concerns about illegal immigration into the country, as well as drug abuse and related offending. These sentiments have been fuelled in no small part by political, media and scholarly discourse that cites police-recorded crime statistics (which have been made available online by the Hellenic Police and the Ministry of Public Order and Citizen Protection) showing a significant growth in thefts, burglaries and robberies over this time span. Between 2009 and 2011, for example, the total annual volume of burglaries and thefts rose by 33%, from 72,658 to 96,925, whilst the respective volume of robberies increased by 41%, from 4,708 to 6,636. Amongst offenders known to the police, Greeks were responsible for the majority of burglaries and thefts, but non-Greeks were over-represented in proportion to their share of the general population. As far as robberies are concerned, however, non-Greeks were both the majority of known offenders and were again proportionately over-represented.

Alas, such data have helped to retrospectively justify what have been longstanding trends of disproportionately high levels of public fear of criminal victimization, but also of public support for the harsh punishment of common offenders, especially of immigrant origin, as this has been practiced by the Greek state for decades now and has intensified more recently. Indeed, over the three decades that preceded the crisis, Greece became one of the most crime-fearing and punitive nations in Europe and beyond, even though police-recorded crime rates in the country were low by European comparison, rose only modestly, and most of this rise was due to offences of little criminological interest (e.g., traffic offences such as speeding and illegal parking) (see further Cheliotis & Xenakis, 2010; 2011).

It is plausible that levels and patterns of public fear of crime, as well as of punitiveness, still remain incommensurate to the actual levels and patterns of criminal victimization. For instance, the occurrence of certain types of violent crime has fallen since the onset of the financial crisis, whilst the percentile rise in the occurrence of other types of violent crime is far less impressive when expressed in terms of absolute numbers and compared to the pre-crisis period. Thus, between 2009 and 2011, the total annual volume of police-recorded rapes decreased by 20%, from 214 to 172, whilst the 29% growth in the respective volume of homicides, from 143 to 184, did not exceed the peak rate experienced in recent decades. Also, the participation of Greeks in thefts and burglaries has risen much more starkly since 2009 than that of non-Greeks, whilst non-Greek participation in robberies actually shrank between 2010 and 2011.

In any case, there are multiple reasons why police-recorded crime statistics in Greece need to be treated with particular caution when used as a proxy for actual crime rates. These range from the reported ease with which the Greek police file unwarranted charges, to their systematic over-policing of immigrant communities (including so-called 'sweep' or 'cleaning' operations and a propensity to stop-search and arrest immigrant individuals to a greater degree than Greek persons), to the tendency of Greek citizens to report crimes to police authorities even when cases are frivolous and their specifics largely uncertain, just as they are more likely to report crimes when offenders are believed to be immigrants (see further Cheliotis & Xenakis, 2011). At least some of these pitfalls could be overcome by comparing police-recorded data against prosecutorial and judicial data for the same period, but the Ministry of Justice has not publicized prosecutorial and judicial data since 2009; the year that it was renamed the Ministry of Justice, Transparency and Human Rights.

Organized political violence by sub-state groups

Perhaps the most dramatic concern expressed by domestic and international commentators about the relationship between economic downturn and lawbreaking in Greece has related to political violence perpetrated by sub-state groups. This apprehension has not been surprising, given that less than a year before the crisis broke the country had experienced its worst social unrest for decades. There had also been a significant re-emergence of covert politically violent organizations since the mid-2000s. Moreover, within a year of the economic crisis erupting, an incident in which a mass protest against austerity coincided with covert organized political violence saw three civilian fatalities (Xenakis, 2012). The most melodramatic prognoses about the impact of the crisis in fuelling political violence have, nevertheless, not yet been realized; not, at least, from the quarters most expected: covert organized covert groups identified as anarchists and far-leftists that are willing to use violence in support of their political campaigning.

Following a series of arrests and weapons seizures in 2010, during the very time frame in which the impact of the crisis was increasingly being felt by Greek society and by the youth in particular, political violence from sub-state covert groups to the far-left of the political spectrum radically diminished. Equally, by summer 2012, there had been no repeat of social disorder to match the month-long unrest of December 2008. On the other hand, covertly organized political violence by the far-right continued the ascent it had begun over the 2000s. By the late 2000s, far-right groups were already bold enough to patrol immigrant-dense districts of Athens in platoon-like formations of around thirty to forty black-clad and capped individuals armed with sticks, and to engage in violent assaults against immigrants and their property in broad daylight (on occasion, also, to do so in front of the police). By 2012, black-clad foot and bike patrols were reported to be regularly carrying out serious attacks on immigrants and their property in Athens.

Over this timeframe, whereas police operations against protesters from the left of the political spectrum escalated – Amnesty International (2012) reported, for example, that the number of cases alleging excessive use of force and other illtreatment against peaceful protesters by the police rose significantly between 2010 and 2012 – the police were accused of failing to take action against, or even to be complicit with, violence perpetrated by far-right groups. Police inaction or complicity has been indicative of the broader reluctance of the Greek state to see far-right and racist violence monitored, prosecuted, or punished.

Unfortunately, despite NGO efforts to draw attention to far-right and racist violence, these issues have commonly been neglected by political, media and scholarly commentators on political violence in Greece, and it was only the success of the fascistic far-right party Chrysi Avgi ('Golden Dawn') in the general election of May 2012 and their ensuing entry to parliament that catapulted organized political violence by far-right groups into the mainstream political spotlight. Even so, a notable degree of ambivalence towards organized violence by the far-right has remained apparent in public discourse, reflecting the breadth of public support that far-right sentiments have gained over recent years. This is a development that has been sustained not only by the exacerbation of domestic socio-economic tensions over the same period, but also by the opportunism of PASOK and New Democracy to exploit xenophobia, and anti-immigrant attitudes more particularly, in their efforts to distract attention from public discontent about the role these parties have played in fomenting financial crisis and in inequitably distributing its negative ramifications upon the citizenry (Xenakis, 2012).

Concluding remarks

As suggested by this brief essay, the relationship between crime and the financial crisis in Greece has been non-linear, irregular, and complex. Core concerns about the impact of economic upheaval upon Greek society have encompassed dimensions of lawbreaking that go beyond property and violent crime, without, however, treating them as part of the 'crime problem'. Furthermore, there are important connections between corruption, property and violent crime, and organized political violence, with the crisis playing a central part in bringing these to the fore. Equally, the linkages between such forms of illegality have been highly politicized, and recognition of this point is vital to avoid analytical entrapment in narrow terms of reference that serve to convenience particular political constituencies. To account specifically for the intensified preoccupation with property and violent offences in recent years in Greece, three factors are of paramount importance: first, that the financial crisis has had a role in fuelling a rise in at least some of these offences; second, that against the backdrop of the crisis, mounting experience of state impunity towards grand corruption scandals has strengthened the need for political elites to divert public attention towards property and violent offences (particularly towards offences attributable to weak minorities); and third, that this imperative has become all the more pressing given the constraints posed by the crisis on the use of clientelism, itself another longstanding means of assuaging socioeconomic strains amongst the public.

Part 3: If These Walls Could Talk

Chapter 8

Testimonies and Appraisals on Athens Graffiti, Before and After the Crisis

Orestis Pangalos

Description

Nowadays, in the Athens of change and transition of day to day individual and public life, of peoples' psychology and of the general atmosphere of the city, we observe an unforeseen concentration of writings (the whole spectrum of graffiti practices and versions) on the city's vertical surfaces, rendering it one of the most "stained" and "saturated" cities in the world.

This can be witnessed along the track line of the Athens to Piraeus railway (ISAP) (in and off the tracks), along motorways like the Attic highway, Kiffisias street and the national highway No1 to Lamia and Thessaloniki, Katehaki Street and the Imittos ring road. This can also be seen in the underground motorways below Syggrou street and their underpasses, in inner city streets like Vouliagmenis and Piraeus street, in special areas, such as Plaka, Monastiraki, Exarcheia and all along the city sectors that lie within these areas, in Keramikos, in Gazi, in Psirri and all over the center of the city, outside gyms, schools and in city squares, backstreets, bus stops and along bus routes all around Attica. Moreover, it can be observed on benches, bar rest rooms, surfaces such as shop window blinds, the showcases of closed down stores, abandoned billboards and plexiglass noise barriers. The same applies to abandoned buildings, both to their external and interior surfaces, to their rooftops and backsides and to trains, as well. Almost every carriage of the state carrier (OSE) and the Athens to Piraeus railway is sprayed all over below its windows. The trains are guarded during the night (but not always) and are not buffed or cleaned up from graffiti, anymore.

With all the above in mind, the scope of this chapter is to isolate the process that caused graffiti to multiply in Athens and investigate to what extent its proliferation is linked to the advent of the crisis and the conditions preceding it and also, to examine whether and if so, in which cases graffiti responds directly or indirectly to the crisis itself. For this very reason, we will have to visit the whole spectrum of intervention practices on city walls and revisit the various terms that have been given to them, so as to specify the case that is of interest to us. Finally, we will attempt to analyze the variety of ways that a piece of work can be termed political and present a number of examples first from abroad and later on from Greece itself, both from the past and today.

Terminology and classification: Graffiti, street art and slogans.

Until the late sixties, the term graffiti was used to describe any kind of older or modern scribbling in public view on archeological sites, monuments and artifacts or in the urban or rural environment, painting, drawing or representation made by citizens, travellers, wanderers, soldiers, (certainly not by an official authority or proprietor). From 1971 onwards, the term is used to describe, apart from the above, the tag epidemic that hit Philadelphia and New York that was carried out by youngsters in their early teens that termed their practice as writing. The tags, soon evolved into large-scale murals on New York's subway system and the practice, in conjunction with the works themselves, formed a whole new culture. The term writing was gradually replaced by the word graffiti, while other terms that were used to describe the movement were the terms spraycan art, subway art, aerosol art, graffiti art, aerosol culture or even, hip hop graffiti.[1]

The people that did graffiti called themselves writers, in the tradition of writing as their fundamental act, that was scribbling-writing, and they are still called so today. From this point on in the text, we will use the word graffiti only to describe the above practice, its works (in their whole spectrum as tags, bombs, train jobs and legal or illegal pieces) and its culture and not other scribbling and practices on the walls (despite the fact that these too are part of the great family of wall scribbling that could be called graffiti).

Jack Stewart observed and studied graffiti since its infant steps in New York City and followed its evolutionary process (in form and content) on the trains until 1978, later doing the first PhD thesis on the subject. Regarding the different scribbling he encountered on the walls, he isolated 5 categories depending on the content of the scribbling-that could also apply in the graffiti that is of interest to us: 1) personal names, nicknames and initials, 2) amorous, 3) obscene, erotic, scatological, 4) intellectual: limericks, folk wisdom, homilies, 5) protest: political, social, religious. In his own doctoral thesis, Stefan Jacobson names graffiti, TTP (from the initials of the fundamental versions of graffiti, namely: tags, throw ups, pieces) so as to differentiate it from all the other earlier versions that he calls TD (traditional graffiti).[2] Susan Phillips divides the different versions into popular and community based graffiti,[3] with the first covering writings from Jack Stewart's categories 2,3,4 and commonly seen on walls, benches, toilettes and the second encompassing all "graffiti" aimed at specific audiences with common interests, with 3 subcategories, those of "hip hop", "gang" and "political". Gang graffiti can be self-referential and it has to do with names, tags and symbols that are utilized to mark areas of the city under their control and influence. On the other hand, for reasons we have referred to before, hip-hop is not the most successful way to describe graffiti. Graffiti, although it refers, by and large, to "internal consumption", by nature appeals to a much wider audience, without excluding a sometimes indirect, at other times covert, obvious or even political message. The political writings on the walls, themselves, are not aimed at a single, specific community since their fundamental intention is to sensitize and inform a much larger audience.

Bypassing the subject of content, we suggest a taxonomy with regard to the techniques and general practice of expression and there are basically three categories, that of graffiti, that of street art and that of the various slogans (all three can have any content. In the first category, we have all graffiti that come from those that practice it (the writers): tags, pieces, characters, be a murals on walls and trains. The basic materials are sprays (markers for tags) and also plastic paints with paint rollers and brushes or improvised fire extinguishers and sprinklers. In any case, there can be a combination of the above media. In the second category, there is the wave of works that are termed "street art". Normally, the above term refers to works that are easily identifiable and can often be reproduced with stencils, stickers, stencils and paintings on pieces of paper (even in large sizes) that can be wallpapered with glue, or brush drawings (but also with the use of sprays, rollers etc.). The range of the above practices can even have the form of sculptures or special screenings.

In the third category, we have the slogans and other writings that do not fall under the other two categories. They usually carry one (any kind of) message and they do not aim at creating a piece of art. However, to the degree that they are poetic and calligraphic (independently but much more in relation to the space and context in which they appear) they can be regarded as artistic or as having an aesthetic function as well. Here, we can observe a sub-categorization with regard to their size: the small ones that appear on benches, bus stops, rest rooms etc. and the large ones that are sprayed on larger surfaces. The latter are in direct competition, regarding space, with the other two categories. The borders between the different categories are often blurry and the categorizations themselves can be deemed subjective and erratic. Frequently, a piece of work can entail elements from all the above categories and can be classified depending on the spectator, circumstance and the creator of the work, in both first categories. At other times, the differentiation of various pieces of work is crystal clear. Examples of pieces of work that can be listed in both categories are the characteristic works of the (famous) Brazilian, Os Gemeos and that of the American, Twist (Barry McGee), from '96-'97 onwards. As mentioned above, the classification is done with regard to the means and materials used and not with regard to content, which will be analyzed below.

The term street art was used for commercial reasons and because of the need to categorize an expression-trend and turn it to a certain kind of marketable artistic genre. Of course, "street art", meaning art of the streets can be a lot more. It can cover a broad range of activities from street theater, puppet theater, pantomime, juggling acts and performances, street music, dance and public screenings to skate boarding, BMX, and parkour. Of course, it covers graffiti too, as graffiti is the principal kind of street and public art. On the other hand, all the above expressions are also forms of public art -another term that can be used to describe the various expressions on the street. However, apart from the forms of art mentioned above –which are, mainly, citizen generated- it also describes every kind of official intervention in public space on the part of the state or private individuals (e.g. from a sculpture or monument to a concert). In this sense, public art is not a certain kind of art, but it is the definition of the location of the intervention –the open spaces of the city. Street art, however, has become an art genre. There are, of course, objections to the use of the specific term. Some use the term "urban intervention art" and others use the term "street marking" to describe both graffiti and street art. The term "urban art" has also emerged to define various activities that take place in or are inspired by the city. It seems that, eventually, we are forced, for reasons of understanding, to use the term, "street art", to cover all kinds of intervention described above. Street art style interventions had already emerged, sporadically, in the sixties, but the new wave began in earnest by writers during their search for new means of expression and originality. Today, it is common knowledge that street art evolved from graffiti. Moreover, the proliferation of graffiti practices prepared the ground for the spread of the new forms of intervention. Street art is, generally, considered more activist, more intellectual, more meaningful, richer in social and political message and much more communicative with the broader audience in comparison to the more "self-related", self-referential graffiti. Often street art is characterized by a more artistic dimension and pop aesthetics and the "ultimate motivation" –and not necessarily a hidden one- is the recognition of the artist and his creations on the streets and his/her ultimate leap to the galleries and "official" artdom (many graffiti writers, also, followed the route of the official art).

Graffiti, on the other hand, evolved primarily around the scribbling of names. Names, that are, often, totally impossible to read. However, their letter connection, their coloring, the selection of additional elements, their application on a train, wall, building or specific area, (meaning, its "grand" background on a secondary level), finally, create an image that exceeds the letters and the name and communicates in its own, peculiar way. We also have characters, whole landscapes and representations and on a parallel level, the expression of personal opinion or social message, either via drawings or via words and phrases that can be read clearly, with big or small lettering, among the more "abstract" letters and their superimposed image.

One of the most prominent differences between graffiti and street art is the fact that graffiti can be encountered everywhere, while street art is, mainly, found in specific areas of the city.

Furthermore, traveling street artists select specific hot spots in the cities they visit, to leave their works of art. Another crucial difference between street art and graffiti is that street art never built hubs or networks of people-creators with special bonds between them like graffiti did. Street art created a new pictorial language but did not help create a new culture (neither it maintained or reproduced the positive aspects of graffiti culture). The above fact has a lot to do with the action and experiencing of the execution of a piece of work, that in most cases (but not always), is much more dangerous and intense in the case of graffiti. On top of that, a graffiti piece demands teamwork and even when the work is done individually, it is done in groups (side by side) and it is experienced collectively (while most street art works are done or credited to one person, take less time to be executed, and are less or not dangerous). That is exactly when graffiti becomes more complex. It is the act and what it signifies and the manner it communicates things, but also the bringing together of people that create relationships and networks that eventually, re-feed the whole scene, the different actions, the forms and the pieces of work that are produced in the interactive journey of art and its culture. In the same time, many graffiti writers avoid the term artist for themselves and state that "they do graffiti, not art".

Of course, as we have mentioned above, the so called "street art" emerged as an evolution of graffiti, in the nature of which, the evolution of media is innate. Innovation has always been its evolutionary feature and every time a new form emerged, it stirred the "status quo" of the times. After all these years, though, we would expect the acceptance of its every evolutionary version. It is ironic that (contrary to Jacobson's term) graffiti is many times referred to as traditional graffiti to differentiate it from street art. Although, many writers, in the natural course of personal evolution (whether in a personal quest or out of commercial ambition) followed the path of street art, many others stood against the new wave. On the other hand, the often excessive attention that street art and street artists received in the past decade, caused intense and at some level, justified resentment, not so much among the globally famous writers and street artists (who shared common space in exhibitions, documentaries and books, anyway) but among the creators that worked in the shadows of global fame and also in the heated discussion that often comes up in the forums of an all the more enlarged audience.

The discussion on the differences and similarities can only be extensive and it cannot end here. Suffice it to say that the streets do not belong to writers alone and neither are they the political privilege of street artists. The former are not more, nor less artistic than the latter and good and bad pieces of work can be encountered among artists of both camps.

The graffiti epidemic in Athens

The reason why walls are so covered with graffiti is highly complex and can be related to current events and also to the conditions and general situation in the period before the crisis. However, it would be a fallacy to claim that there is a general tendency of direct, theme oriented response by graffiti writers to the crisis. Besides, many of the graffiti pieces that we can observe on the walls, today, were not done recently and certainly not in the two years that the economic crisis has really made itself felt and has become the talk of the day (in a report of the English speaking news network of Al Jazeera that was aired in October 2008 –meaning, just about when people in Greece started talking about the crisis- there is mention of the problem of excess graffiti in Athens).[4] Graffiti, just like the crisis, is a process that takes a period of years to unfold and cannot be isolated to a specific moment or some months. It has its ups and downs in intensity and has to be seen in the depth of half a decade. Every two years in Athens, we can observe a graffiti eruption that drags along many followers and for half a year it remains at a peak. However, at present, it is in distinct recession.

What is remarkable about graffiti in Athens in the recent years is the fact that there is a strange, general tolerance and acceptance of it, by society in general and by the authorities and the police in particular (that seem not to pursue a hard line towards writers). The reasons behind this are the following: On the one hand, the funds to erase graffiti are simply not there (and this applies to both the state and private sectors). On the other hand, the social problems all around the city (bearing in mind the general degradation of the urban landscape) do not make persecution of graffiti writers a priority. However, there is another element in play that is the product of processes that took years to ripen and that is the gradual assimilation of graffiti into the cityscape, the familiarization with its presence and its social acceptance as something mainstream and harmless (something indifferent or even beautiful), that has led to its excessive proliferation in Athens. All that, apart from the local framework, has a lot to do with the global spreading of graffiti and its ecumenical language, art and culture. However, in most countries of Europe and in the USA, it is still prosecuted in a very harsh manner.[5]

Graffiti proliferation and the reasons behind it

During the eighties and nineties and up until 2000, a spray can was associated, in the common mind, with rebelliousness, political slogans and the social and political margin. This, in conjunction with a deeply rooted resentment, by the police, towards the youth and any kind of new ethic (a characteristic of which was the exercise of verbal and physical violence and general harassment, on the part of the police, towards anyone that had external stylistic differences compared to the general public) could lead to all kinds of trouble. The contact with the police could result in verbal assault, a vindictive arrest at some police precinct, and a couple of slaps on the face or even a proper beating or formal prosecution in court. In the last case, the accused faced prosecution for violating legislation on means of facilitating the dissemination of ideas (a charge identical to the one for illegal poster sticking) and aggravated case of damage (but in no case has there been use of the police archives to press charges against a graffiti writer for his total work or a recursive fine for previous violations). Today, regardless of the dramatic increase of uniformed policemen on the streets (contrary to the past and what is happening in other countries where there are special police detachments that deal exclusively with graffiti and writers are fined exorbitant sums of money for their passion) a writer can work unhindered, even in broad daylight (with indifferent passers by or onlookers checking out "how it's done") and this makes someone wonder how things have changed so profoundly in such a short amount of time. Gradual tolerance, usually, goes through different stages. One of them, surely, is the legal version of graffiti and this was the exact way it blossomed in Greece, especially in schools, stadiums and gyms.

During the 90s, in the largely impersonal school environment with the gray buildings, schoolyards and railings, school kids demanded, through their councils, to cover all those gray walls with graffiti. This happened within the framework of appropriation of the school (something connected with the school occupation wave of the time), for reasons of school prestige towards other schools, but, mainly because graffiti, being something novel, in color and message, was very appealing. Gradually, a large number of schools got graffiti sprayed all over them and many more were on the waiting list for a permit to receive their own coat of graffiti paint. In a sense, graffiti got a paradoxical start, with all those graffiti permits at the various schools and then at stadiums and gyms. On the streets, it was quite a different scene, with the police appearing fast enough to put a rapid end to any public spraying, on conspicuous public and private property that lasted long enough. Even at schools that had issued the relevant permit, a simple phone call was all it took to get a patrol car on the scene. On the other hand, there were cases of store owners that asked for writers who had done pieces at some school, to decorate their store internally or externally.

Another phenomenon of the time was various graffiti festivals. Different municipalities organized graffiti festivals that were relatively cheap, in terms of cost (since they only purchased a number of spray cans) and at the same time, extremely popular with children and a good promotion for the municipalities themselves. Graffiti was proven to be less costly than the constant whitewashing of wall surfaces around the respective municipalities since the various pieces done were largely respected and left alone by the slogan writers and since the number of graffiti writers was relatively small (and Greek graffiti was in its infancy), they stuck to the allocated wall surface for their creations. At the time, graffiti was, by and large, concentrated in specific areas and was, in a sense, more or less, controlled. Between '95 and '98, there were festivals in Kallithea, Volos, Kalamaria and permits for graffiti pieces were given in Nea Philadelphia, Glyphada, Vyronas, at the Hippodrome and at schools all around Attica.

1998 is the turning point in the history of the propagation of graffiti in Greece with an international festival at Thission in Athens, where many people get the chance to come in contact with graffiti itself and get to know graffiti writers from all over the world. In a parallel level, it was just a question of time till graffiti took on its illegal form and with it its vandalistic (not necessarily less visual, but definitely more authentic) versions. In 2002, 2 years before the Athens Olympics, there was the cultural Olympiad –another great step towards the institutionalization of graffiti. The various festivals, although they do not promote the fundamental graffiti version, that is being on the street without anybody's permission (but "the right way to do graffiti" according to the minister of culture of the time), are a great opportunity for people to come in contact with graffiti and great meeting places for all those, like-minded, writers that did not have the chance to get to know each other, previously. Therefore, the festivals brought about the concurrent projection of a false image of what graffiti is all about and its partial acceptance by the public. In 2005 and for some years after that, it was the free press, the media in general and the galleries that gave fashion and celebrity status to street artists and street art & graffiti, in general, in Greece. In the atmosphere of the time, graffiti was encountered everywhere. It now can be seen on TV, in various products, in advertising, in clothing and school equipment as a result of the global expansion of graffiti and its ubiquity in modern culture.

Gradually, we "have become used to" graffiti for the above reasons and because graffiti does not stand out, anymore. When city walls are covered all over, then there is no "aggravated case of damage", anymore, since there can be no damage to something that is already damaged beyond repair. Also, the visual noise that is caused by graffiti is almost undetectable in the general visual noise that characterizes Athens. Graffiti adapts to the chaotic landscape of the city and to the tendency of its inhabitants towards indifference and depreciation of public space. It could be set within a framework of other irregularities (violations of the legislation concerning outdoor advertising, shop signs or illegal construction) that are eventually overlooked on a grand scale. In the same way, the police or those responsible for their operational orders have gotten used to graffiti. On the other hand, the rise of the crime rate and the high incidence of violent outbreaks, the streets that are full of homeless immigrants, beggars, people pushing carts full of items retrieved from garbage cans, prostitutes, local homeless and poor drug users and the widespread poverty and disorder, with the daily suicides and rapid degradation of daily life (along with the mass terrorization of the public by the media) simply make graffiti less than obvious and dealing with it far from a priority at the moment.

The present tolerance towards graffiti could signify an advance in society but also an involuntary acceptance of its presence. It could mean a positive approach and at the same time, habitual living among these images; liveliness on the streets or surrender to an uncontrollable situation - a grave case of indifference, but also a sign of weakness that prevents from giving priority to its crackdown. This applies to the center of Athens but also to streets that lie in other areas within the metropolis.

Back to the crisis. Does graffiti respond to it?

In the general conjuncture of the crisis, of the austerity programs, the wave upon wave of measures, the "national depression" and the omnipresent repression, one would wonder what the reaction of the people is, especially bearing in mind the tradition of the Left, the social movement and the antiauthoritarian block, as they appear in the political history of the country. Their roots lay in WW2 and the civil war that followed it, they continue in the period preceding the dictatorship of 1967-74 and the struggle against it, climaxed in the post-junta period and reached a critical mass with the high school and university student demonstrations and also the "December" riots. A simplified projection of the previous would possibly include the "indignant movement of the squares" or the recent elections.[6] Apart from what the reaction of the people to the new era is, one would also wonder how this is reflected on the walls, among others via the practice of graffiti that we are trying to examine.

Earlier on, we stated that a graffiti response to the situation is not that direct and surely it is not a massive one. I would also add that there are political graffiti pieces on the walls, but they date before the crisis. The fact that they are numerous is owed to the perseverance and consistent action of the few that are responsible for them. Moreover, when it comes to young people in general (notwithstanding the tradition of the left and the present situation) nobody can claim, with any given certainty, that they are politically aware and active.

As for the ones that did or are still doing graffiti, the youthful aura of restless search it entails (its artistic aspect, the framework of petty lawbreaking, the confrontation with the authorities, the face off with danger and the whole contact with the streets) theoretically, at least, places them among the rebellious spirits (something that can vary depending on the geographical area and the times). On the other hand, graffiti is part of the broader social fabric of its time and in general terms constitutes a part of society. If a part of society deals with common issues (especially when it actively participates in public politics) then the same goes for the members of society that do graffiti, which is part of public political expression at large. Let us examine, however, what political graffiti is and analyze some of its manifestations.

The range of the political in graffiti.

At this point, it would be useful to examine three fundamental concepts in the foundation of graffiti, concepts that cannot be conceived separately from each other. a) The deed (the act, the praxis), b) the works, and c) the culture (and the whole practice). Along with the deed come the works and the two of them, combined, feed the culture that re-feeds them in a bi-directional manner. From the nature of the deed, itself, someone can discern the basic characteristics of the magic of graffiti. The deed breaks the law, disputes ownership, exercises spontaneous critique on architecture, on the urban landscape and on society at large. Among other things, it is an existential statement, a cause for wander and adventure in the city, a cause for access to out of bounds areas, reclamation of public space, a game of challenge with danger and all forms of authority, a way to combat boredom, an opportunity for self-education and self-awareness, a chance to create a visual language, create social relations, become part of a group and community, communicate with friends but also with the urban public, give "a present" to the city and finally, create culture. Above all though, it is a fun deed, not only for the moment of the deed itself but also for everything it signifies and what precedes and follows it.

Taking part in the budding graffiti culture since the early years, the writers overcame fundamental discriminations and as a result, children of every race, religion, economic or social class, age and ideology found themselves in the same community. Very soon, graffiti spread worldwide and the formation of international networks of communication was the next natural step. The works (in unity with the deed and the culture) can automatically be termed "political", based on what we have stated above, irrespective of what they write or portray.

Furthermore, we have referred to graffiti culture as the whole practice of graffiti. In tandem, the writer, as carrier of the culture, acts as a political being: (s)he creates relationships, learns how to do graffiti, (s)he teaches others, (s)he practices, (s)he identifies potential targets, (s)he wanders in the city (until he does the deed), (s)he studies graffiti, (s)he talks about it with others, (s)he takes pictures of works and (s)he is real (in which ways). Will (s)he participate in a show or not (and in which particular show), will (s)he talk to the police or not, will (s)he look for publicity outside graffiti circles or not, will (s)he talk to a journalist or researcher (and to which one), will (s)he agree to do a paid job or not (will say yes or no and to which one) and will (s)he offer to the community and culture (how?). Finally, it is the way all that is incorporated in the individual work of every writer.

The above thoughts reveal the complexity of the matter and help us distinguish the processes that render graffiti as a whole, "political", so that we can examine the topics of the works in a more specific manner. They also help us discern what the walls communicate, even in the case of color and illegible letters and words, which remain hidden and indiscernible at first sight. After all that, it is easier to state that, in a sense, the message of graffiti is graffiti, itself. The message lies in the fact that it is there. Its relation to politics can be found exactly in that fact (the same way it can be found in jazz or punk rock). The above is a template of the dynamics... but the world of graffiti is far from perfect. As part of modern society, as we have stated before, it suffers from the pathogens of competitiveness, selfishness and backwardness. The first two of these three pathogens are part and parcel of the nature of graffiti and constitute basic elements of its evolutionary process. However, when they are minimized or overcome, there is limitless potential for flourishing relationships and positive, creative movement.

The case of political graffiti

Graffiti works can be deemed "political" on account of their content and they cover a broad range of expression, from simple messages, comments and personal opinions to direct social or political criticism and even, overt propaganda. It can take the form of an awareness call, information about an event, a call for support, solidarity or opposition and hate, a call for prisoner release or be a vehicle of propaganda, ideology, politics and militancy, often times, incitingly or imperatively or be a comment on any current affair ("fuck this", "against...", "fight...", "this sucks"), against nuclear power, summit meetings, ministerial decisions and legislation, military operations, authoritarian regimes, racism, sexism, the Nazis and of course the police or pro human rights, conservation, etc.

The message can be written in capital, oversized graffiti style letters or complementary phrases next to a graffiti piece, or as complete thematic works, or isolated characters, or colors thrown all around, aggressive drawings and expressive ways (color combinations, shapes, symbols, faces, silhouettes and expressions, always in relation to the location, the part of the city and the part of the wall, the conversation with the landscape and the times) that convey visually what the writer feels, even if this means the creation of a, not readily legible, piece of work. The political comment or the topic of a piece of work, is highly dependent on the writer's awareness, extent of knowledge on the specific theme and manner in which he converses about it, but also on the theme he attempts to tackle, that sometimes leads to a successful outcome and other times it does not (the success, every time, depends also on the recipient of the message). This is where we can raise the question of "quality" and the "successful" way of putting a message across, to touch another issue that cannot be analyzed extensively.

A reference to "professional politics: It goes without saying that it would have been impossible for graffiti not to be re-appropriated by political (and governing) parties, in their campaigns, functions, leaflets, to boost their public image as "being close to young people". In the past, a number of parties have not just funded, but also organized, graffiti festivals. Also, various other groups (not writers) borrow a leaf from the great graffiti book to write their slogans, accordingly. Features of the philosophy and style of graffiti (big outlined letters, fill in strokes, two color jobs and a "light" form of calligraphy) are seen in pieces done at conspicuous parts of the city, to advertise political parties and fractions. Even religious, football related as well as commercial (clothing, car and life insurance ads on the highways) slogans in graffiti style can be found, all around town. The fact that these are not done by writers (even when a writer is "commissioned" to do such a piece) excludes them from classification as graffiti, for the time being. Lastly, someone can even observe patriotic and nationalistic graffiti, all in the framework of competition for, free for expression, public space.

On another level, graffiti that mocks advertising signs and those done on bank, department store property and buildings that symbolize any form of economic and state authority, remind us that graffiti is an innate critique on public space, on architecture and society, generally. Even through the filter of boredom in the modern city that the masked interviewee of Al Jazeera refers to in 2008, political graffiti can find a way to sprout. Naturally, a writer does not do political graffiti, exclusively, but such pieces can pop up in his repertoire as frequently as he chooses to –even if for only once in his career- even if he does not, in general terms, deal with politics. On the contrary, there are writers that are into politics and social issues but that trait is never exhibited in their work (in form of any clear message), which simply focuses on the writing of their name.

Examples of political graffiti

There are examples of political graffiti from all periods of graffiti and all places. "Hang Nixon", written in large lettering by the pioneer Mico (1974), on one of the cars of the New York subway system is one of the first and most famous cases of political graffiti, while many of the graffiti pieces of the time, sported the caption "Free Puerto Rico" next to the super sized letters of the name of the writer. However, it is the political atmosphere that sets the framework for things to happen and ultimately, sets processes in motion. The writers, Phase II, Bama, AMRL, Wicked Gary and Lee 163rd (pioneers of the first years of graffiti, 1969-71) state that they were fully aware of the political and social upheavals of the time and their catalytic influence on their daily lives, their personality and the birth of the graffiti scene. "The "Black Panthers", the "Young Lords" (a movement of Puerto Ricans similar to that of the Black Panthers), the civil rights movement, the Vietnam war, were all there" as they, characteristically, say.[7] It would be of interest to refer to the fact that the writers of the first generation of graffiti were kids, aged ten to sixteen, most of them of African or Latin American descent that came from the most degraded neighborhoods of New York city. A bit later, during the crisis of 1973-74, came the years that were to be known as the "golden" years of New York graffiti that were characterized by its endemic proliferation, continuous development and consecutive innovation in the works.[8]

On the fourth page of one of the most important books in the history of graffiti (*Spraycan Art*, 1987) there is graffiti against Apartheid and on the third there is one that reads "Jungle city". In another graffiti, in the same book, we can read in small lettering "the fun and laughter will never happen if graffiti stops". On the cover of *Subway Art* (1984), although we can only read names and words, we can clearly distinguish the words "Revolt, Crash, Wreckonize, Crasher, Kid, Poem, Heart, Mark, Panic, Spank, Pot, Booze, Kidish, Dude, Pain". In the book, someone can see that graffiti is not just the writing of names. In 1978, Lee (Quinones) sprays whole lines of subway cars, from top to bottom, inspired by daily life and current affairs, talking in a very imaginative way about the urban environment, the Cold War, nuclear weaponry and other political and social issues, but also about the nature of graffiti, itself.[9]

In the Europe of the 90s we have many similar examples. It would be helpful to note that in the political spectrum, there have been graffiti pieces by the ABC of Munich, the Danish Tele, the Spanish Chinijos del Millo, the Italians Volkswriters, and the Belgians 2T, only to mention a few cases amongst many. There have also been common topics for many, for example, works against the second war in Iraq, pieces regarding the victims of 9-11, while there is also the subcategory of the painting of caricatures of known political and other personalities. It is worth mentioning two graffiti magazines (Non Stop –Switzerland and Art Unique –Germany) that had political issues on their covers and pages. One last example could be the German crews in Dortmund in 2012 that refer to political affairs (on trains) with an authentic graffiti style, technique and modus operandi.

Political graffiti in Athens

Athens and Greece are no strangers to political graffiti. There have been political statements on the walls of Athens and other Greek cities by many crews and individual writers, but crews and writers such as 114, NDA, Pete, Deck, Antiea, Javaspa, 381, count amongst those who have consistently used graffiti as a vehicle for clear political messages, while lately the words "wake up" or "haters" pops up on many walls.[10] However, what could the position of writers and their works be in the recent atmosphere of public dialogue and general assemblies, occupations of public buildings and public space in general and the revival (and absolute necessity) of a collective spirit? In an episode of the popular TV show, "Wonderful World",[11] dedicated to written walls, a writer (who hid his face and identity) was asked what the message of graffiti on the walls could be. His straight answer was that "the basic message and essence of the matter is that we claim everything for everyone without asking for anything back", words that would have been unthinkable to hear about graffiti on prime time TV in the past.

In lieu of a conclusion and to respond to all the above, we will make use of the contents of the three DIY graffiti magazines that circulated in Athens in the last two years. Naturally, magazines cannot give an authentic picture of the scene in all the walls of the city. There is always selection and sometimes there are pictures of pieces that are hidden or have since been covered, erased or done on trains that are not accessible to the wider public. All the same, they show what the current trend is, they reflect on a given situation and they also help form a trend. The last three magazines that were published are called: *Outsiders* (2011), *Dopamine* (2012) and *Pisa* (Tar, 2012) – all aggressive names for magazines that contain exclusively illegal material. All three, opt for the hard way, meaning there is no advertising at all on their pages (which is the norm for magazines of this type). The introduction in *Outsiders* informs us that: "We support any illegal activity. We are responsible for the flicks and actions we present you in this issue. We agree that writing on the wall damages others property but this is the only way writers remain in this game. This is graffiti. Hope you enjoy this first issue. The best are yet to come!"[12] In *Dopamine* the one and only text wants to talk about "graffiti and lost meanings": "...we were not raised in playgrounds, nor in an "ideal" environment, but only in ramshackle parks with all elements of decadence present and among cement monstrosities that bear no resemblance whatsoever with the idyllic scenery we see in movies. For these and other reasons we sought and are still searching for another kind of entertainment. In short, for us "train guys" and street-bombers, writing is not a safe "art"; it's not the "legal jobs" and the original "styles". It is the need for our everyday fix of adrenaline offered by the fear of an arrest or accident. That's the way it stared, that's the way we got to know it and that's the way we live it. Graffiti is and will always be illegal".[13]

For Tar, after the observation that the regurgitated word "crisis" is not simply financial but "a profound crisis of a whole culture", there is mention of "the return of graffiti on the streets". Tar was the fruit of the cooperation of many people that are active on the streets. Their views, works and action did not "result from the current conditions of crisis", it is just that "now, there is more space". The work, texts and tributes, presented in the pages of the magazine portray the broad range of political graffiti, in the best possible way. In the pictures we read, among others, "forever", "holiday break up trauma", "poison", "intifada", "we are the kids", "aller retour" on an abandoned bus, "you look stupid from up here", "merde", "What's next?" (on a train) commenting on a huge representation of a tsunami and nuclear disaster, "on va tous crever", "we're all going to hell for this", "I don't want to be art", a huge mural on a train with a couple kissing and their dialogue: "Oh, Jane all I want to hear is those 3 little words"...and her answer "Agitate, Educate, Organize", "It takes a nation of millions to hold us back", "acab", the comments: "Agents provocateurs do not wear face masks, they wear ties" and "refugees welcome, tourists fuck off" accompany two other graffiti pieces, "Greek time zero", "free Gaza", "Stand up and fight" next to the Black Panthers of the Mexico Olympics, "capitalism" written in capital letters and a huge excrement painted on top of it, "If I can't dance it's not my revolution", "born like this", "kids of the ghetto", "hell", "runaway", "we're all immigrants", "1984".[14] Apart from the written texts that accompany them, the graffiti pieces themselves are wild and aggressive with "dirty" lines, chaotic drawings and enigmatic, warlike figures. In the tributes, we can see observations and photos from journeys within Athens, ramblings in the sewer system of Athens and various basements, atmospheric collages from the urban wanderings of the writers and a collection of photos of dead animals in the city. The first picture that can be seen by opening the magazine is the picture of a riot policeman, covered all over with pink paint, sprayed from an improvised fire extinguisher, during one of the demonstrations in downtown Athens.[15]

In the "editorial" we can read: "...At the same time we have another goal. To abolish the stereotype saying that graff is only a matter of style, cut off from the lives we lead—, our personal quests, our loves, our hatreds and our relationships. This is the kind of graffiti we care to demonstrate, this and the communities that give birth to it every day again and again. Communities that -no matter the cliché- produce life in contrast to the dominant misery..." And on the last page, they conclude simply that "it is for the company, it is for fun. Not to feel alone in the city…".[16]

There is one thing that has always been very difficult (even impossible) to do with graffiti and that was to foresee its evolution. However, the recent history of Greek graffiti has shown that we observe a certain consistency when it comes to political (and not the narrow minded, shallow, quasi-politicized) graffiti. The traditions that were born with graffiti, especially in circumstances in the past, that carried a political and emotional weight, but were a far cry from the state of emergency we are experiencing today, allow us to risk a prediction that there will be political graffiti in the future, in all its forms, variety of expression, and degrees of spontaneity and consciousness and that the course already taken will carry on to the next level. This course, even though it is not a steady process, (stability has never been the principal characteristic of graffiti, part of the charm and dynamic nature of which has been its polyphony and dramatic fluctuations) along with the ever-expanding graffiti communities and life within them, will continue. 'Graffiti has always been company, neighborhoods, relationships and networks of people'.[17]

Within the framework of the social crisis, life becomes harder and on the one hand, there is an emergence of antagonism, violence, hate and intolerance and on the other, the creation of networks of solidarity, cooperation and positive moves. The optimistic view of graffiti and its unique ability to bring people together, regardless of its content, should be seen in this context. The crisis will not end today, nor will it end in the near future and even when it is overcome, there will still be injustice in the world. At this moment, in society in general and also in graffiti, that is our topic of research, there are processes in motion that have not made their presence felt on the map yet, but they will do so –with a still undefined manner- in the future.[18]

Chapter 9

Re-image-ing and Re-imagining the City: Overpainted Landscapes of Central Athens

Pafsanias Karathanasis

Image 4: 'Overpainted' walls in Exarcheia area (central Athens), August 2012. Graffiti 'through ups', anti-Nazi drawing, a paste up with a boy character and the question to the public: 'Should We Open Governments?'

The walls of central Athens have always been written and painted to some extent. However, in the past few years that mark the period of the 'Greek crisis', certain areas and many walls of central Athens have been literally overpainted. The practice of painting and writing the city public walls, and other surfaces, seems to have 'grown'; more people got involved in it and the different, but increasingly radicalized works on the walls are becoming more visible in the everyday landscape, affecting the experiences of the people who use the city and feeding with alternative images and meanings the political imaginary of resistance. In the changing everydayness of the public space of Athens during the 'crisis', in which are reflected the governments' austerity measures and the cuts in social welfare under the lead of the IMF and the EU, the practice of writing and painting the public walls contests the dominant media representations of the 'crisis' and actively produces counter discourses through visual culture.

Image 5: Exarcheia area (central Athens), December 2011. Characters on a wall having their faces covered. The female character on the right holds a hammer and next to her is written 'Classes War'. Headscarves or gas masks are common elements in the works of the past five years in Athens, which reflect the clashes with riot police and the heavy use of teargas during the demonstrations.

> THINGS CHANGE RAPIDLY. Used up words like crisis and depression have taken hold of everybody's mind. (…) As far as graffiti is concerned, the change is totally obvious. Painted trains, walls, window screens –a multicolored collage taking over the city, a threat that state as well as private individuals are no match for. (...) Every effort made for 'cleaning the place up' has become just a memory. Everything is overpainted –a heaven for writers– and we really feel like home. (*Pisazine*, 2012, p. 3).

These are the starting words in the first issue of the recently published graffiti magazine '*Pisazine*'[1] published independently in Greece by people who write and paint the public walls of Athens (and of the other major Greek cities). With these words the actors (and authors) point out different interpretations and representations of the 'crisis' by the people who live, spend time, socialize and, like themselves, have been socio-politically active in changing the everyday imagery of the Athenian public space.

Image 6: Stadiou Avenue (central Athens), March 2011.
Mix of styles, on top of a street art piece depicting people facing each other, a protester wrote: *'Class VS Class'* during an anti-government demonstration on the 7th of last February.

The overpainted cityscape mentioned in *pisazine* is the material outcome of the growing practice in Athens during the period of the 'crisis'. The practice of painting and writing includes several aesthetic traditions and styles of visual urban intervention, which reflect different ideas and cultures. Hip-hop graffiti, political slogan writing, as well as iconic works of the post-graffiti tradition, such as stencils, stickers and paste-ups, they are all merged together, 'occupying' the public walls and creating the overpainted urban landscapes of today's Athens. Newcomers in this visual culture of urban public space meet those who have been already out 'in the field', and besides the aesthetic and cultural differentiations reflected in their works, they are connected by the common experiences of radicalized intervention in the changing and often violently controlled public

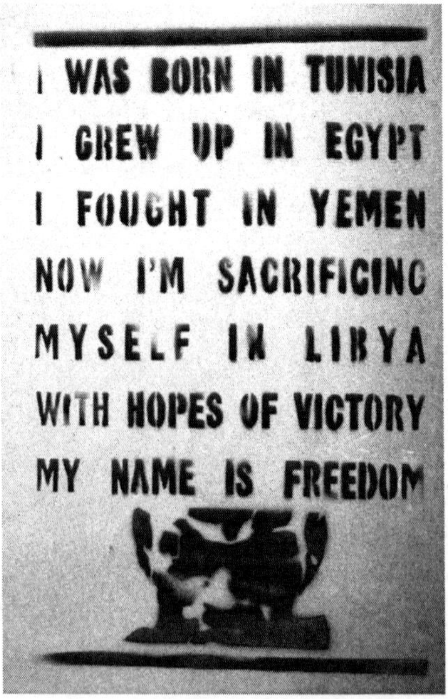

Image 7: Stencil in Ermou Avenue (central Athens), January 2012. Referring to the recent uprisings and revolts in the Arab world connecting them with the political situation in the Western World.

space of Athens. Graffiti writers, street artists, radical protesters, post-graffiti interventionists and activists, all together connected by the use of public space, practice their right to participate in the visual production and reproduction of the public urban spaces, imagining, altering and affecting directly the everyday urban landscapes they use and experience.

In this way, they create 'practiced places' in the city – de Certeau's understanding of the lived and experienced everyday city space (1988, p. 117) – resisting the control mechanisms of the sovereign power in the public space. Moreover, they form 'communities of practice'[2] between people and groups that are active in the public space, and they produce contemporary visual culture, which is increasingly 'occupying' the surfaces of the city. Different actors materialize their alternative sociopolitical ideas and images to the lived environment of the city and actively resist the dominant regimes of visibility by practicing their radical identities through their counter-practice on the public walls.

As Hagi Kenaan argues, the sovereign powers around the world did not limit themselves to shaping the actual appearance of the city, but also 'insisted on controlling the sphere of the imaginary onto which the city opens up' (2011, p. 105). It seems that during the period of the 'crisis' sovereign power in Greece has lowered its control on the public walls of the city. Either because 'they are broke, or they have bigger problems to face', as the authors of *pisazine* say, the authorities of Athens do not seem to have the capacity or the will to 'fight' graffiti at this period. However, this is not merely the reason for the growth of the public painting and writing practice. During this politically intense period it seems that the practice itself is being transformed, acquiring different political dynamics in the changing urban everydayness of the 'crisis'. More people talk about what they see on the walls, take pictures of the works, distribute them through the Internet and widely reflect on the ideas and meanings presented to the public on the walls.

If Kenaan is right that the 'official de-legitimization of painting and writing on the street not only serves to protect public or private property, but is first and foremost a prohibitive measure taken against attempts to undermine the regime of imagination imposed by the sovereign power' (2011: 105); then the people who write and paint the walls of Athens are exploiting the occasion resulting from the 'crisis', to *re-image* and *re-imagine* the city, adding to the political dynamics of the practice. Through the intense and illegal painting and writing the city the community of practice performs directly the 'right to the city', to use Lefebvre's phrase,[3] which as David Harvey argues 'is far more than the individual liberty to access urban resources: it is a right to change ourselves by changing the city (...) the freedom to make and remake our cities and ourselves' (2008, n.p.).

Chapter 10

Mapping the Geographical and Spatial Characteristics of Politicized Urban Art in the Athens of Crisis

Konstantinos Avramidis

Setting the Scene: On the emergence, spread and legitimization of the crisis

Craig Calhoun (2011, p. 9) notes that 'the word 'crisis' can easily be abused' mainly due to its urgent nature. He also pinpoints the fact that the 'very naming of crisis', its constant repetition by politicians and the media, along with the widespread usage of the term from a substantial part of the population, helps to constitute and legitimate it (Calhoun, 2011, p. 10). More than thirty years ago, Hall et al. (1978), using as their starting point the 1972 'mugging' panic in Britain, suggested that the social alarming of the time had all the characteristics of a 'moral panic'. Stanley Cohen (2011, p. 1) described moral panic as 'a condition, an episode, a person or a group of persons…a threat to the values and the interests of society'. Moral panics are often presented in stereotyped form by the media and experts are called to introduce diagnoses and solutions in order to deal with the emerging condition (Cohen, 2011, p. 1). In these 'exceptional moments', statistics are utilized to justify the draconian tactics and strategies that are to be adopted to ensure a new ordering and social security.[1] These periods of crisis - and Greek society seems to live such a period - result in the reduction of guarantees and rights, which in turn ignite political clashes. This dismantling of the welfare state and the subsequent decrease of living standards in Greece, along with the rocketing of unemployment rates, triggered a generalized civil distrust towards the system as a whole.

In this context, Greek citizens' trust in institutions and political system is depleted. This distrust manifests as civil disobedience which is interpreted by dominant groups as hurtful of the Greek image in general and Athens' in particular. This is probably the reason why a 'clearance' (e.g. from immigrants, new homeless etc.) in the Greek capital is increasingly promoted. More often than not, during such times, certain voices are regarded as valued and accepted, while others are not. This civil exclusion from the dialogue that forms the public agenda can be seen as indicative of the delimitation of public sphere. This is perhaps why the process of both transmitting some information and suppressing certain others, may take a violent form within a time of crisis (Avramidis, 2012), while the control over public discourse has increasingly become the bone of contention amongst dominant and subordinate groups. Amidst this politically unstable condition, which is underlined by two elections within one month (May-June 2012), citizens, being unable to comment on this unprecedented situation, are struggling to locate - or even to construct - spaces that will allow their voices to be heard.

In search for social space: exclusion and construction of publics

It is widely accepted that dominant cultural institutions (such as the media) promote certain viewpoints and, by doing so, establish a dominant understanding of local circumstances. However, the uncertain political situation in contemporary Athens finds the Greek society, and especially the youth, struggling to voice their frustration and alternatives as a result of their exclusion from the public discourse. This is probably why protests and rallies take place with a significant frequency. Nonetheless, these actions should be seen as part of a multifaceted network of resistance, where information and ideas are voiced in order to reach a public and to mobilize it accordingly. During this struggle for social space, information is transmitted through various forms, both physical and digital, which are operating as alternative public arenas.

In order to characterize a form of communication as 'alternative' and 'unofficial', or even 'counter' and 'subaltern', it presupposes that we consider another type as 'mainstream' and 'official'. This means that a certain type of political communication is imposed from above by professionals and, as aforementioned, does not express the views and demands of some citizens. In this battle of interests and purposes, these alternative communication channels are born and evolved. Besides, as Chaffee (1993, p. 3) argues, 'societies evolve communication systems that allow governments, organizations, and individuals to present their views, demands, needs, and ideas'. Thus, it is not surprising that new communication practices are formed, while some more 'conventional' ones re-emerge. In the latter category lies the practice of political wall writing, which has boomed since the beginning of the crisis, probably because graffiti 'gives expression to groups that otherwise could not comment upon or support current or perceived social problems' (Chaffee, 1993, p. 3).

The intensification of the politicized wall writing phenomenon (since the 2008 Greek Youth Uprising) in contemporary Athens has gradually transformed the urban landscape into 'a platform for negotiation and dialogue' (Tsilimpounidi & Walsh, 2010, p. 111). This innovative and provocative type of graffiti 'filled in the gaps of culture's hegemonic discourse' (Tsilimpounidi & Walsh, 2010, p. 111) and, by doing so, became a social space where unquestioned issues were raised and rights were exercised. Since the right to the city 'is dependent upon public space' (Mitchell, 2003, p. 5), this creative reclaim of the streets in contemporary Athens should not surprise us. Given that 'in the city, different people with different projects must necessarily struggle with one another over the shape of the city, the terms of access to the public realm, and even the rights of citizenship' (Mitchell, 2003, p. 18), the city is an ideal place for both hegemonic views and their contestations to be expressed (Cresswell, 1996). Considering that, it might be argued that political graffiti does not initiate a new discussion about public space but brings into the foreground an existing one that is associated with the 'democratic' city (Mitchell, 2003, p. 4). 'Democratic' refers to those places that are open to multiple meanings and encourage debate and negotiation (Harris, 2006, p. 101).

The purpose of this article is not to address the notion of 'public' at large; it seeks to identify how graffiti can be seen as a 'public address' (Iveson, 2007) and its association with the contemporary pressing situation. Seen as a record of popular history (Chaffee, 1993, p. 4), in the changing patterns of graffiti writing we may read the struggles over the transformations currently taking place in a social, cultural and political level. What I argue is that, in these wall inscriptions, we may identify the shifts in the dominant public narratives and their oppositions. In other words, we may understand the counter-hegemonic discourse; an alternative narrative of what is going on in Greece nowadays. Through their creative way in initiating conversations, in these writings we may identify the lack, the need and the struggle for social space, communication and representation. My line of thinking is perfectly aligned with that of David and Wilson (2002, p. 7), according to whom graffiti should be treated as 'symbolic expressions that facilitate the transmission of ideas ... [as] a result of relations between people, places, and things that have emerged from historical circumstances'. This given, the question raised here can be put as follows: can the urban condition and spatial practices - such as graffiti - reveal the current Greek 'transitional' state? Does this situation influence the way people operate in and through the city? By studying the behaviors and intentions that are shaped through this social condition, in the case of political graffiti in Athens I seek to find some answers to the aforementioned questions. To do so, I explore how urban artists transmit and circulate their views by forming publics through 'public address' (Iveson, 2007). What their (counter)publics are and how they come into being, enabling them to effect the mainstream public sphere, are also under consideration. Then, I investigate the geographical and spatial expression of political graffiti to finally capture how urban artists, through their innovative urban cartography, vibrate the resting dominant public sphere, opening paths of increased civic inclusion.

Since every struggle in the city is materially grounded and geographically expressed, my main claim here is that through graffiti 'new modes of living, new modes of inhabiting, are invented' (Mitchell, 2003, p. 18) that contain forms of reclaiming the city and are influenced by the current 'emergency state'. By exploring the ways in which these urban interventions engage with, or seek to alter, existing social conditions and communication practices, we might understand how they take the form of political mobilization or spatial contestation, illuminating alternative visions of urban life.

Inventing publics: politicized urban art and the process of 'public address'

It is important here to point out that every public form of wall writing is not graffiti. 'There is a difference between slogans, wallpaintings and graffiti. What makes the difference is neither the means nor the aesthetics of the pictures, but the topics, the intention of the agents and their potential audiences' (Avramidis, 2012). Bearing that in mind, the terms 'graffiti', 'wall writing' or 'urban art' will henceforth be used in this article to describe the most common forms utilized for political communication and opposition, namely two specific types of writing: political graffiti and slogans.

Political wall writing, especially during periods of crisis, is neither a Greek phenomenon nor a new one. For instance, Armando Petrucci (1993, p. 3), referring to the intensification of hand-written epigraphy phenomenon during the period between the eleventh and thirteenth centuries in Italy, notes that it 'correspond[s] to the urban revolution taking place in the cities and to the consequent discovery of the civic and political function of outdoor urban space'. Nonetheless, the importance of walls as spaces of resistance has gradually increased, especially during contemporary era. This is the case as the established groups tend to use more effective and sophisticated ways to circulate their ideas such as the mass media (Karathanasis, 2010, p. 318). Anne Cronin, referring to advertisement and graffiti, argues that 'both these hegemonic and counter-hegemonic practices are able to function precisely because urban space is a site of multiple and contested meanings, visualities, and practices'. Cronin continues to suggest that 'they draw on 'the street' not merely as a location or space, but as an idea, an aesthetic, and a potential' (Cronin, 2008, p. 75).

One of the most powerful features of wall writing is that it cannot be easily avoided, since it is a surprising intrusion in our daily urban visual experience. As such, intentionally or not, many of us become the potential audiences of these extraordinary public discussions. Johanna Drucker (1998, p. 90) points out that the written language in the landscape 'represents an invisible conversation: someone is speaking, someone is being addressed'. Since a specific space and time are required for a conversation to take place, graffiti could not be an exception. However, its nature is 'distinctively different from the here-and-now of a social locale' (Brighenti, 2010a, p. 11).[2] Wall writing is a mediated public communication that invents 'a public' that differs from 'the public sphere'.

As Alan McKee (2005, p. vii) argues in his introduction to this topic, 'the concept of the 'public sphere' is a metaphor that we use to think about the way that information and ideas circulate in large societies ... for thinking about how democratic culture should work'. Jürgen Habermas (1989) described *the* public sphere as an arena accessible to all citizens, where they can debate critically on issues of common interest. For him, the public sphere is the space between public power and private life. However, many recent scholarly works which study the (trans)formation of public sphere have directed their enquiry towards the multiplication of public sphere (Asen, 2000; Fraser, 1990; Warner, 2002). These studies, to a great extent, have criticized the universality and singularity of the notion of bourgeois public sphere (Habermas, 1989), according to which all citizens can potentially voice and debate their common concerns and be critical of the state actions. This shift towards multiplicity of public arenas has been generated by the realization of sociocultural diversity and communication complexity, since 'a single, overarching public sphere ignores or denies social complexity insofar, as it invokes a notion of publicity as contemporaneous face-to-face encounters among all citizens potentially affected by issues under consideration' (Asen, 2000, p. 425).

In her influential text *Rethinking the Public Sphere* (1990), Nancy Fraser recognized the fact that the male bourgeois public sphere excluded other marginal or/and oppressed groups from articulating their particular concerns, and she claims that those in the latter category form public spheres of their own. These 'subaltern counterpublics', as Fraser calls them, are 'parallel discursive arenas where members of subordinated social groups invent and circulate counterdiscourses to formulate oppositional interpretations of their identities, interests, and needs' (1990, p. 67). More recently, Robert Asen (2000, p. 425) argued that 'counterpublics signal that some publics develop not simply as one among a constellation of discursive entities, but as explicitly articulated alternatives to wider publics that exclude the interests of potential participants'. He believes that counterpublics are formed to overcome these exclusions. Asen directs most of his enquiry towards the discursive quality of counterpublics, focusing on the identification and articulation of exclusion through alternative discourse practices. He also pinpoints the fact that the 'deliberative processes in public spheres tend to advantage dominant groups and to disadvantage subordinate groups' (Asen, 2000, p. 428). In this context, echoing Fraser, he supports the view according to which subordinated groups form counterpublics and engage in alternative communicative processes so as to bypass the supervision of dominant groups (Asen, 2000, p. 428).

Thus, it might be said that counterpublics[3] are mainly oppositional networks of communication that are formed by those excluded, deliberately or not, from the mainstream public sphere and its hegemonic discourse, through which they strive to express and circulate their common concerns, aiming to influence the dominant public sphere and to inform a wider public about their views. Counterpublics should be distinguished from social movements, protest groups and subcultures,[4] despite the fact that a part of these public formations are closely associated with some of them. The development of counterpublics is quite a common practice in periods of crisis, which are characterized by civic mobilization; it enables participants to circulate their discourses and to interact with prevalent public sphere, beside the latter's fortified status.

Considering that, those who engage in political wall writing can be seen to form a counterpublic, since '[it] is not a strict or bounded community, it is always territorially spread and its communications are mediated' (Brighenti, 2010a, p. 18). Apart from its internal dynamic for communication beyond the mainstream supervision, the politicized graffiti counterpublic of Athens is highly external since it 'addresses' its views to the city as a whole.[5] How a counterpublic is energized? 'Like all publics',

Michael Warner (2002, p. 120) suggests, 'a counterpublic comes into being through an address to indefinite strangers'. Graffiti writings 'do not exist by themselves, but they happen ... via transmission and perception' (Belting, 2005, p. 303). This given, the publics that these messages form should be conceptualized similarly since, as Warner notes, 'a public exists only by virtue of address... commence with the moment of attention' (Warner, 2002, p. 88).

The public, or rather, every public,[6] is supposed to be a social space that is formed for interaction and debate on issues of common interest. However, this conceptualization of the notion, as Andrea Brighenti (2010a, p. 18) notes, 'remains spatially and materially blind'. Since 'one cannot be the public, one can only be in the public', the role of materiality in publics' formation is crucial, because they are 'inherently mediated' (Brighenti, 2010a, p. 20). [7] Thus, the concept of (counter)public as described here, cannot be examined merely through a spatial lens or a social one, as it refers to both spaces and relations and subsequently it has both material and immaterial hypostasis. Publics emerge in a cultural, temporal and spatial context.

Kurt Iveson, in his recent study *Publics and the City* (2007), bridges the gap between the material and immaterial dimensions of publics and public space through the notion of 'public address'. He identifies the limitations in the conceptualization of public space both in 'topographical approach', which refers to specific kind of space in the city which is dominantly considered as 'public', and in 'procedural approach', which refers to space that is 'put to use at a given time for collective action and debate' (Iveson, 2007, p. 3). Instead, he counterproposes a less static model of public space that emerges upon 'public address'. Iveson redefines the notion of 'public sphere', bringing into the foreground the importance of city and the 'affordances' of specific urban sites to operate as channels for public address (Iveson, 2007, p. 13). The affordances of an object or environment are its embedded properties that allow and furnish an individual's action (Gibson, 1986, p. 127). This given, no space is privileged or underprivileged in the public formation process, since 'publics have no proper location' (Iveson, 2007, p. 13). For Iveson, the power of specific urban sites to be either beneficial or hostile for certain kinds of public address and public making lies on 'the appreciation of [their] different opportunities' (Iveson, 2007, p.13). Besides, there are many and different ways to address a public; each choice of form, place and style carries not only risks and costs but also potential major gains in the type of public it may shape (Warner, 2003, p.14). Essentially, urban artists search for and consequently select and intervene to those places that 'afford' and fit their requirements.

It might be argued that an urban space or artifact becomes public when it is transformed into a channel of public address. Therefore, when graffiti addressees are engaged in the process, they already imagine well in advance their potential receivers, which are commonly personally unknown. In this respect, their public space 'is not a place, but situations for engagement' (Stara, 2009, p. 233). Thereby, by imaging their audiences in advance, they form counterpublics through public address; this is how graffiti (counter)public is formed and this is how, in turn, their public space is conceptualized. Acknowledging the importance of particular urban sites, and their potential combination with other sites or mediums,[8] practitioners of wall writing seek to sustain and enlarge their public address through them.

The geographical and spatial expression of politicized urban art

According to Lefebvre (1996, p. 109), 'the city is the projection of society on the ground'. Thus, the city is the place where both dominant views of society as well as their contestations are inscribed. Considering that urban space[9] is not the sum of abstract geometrical points and locations but places of meaning, since 'they have distinctive meanings and values for persons' (Tilley, 1994, p. 15). Hence, urban spaces are the sites where many, and often conflicting, meanings and values meet. The way people think of space matters as it influences the way they act upon it. Thus, space should not be considered a static or neutral entity but constantly changing and dynamic. According to Doreen Massey (2005, p. 9), space should be recognized as 'product of interrelations', as 'the sphere of the possibility of the existence of multiplicity', always 'under construction'. For her, space is the dimension of the social that is always open to multiple meanings.

However, more often than not, some meanings are regarded as 'inappropriate', and consequently excluded. Tim Cresswell (1996) examines the situations where things appear to be 'wrong', or 'out of place'. In other words, he explores the geographies of deviance (or 'heretic') to unveil the dominant (or 'hegemonic') geographies, which are imposed through the 'naturalization' of space and its expectations. Of course, different people think of and act in space differently, forming different geographies, since every 'counter-', 'sub-' or dominant culture is socially constructed, geographically expressed and spatially constituted (Jackson, 1989: 3). Hence, Cresswell questions the 'taken for granted' relation between place and behavior and explains the importance of place as 'a powerful force in the ongoing hegemonic and counterhegemonic struggles' (Cresswell, 1996, p. 13). Thus, we may argue that inclusion and exclusion, resistance and acceptance are always present in urban social spaces. Considering that, graffiti can be seen as a 'resistance to sociogeographical exclusion' (David & Wilson, 2002, p. 43).

The plurality of cultures and the multiplicity of meanings assigned to certain places, leads Cresswell (1996, p. 13) to talk of the city as 'text'. David Frisby (2002, p. 15) identifies a few presuppositions that underpin the notion of the city as text, amongst which are 'textuality', 'language', 'reader(s)' and 'legibility' in principle. However, according to Frisby, the later presupposition 'does not exclude erroneous readings'. Some of these 'erroneous readings' could also been seen through the 'heretic' lens. Cresswell uses the city-text analogy to underpin his argument that places become meaningful through practice, which is simultaneously both a form of production and interpretation; a writing and a reading. To extend Cresswell's point, we may recall Roland Barthes' words in his text *The Death of the Author* (1977), in which he suggests that the true locus of writing is reading. In his viewpoint, 'to give a text an author', in our case to associate a single meaning to specific place, 'is to impose a limit on that text, to furnish it with a final signified, to close the writing' (Barthes, 1977, p. 147). Place neither has a specific and solid meaning nor is this meaning produced through a linear route; place as text is written and re-written every time different people read it differently, since 'the reader always constructs a new text in the act of reading' (Hill, 1998, p. 26). However, dominant social groups and cultural institutions employ their cultural influence in a downwards direction and establish a 'preferred reading' (Jackson, 1989, p. 3),[10] imposing, at the same time, their values on space. Thus, when someone regards one reading as 'normative' and another as 'incompatible', then the latter reveals the contested interests in preserving or excluding 'a particular set of meanings' (Cresswell, 1996, p. 59).

Every single agent, who acts either antagonistically or normatively, reads a particular spatial text and reacts according to needs and ideology. Those who engage in political wall writing draw attention because they choose to interpret space differently, and thus, 'by disobeying the expectations of place, provide a heretical reading' (Cresswell, 1996, p. 165). This 'misinterpretation' of proper or dominant spatial meanings provides the field through which new modes of spatial inhabitation and communication emerge. Considering that, urban artists' 'transgressive' geography becomes a tool of creative resistance,[11] counterpublic making and communication with peers and the like. It should be noted here that all 'heretic' geographies critically encounter existing orderings; they do not replace them or construct their own (Cresswell, 1996, p. 166). This is perhaps what Mitchell (2003, p. 81) describes as 'conflict over the legitimacy of various uses of space'. By manipulating the power of geography, wall writers question the latent, well dressed under naturalization, character of dominant topographies. Besides, the 'normal' is defined by its opposite: the abnormal; what is considered 'out-of-place' unveils what is 'in-place' and vice versa (Cresswell, 1996, p. 49).

What do graffitists gain by adopting a 'transgressive' attitude? The ensured anonymity, along with the ephemeral and illegal nature of this practice, provides producers with the necessary autonomy and freedom to avoid any visual and communicational discount (Avramidis, 2012). Rather, for Gonos et al. (1976, p. 42), the aforementioned allow them 'opportunities to use language, and present beliefs and sentiments, which are not acceptable in ordinary social life'. This illicit – but quite safe[12] and economic – practice, 'usually undertaken beyond the gaze of censoring authorities' (David & Wilson, 2002, p. 43) and by manipulating certain mediums together with the dynamic of the 'street', manages to address particular audiences[13] and excludes those that could be potentially hostile and hurtful in their counterdiscourse circulation (Iveson, 2007, p. 143).

Since urban art is produced freely, avoiding any potential censorship, the oppositional views on this practice should be mainly seen as 'struggles over its circulation as a form of public address' (Iveson, 2007, p. 143). These illicit public and politically oriented inscriptions are usually seen as 'out-of-place' (Cresswell, 1996), as 'property damage, cause and consequence of urban decay' (Iveson, 2007, p. 116). But as Cresswell argues, 'it is only superficially the material defacement of public property that is at stake; the real issue is the image of the city' (Cresswell, 1996, p. 46). These writings supposedly enhance the 'feeling' of crisis and hurt the image of the city, signifying that Athens, as a capital, and thus Greece as a whole, is out of control, lawless and chaotic. They seem to signify a loss of control on the authorities' behalf, but as Anne Norton (2001, p. 193) argues, 'they object to graffiti not on aesthetic ground but on semiotic one ... they oppose on what the presence of graffiti signifies'. Examples from the recent history show that graffiti intensify, both in numbers and content, in various cities during periods of crises (e.g. 70s NY City, 80s London). It has also been observed that graffiti occurs at those districts that experience the most severe problems during this transitional state. This also seems to be the case in some areas in Athens such as Exarcheia and Psirri districts as well as along Piraeus and Panepistimiou str., which host respective emergent social conflicts and currently experience the greatest economic and social pressures. In this context, it is not surprising that some of these districts have become objects of architectural competitions[14] or urban regeneration programs, so as to re-establish a 'correct' image of the city.

Urban artists challenge public space by writing publicly things that meant to be private. Moreover, by marking places they do not own, graffitists claim ownership and make apparent that 'those with more property may also have more speech' (Norton, 2001, p. 194). However, apart from these oft-cited observations, urban art can be seen as something more than a symbolic declaration of power from subordinate groups; it is also 'an expression of resistance' (David & Wilson, 2002, p. 45). Studied as such, urban art 'can be used as an unobtrusive measure to reveal patterns of customs and attitudes of a society' (Stocker et al., 1972, p. 356). In our case, these writings offer a revealing insight not only into the communities that produce them but also into the relationship between graffitists, hegemonic relations and urban space. Through their -often unflattering- point of view, they become an important and unfiltered source of information concerning the social and spatial attitude of a hidden side of Greek society.

Echoing Stocker et al. (1972) and Gonos et al. (1976), David and Wilson (2002, p. 44) argue that graffiti is socially produced and thus sensitive to societal change, while observing that the need to write particular types of graffiti is constantly changing. Here then, it is worth mentioning that Drucker (1998, p. 90-92) identifies two categories of signs in urban written language: one that derives from the material form, meaning recognizing the 'features of the method of production', and the other that derives from the linguistic form, namely such 'current slang, obsolete jargon, newly coined words' and so on. Then, both material and linguistic forms, meaning both the way of production and language used, can place a sign – in our case graffiti – in a temporal frame since it carries 'information about [the producer's] intention'. Thus, in the writings of these anonymous public commentators, we may identify the struggles over the current transformations in Greece.

Image 8: 'We are all immigrants'.

Graffiti piece at Victoria Square. Artist: JNOR. Photo: Author's own.

Considering that, observing and studying graffiti may reveal both the social and cultural transformations in contemporary Athens and the shift in spatially expressed resistance patterns, which are embedded in the current socio-political condition: the exceptional state of crisis. Hence, it is not surprising that many urban artists choose counter-memorandum topics. For example, a slogan on a public building at Panepistimiou str. says 'For sale', referring to the planned privatizations, while a few meters farther another one writes 'No more rescuing', referring to the financial rescue package. Since the current crisis is not merely financial but also social, the topics chosen are also concerned with civic exclusion, human rights and the impact of crisis on citizens' lives. For instance, a political graffiti by Jnor at Victoria square, where an accumulation of immigrants has occurred,

Image 9: '& Health Kaput'.

Graffiti piece on the abandoned building of the Social Insurance Institute at Piraeus str. Artist: Bleeps.gr. Photo: Courtesy Bleeps.gr.

depicts a woman wearing burka and reads 'We are all immigrants' (Image 8). Apart from the topics, the visual treatment of the messages is extremely crucial (Chaffee, 1993: 6-7) to communicate them more effectively, while positioning seems to be chosen either to be highly visible or symbolically. For example, a piece by Bleeps.gr which is symbolically placed on the abandoned building of the Social Insurance Institute at Piraeus str. represents a man on crutches and writes '&health kaput', referring to the cuts and reforms in the Greek NHS (Image 9).

A piece by Paul at Monastiraki district shows a shocked young woman together with the last words of a man who committed a politically motivated suicide[15]:

> Ladies and Gents, welcome to metropolis of chaos! Install security doors and alarming systems, lock yourselves in, open your TV and enjoy the spectacle. The next rebellion will be much stronger as our society rots… Get out in the streets next to your children and claim your stolen lives. Remember that when you were young you also wanted to change the world (Image 10).

The aforementioned examples are indicative of both the topics and the tactics adopted by Athenian street artists. They illustrate how over the last years Athens' walls have become 'witness surfaces' (Chmielewska, 2008) of the political transformations and social demands generated by the crisis; how graffitists manage to invent publics so as to get their messages across by adopting 'transgressive' attitudes.

David and Wilson argue that the shift in the customs and attitudes of place marking tactics 'imply changes in social circumstances' (2002, p. 45). Operating beyond any social constraints that could potentially limit their communicative power, graffitists do not mirror the established cultural norms

Image 10: Stencil at Vlahava St, which partially reproduces Savvas Metikidis' suicide note. Artist: PAUL. Photo: Author's own.

and power relations; contrary, they inscribe an alternative set of values on urban spaces and take advantage of the opportunities that those spaces afford to form a desired audience and circulate a particular discourse. Thus, by writing the city and inscribing new meanings, urban artists 'invent' space 'in which [their] rights can exist and be exercised' (Mitchell, 2003, p. 81). This given, following the intensification of the political graffiti phenomenon, we might argue that the ambivalent crisis environment cultivates such modes of conduct on rights claims, which derive from a respective lack. In other words, as heretic geographies increase, they reveal the hegemonic crisis. Of course, urban art should not be seen as a practice which intends to provide answers (Cresswell, 1996, p. 166); political writing challenges and poses questions, and in the process can be seen as a response to the lack of expression, creativity and political struggle in urban space, by envisioning a polyphonic and more democratic space.

Remapping the city: Athens' walls as contestable spaces

Walls dictate both spaces and behaviors in urban environments. They are a tangible method to govern and regulate activities, an efficient way to impose order and restrictions in physical space. This is probably why they are historically perceived as artifacts of exclusion par excellence, but they also 'tend to become part of the unquestioned, naturalized background of the here-and-now of a given urban environment' (Brighenti, 2010b, p. 323). However, this conceptual simplicity of walls, which derives from their unquestioned nature, is constantly challenged in and through practice. Thus, reading political graffiti as a heretic usage of Athens' walls, this study suggests a new 'mapping' of the urban social-cultural conditions. The term 'map' is used here to describe 'any form of representation that reveals unseen space, latent conditions or narratives in and of the city' (Brook & Dunn, 2011, p. xiii). Hence, the graffiti mapping reveals heretic interpretations of the current social-political phenomena and contexts. By making visible their own discourses and narratives of the current social and political situation, graffitists reveal the latent meanings of walls and the like. In this respect, urban walls are conceptualized here as 'public spaces' that are energized by short- or long-lived marks, meaning through public address.

Hénaff and Strong (2001, p. 4) suggest that public space is 'always contestable, precisely because whereas there are criteria that control admission to its purview, the right to enact and enforce those criteria is always in question'. Considering that, Athens' walls exist under a contested state because they have gradually become open to new interpretations and uses: they have been transformed from devices of division and exclusion into artifacts that permit -and maybe enhance- social interaction and communication, thus becoming spaces of social life and inclusion. Practitioners of political graffiti saw these liminal spaces not as 'property', but as a medium for circulating their messages and counterdiscourse with each other and a wider public (Iveson, 2007, p. 116).

Over the last years, Athenian walls became the raw material through which views are expressed, demands are voiced and rights are exercised. Considering that, political graffiti can be seen as visual urban documents that reveal the current Greek transitional state. Of course, this type of wall writing is a not a cause, but a symptom of the crisis; it is another testament of how crisis is manifested in everyday life. Through their polemic and opportunistic relationship with specific urban components, urban artists forged an unofficial network that operates as an alternative communicational venue through which they discuss, are informed and comment on their perceived reality. The presence and spatial proliferation of these marks not only change the visual image of the city, but also the ways single individuals and informal groups manipulate and interpret the city and its artifacts in order to communicate their views. Political wall writing in Athens can be seen as a practice that upsets 'the indistinct order of urban space with the 'forces of exception'' (Brook & Dunn, 2011, p. 184). Through a tactical use of specific urban artifacts and by manipulating their communicational power, wall writers filled in the gaps of hegemonic discourse. By doing so, the margins invaded the center, the personal has been transformed into common, the unquestioned became contested, and, in the process, a new counterhegemonic reality gradually emerged.

Through this discursive lens, political graffiti can be seen as a heretic reading of the city; a remapping of the emerging urban condition through which a new culture of public use is cultivated. Undoubtedly, the 'emergency state' in Athens leaves a lasting footprint on urban space and people's lives. Even though 'crises constrain our choices', political graffiti, by its marginal position, calls us to focus our attention on the narratives and latent conditions now operating in Greece so as to re-conceive the current situation as a 'state of emergence' and to re-imagine our 'possible futures' (Calhoun, 2011, p. 42). Athenian graffiti are not only indicators of the crisis in contemporary Greece but also an expression of an emerging urban culture, which invades and, in the process, renews the identity and the image of the city. Politicized graffiti are personalized micro-geographies of resistance to the overwhelming forces of crisis.

Chapter 11

Art and Politics: Bleeps' Politically Charged Paintings on the Walls of Athens

Konstantina Drakopoulou

According to Arthur Danto's classic essay, *The Philosophical Disenfranchisement of Art*, (Danto 1986), there is an attitude of neutralization that renders art and philosophy 'impotent' to 'make anything happen' in the world.

> Danto then considers Marxist and other theories of *deep history*, which, in removing art from 'effectiveness' at the structural base, again either disenfranchise art or fail sufficiently to distinguish art from any other form of social expression. Art, in these theories, is now stripped not only of its power but also of its particularity. Moving then to *surface history* Danto reminds us once more that it is simply a matter of fact whether art makes anything happen. He doubts that art can 'save the Jews' or 'save the whales' directly; but he does consider the possibility that art might communicate indirectly what cannot be communicated directly (Goehr, 2005, p. 481).

Through elements that give us a glimpse of what a radically oppositional culture could look like, art, and especially public art placed within the interruptions and interstices of social life, offers a glance of freedom against oppressive political power.

It is well known that the post-war period attributed to modernism a vanguard role, both in the political sense and in the sense that it claimed that art was capable of reuniting humans; that art was able to release hidden potentialities in the human being. However, at the end of the '70s this transcendentalist approach that mythologized innovation and individualism in the name of creativity was replaced by a new practice according to which the artist became a manipulator of signs more than a producer of art objects, and the viewer an active reader of messages rather than a passive contemplator of the aesthetic or consumer of the spectacular. Many artists of that period were influenced by the theories of Jean Baudrillard, who asserted that we experience a 'hyper-reality', a world in which images no longer represent a real object, but referred the viewer to another image, then another, in an endless sequence. It is about a world where simulation was not the pretense of a real experience, but was simulacrum itself the only kind of reality we could hope for.[1] This condition inevitably recalls one of the more fashionable themes in contemporary postmodernist theory, that of the 'death' of the subject itself and the accompanying emphasis on the 'decentering' of the formerly 'centered' subject.[2] The end of the bourgeois ego or monad means not only the end of style, in the sense of the unique and the personal, but also much more. Frederic Jameson claims that it brings about the waning of affect liberation from anxiety and from every other kind of feeling as well, 'since there is no longer a self present to do the feeing' (Jameson, 1992, p. 1074-80). Yet the manipulation of what already exists, be it capital or cultural signs, and the end of the autonomous bourgeois monad or ego create a number of troubling questions in regard to the political significance of art: How can artists address the world of the simulacrum? Is it possible to represent a simulation? The practice of simulation can also be seen as an endorsement of the culture of simulacra. But is such an endorsement desirable, if, as neo-Marxist theorists believe, post-industrial culture constitutes a further level of social alienation?

Hal Foster tries to reconcile these contradictions by identifying two types of postmodernism: a postmodernism of complicity in contemporary capitalism, and a postmodernism of resistance to it (Foster, 1992, p. 1065-66). He dismisses postmodernism as relativism, as pluralism-a notion that all positions in culture and politics are now open and equal, that 'anything goes'. The argument that the 'end of ideology is here,' is simply the inverse of the fatalistic belief that nothing works, that we live under a total system without hope of redress the ideology of late capitalism. In cultural politics today the postmodernism of reaction includes a neoconservative tendency that severs the cultural from the social and confounds the practices of the one (modernism) with the ills of the other (modernization). Accordingly, an 'adversary' culture is denounced while the economic and political status quo is affirmed. In opposition,

> a resistant postmodernism is concerned with a critical deconstruction of tradition, not an instrumental pastiche of pop-or pseudo-historical forms, with a critique of origins, not a return to them. In short, it seeks to question rather than exploit cultural codes, to explore rather than conceal social and political affiliations (Foster, 1998, p. ix-xvii).

Within the framework of postmodernism we could also posit Bleeps,[3] the Greek artist who works in the pubic space, and especially on the walls of Athens, expressing the overall spirit of suppression as well as the general dissent and the intense social upheaval that prevail in Greece in the last few years of the global financial crisis. However, we should proceed very carefully and espouse Foster's distinction between a postmodernism of reaction and a postmodernism of resistance. Thus, Bleeps' pieces arise as a counter-practice to the 'false normativity'[4] of a reactionary postmodernism; however, he does not reduce modernism to a mere style but he consciously assimilates some of its fundamental practices such as: the formalist concerns with innovation and the faith in genuineness and originality as important values in the creation of an unrivalled personal style.

He relentlessly experiments with different styles, non-artistic made and found materials (*objets trouvés*) assembled into his works in public space and onto canvas. His choice to incorporate materials of waste and impoverishment (cardboard, adhesive tape, rags, gadgets, plastic wrap, etc.) generates an asceticism that can be understood as the political radicalization of a programmatic poverty of means; these transitory objects, or rather, non-objects since they are made to be thrown away manifest the transition from cultural representations in the bourgeois public sphere to those of a newly emerging proletarian one, in which artistic production promises the future equality of the constitution of the subject within the collective. Moreover, even on the basic level of materials, Bleeps' work reflects upon the concept of value in artistic production, and on its continuous shifts between cult value and use value, between exchange value and surplus value, between exhibition value and sign-exchange value. Bleeps not only foregrounds the work's perishable nature but also regards vandalism as one of the many possible responses to his public creations. After all, the attraction and deployment of debris, i.e. the *assemblage* technique, have remained tropes of modernity, and even ascended to a central avant-garde strategy. Since then, this strategy has expanded its spectrum, and in Bleeps' work shows a resistance against accelerated production and total instrumentalization; it articulates clear political commentaries on the late capitalist overproduction and its systematic destruction of resources, albeit without being devoid of humor.

By locating his works in public space without any evidence of a legitimizing institutional frame he instigates a new type of value, different form the market value, and integrates a certain kind of activism, of struggle in his art; when an artwork is in a public space it is important to provide the choice not to see it or not to use it; however, passers-by often remove and take the kind of disposable materials Bleeps works with to them. At this point, we can reflect upon the role of the participatory spectator in Bleeps' works: The social environment the pieces create triggers the involvement of the passers-by; they decide whether to destroy the works or to maintain and animate them, and thus they create a social relationship beyond them; it is as if the artist cannot avoid investing the works with some kind of social contract and therefore people are likely to read them as some form of artist-activism. In this sense, Bleeps' public art is not merely art in the public space, but art that institutes a public space, a space of common action among people. According to Chantal Mouffe, the artistic activism has definitively an important role to play in the creation of an agonistic public sphere (Mouffe, 2000, p. 1-17).[5] The agonistic approach is particular suited to grasp the nature of these new forms of artistic activism. It aims at giving a voice to all those who are silenced within the framework of the existing hegemony; it foments dissent; it makes visible what the dominant consensus tends to obscure and obliterate; it increases the capacity to think politically and to make a choice between conflicting alternatives. Nevertheless, Bleeps' critical art does not offer a manifestation of refusal, an expression of the absolute negation. It is important to see that his critical practices are not practices of denunciation. Denunciation is just asserting the belief of the people addressed, it doesn't really change the way we see things. The artist instead goes a step further and makes the viewer ask questions on the financial crisis in Greece, on the urban poverty and political exclusion, on unemployment and bad health services, on all that informs the narrative of Athens' decline; he does not provide answers; he does not tell him or her what to think; he creates other forms of consciousness, not simply lifts false consciousness by denunciation, and most importantly he does not approach the political discourse in moral terms.

In accordance with Mouffe's further argumentation, I will stress her illuminating thesis that we should not see the relation between art and politics in terms of two separately constituted fields: art on one side and politics on the other, between which a relation would need to be established. As Bleeps' work manifests there is an aesthetic dimension in the political and there is a political dimension in art. By putting aesthetic means at the service of political activism, this 'artivism' can be seen as a counter-hegemonic move against the capitalist appropriation of aesthetics in order to secure its valorization process. 'From the point of view of the theory of hegemony, artistic practices play a role in the constitution and maintenance of a given symbolic order or in its challenging and this is why they necessarily have a political dimension. The political, for its part, concerns the symbolic ordering of social relations, '*the mise en scène*', of human coexistence and this is where lies its aesthetic dimension' (Mouffe, 2007). Politicization in Bleeps' pieces is achieved with the means of a criticality that would have governed conceptual and post-conceptual works. The objective of his work is to occupy the public space in order to disrupt the smooth image that corporate capitalism is trying to spread; hidden locations, abandoned buildings or walls located on the edges of Athens, all these transient spaces where the city's borders tend to blur, also offer a fertile ground for his activity since visibility is not a precondition for understanding it, nor is agreement on a certain political goal; rather the willingness to reflect upon current political and economic issues is essential.

Writing/speech and images are inextricably linked and constitute a central practice to Bleeps' activity. As he personally claims: 'My work is a social diary on public display'.[6] Equating the public sphere and the public square Bleeps implies that the shared public space of the city could be 'read' like a newspaper's politics-reporting section. On one side there is a 'preferred reading': the official argumentation within the mass-mediated public sphere stresses that the reason for the existent situation does not lie in the widespread political corruption and mismanagement, but in a process of unrestrained spending and failure to implement financial reforms which left Greece badly exposed when the global economic downturn struck.[7] On the other side, according to prominent economists the current crisis should be seen as a systemic crisis of a particular form of capitalism, namely neoliberal capitalism. The systemic crisis can be resolved only through a major restructuring of the system and not through appropriate state bailouts of financial institutions and the imposition of some new regulations on the financial system.[8] The preferred reading has been contested by mass protests and riots in Athens and other cities, in an attempt to disrupt the planned invisibility of a different discourse on economic, political and institutional crisis.

Other issues of Bleeps' pieces that trigger a number of insights concern iconographical and morphological aspects, and since I am an art historian, this is the field on which I have more to contribute. By using a visual vocabulary directly concerned with representation, this kind of representation borrowed from the mass culture-film most particularly-the artist employs a strategic parallel with that of a group of artists in the '70s analyzed by Douglas Crimp in his essay 'Pictures' (Crimp, 2005, p. 17-30).[9] I will recall the art historian's thoughts because his conceptualization of representation can be applied wisely to Bleeps' problematic. It is about a kind of representation that the artist sees as an inescapable part of our ability to grasp the world around us. Representation emerges in his pieces not in the familiar guise of realism but with certain autonomy, freed from the tyranny of the represented; that's why there is no formalism any more, nor is it productive to speak about style in regard to his work. His pictures show an important connection with questions raised by Surrealism and Pop. However, the primary issue in his work is the structure of signification, with that distance that constitutes our desire. Hence, his pictures maintain an allegiance to that radical aspiration that we continue to recognize as modernist. On the other side, by using an iconographic pastiche, as described by Jameson (Jameson, 1998, p. 131-134), i.e. representational elements stemming from popular culture and artistic tradition, the artist seemingly approaches the postmodernist condition. The truth is, however, that he does not use this common practice of postmodernism because he believes that it is no longer feasible to achieve any new personal style. Unconstrained by the history of painting he oscillates between modernism and postmodernism; he is uninhibited: he does not worry that figuration might look reactionary, or that abstraction could be merely decorative. He has formed his own stringent criteria by which he evaluates his pieces and therefore has confidence in his own paintings' quality. In short, he always maintains a strong spirit of independence and follows a highly individual course. Bleeps works with representation and let representation remain what it is: the vessel in which the work is contained. It is in this regard, that we can understand his indifference about the formal quality of his pieces (perspectival and anatomically correct drawing, texture, linear quality, color, shape, compositional balance, etc.). His almost fanatical insistence on withholding conditions of quality from the work of art is of particular importance to understand the consistency of his artistic activism. Bleeps believes that a socially enforced absence of subjectivity has to be matched with an absence of privileged forms of artistic articulation.

The embedded texts in his pieces do not operate as an autonomous or unified object, but as a set of relations with other texts: Bleeps often uses the principle we know as intertextuality, the principle that poststructuralists label Text or Writing (Barthes, 1972). Through the recording of the signified, the insertion of word games, Duchampian anagrams, well-known emblems and symbols, and allusions to the mass culture, Bleeps creates visual-verbal hybrids; just the kinds of instances of an intimate inter-medial collaboration between the linguistic and the visual that generated levels of meaning inaccessible to each alone. Thus, by avoiding the trap of binary thinking established by the dominance of language over consciousness he seeks to challenge the conventional scope of language, upsetting and confusing meanings and usage. Bleeps' pieces reveal meanings and power relations that develop within urban landscapes; simultaneously he takes our political awareness a step further. He provides insight into how rights-claims and economic systems are frequently situated in the internal public spaces of the policy process and on how these spaces condition the possible outcomes of such processes. Of particular importance is also the function of the captions combined with the pictures or added to the digital photos the artist uploads onto his personal website. The textual, hand-drawn enunciations invoke an additional tension of urgency, incompetence and poverty of means. Referring again to Crimp's renowned essay, we could similarly reflect upon the lack of an obvious single meaning, and upon open narrative structures in Bleeps' images:

> Artists subvert the standard signifying function of the pictures tied to their captions, their commentaries, their narrative sequences-tied, that is, to the illusion that they are directly transparent to a signified [...] The caption doesn't state the signification of the picture; rather it provides the image with a meaning that it would not otherwise have. The picture is not transparent to such a meaning, while the caption is often self sufficient, has meaning with or without the picture. Can the picture itself be said to be intrinsically without meaning? (Crimp, 2005, p. 20).

Bleeps also leaves the question open. Furthermore, the inescapable *semiology* of visual production is-not unlike in Conceptual art-celebrated as a triumph of language over the primacy of painterly matter. From an art historian perspective I could say that Bleeps' idiosyncratic representation inscribed in the horizon of sophisticated textual references manifests a striking characteristic: the re-materialization of Conceptual art.

A further point is the misleading classification of Bleeps' work as street art. His reputation as a street artist, assigned to him by the commercial media, has been based on the fact that his pieces are situated illegally on public walls; involve an element of storytelling and figurative subjects; are executed with materials and techniques commonly associated with street art such as stenciling; and are accompanied by his signature. However in my opinion, Bleeps' work cannot be classified under the generic term-of-convenience street art and any resemblance between him and the street artists does not extend beyond trivial similarities. The name refers to a certain persona; not a tag; his iconography does not pay homage to street life and street existence, and the pieces are not designed to interact with the natural and architectural characteristics of the site; additionally, the artist departs from the thoughtful aesthetic, the style ornamentation, so characteristic of street art, intending to improve the look of the piece. On the contrary, as previously mentioned, Bleeps uses a self-conscious 'bad' painting technique exemplified in 'unlovely' paintings that translate his concerns about the present politico-economic condition and his general existential unease into expressionist visual terms (hard outlines, bold flat colors, non-perspectival space, simulated infantilism, anatomically graphic and distorted figures); his pieces are content driven, coded and oblique: disjointed compositions and textual cut-ups form multi-layered connotations; unlike the common trait of the street art, the *direct expressive thought* that utilizes words and ideas simply and economically, (Chaffee, 1993, p. 8-9), so that it can be easily understood by any casual observer, Bleeps' paintings do not rely on the viewer's grasp of an ostensible meaning. There is openness here for further interpretation, a need for contemplation that alters the length of time usually spent by the passerby with street art. The compositions are not designed to be taken in briefly by a viewer surprised by a masterpiece on the walls, as is the case with the street art (Lewisohn, 2008, p. 127). On the contrary, with its endless uncontrollable proliferation of information, its vast range of national and international historic topics, its sheer integration of objects and materials Bleeps' work reveals intensity and complexity that affects the time of its reading and absorbs the viewer to sustain engagement over time.

By symbolically signifying his paintings Bleeps is not identifying them as his own. On the contrary, his signature, written in the plural, conveys the contribution of his assistants and thus subverts the notion of ownership of ideas. He indicates that the pieces are executed by a loosely formed collective. The collective is predicated on a collaborative attitude ranging from exchanging ideas, providing help, materials and tools, to offering inspiration, companionship and animating the whole activity. Bleeps.gr ostensibly operates like a graffiti tag; it circulates too publicly in the physical territory of shared public space as well as in the mass-mediated sphere, and too fast to earn the unmitigated approval and respect of the appropriate validating bodies: the graffitists, street artists and the general public, nationally and internationally. Moreover, the signature alludes to Bleeps' website in an attempt to undermine the traditional practice of the artist's signature, which constitutes a decisive mark of authorial presence, a vestige of Western cultural property. The free distribution of his works via social networking services on the Internet is in accordance with the theorists of the cognitive economy and the digital commons as 'information and knowledge resources that are collectively created and owned or shared between or among a community and that tend to be non-exclusive, that is, be (generally freely) available to third parties. Thus, they are oriented to favor use and reuse, rather than to exchange as a commodity'.[10] In agreement with the aforementioned tendencies Bleeps asserts that immaterial products only function to their full potential when they are shared in an open way. Sharing it with other people does not diminish the usefulness of an idea or an affect. On the contrary, it becomes useful only by being shared in common. Bleeps proceeds here from the thesis on 'the common' defined by the political philosophers Antonio Negri and Michael Hardt in their widely known book *Commonwealth*. They both consider the common as the commonwealth of the material world, and 'more significantly those results of social production, that are necessary for social interaction and further production, such as knowledges, codes, information, and so forth' (Hardt & Negri, 2009, p. viii). Following this argumentation the artist focuses his practices on interaction, care and cohabitation in a common world. In his hands, political philosophy and art become *machines de guerre* that help him to fight for his ideas, to act and create, to overtax himself again and again.

A significant piece 'The Bailout Sleep' (2012, Image 13) exemplifies Bleeps' procedure to turn the image into a perceptual puzzle.[11] The scenery consists of drawn and stenciled references to Ancient Greek architecture, as well as of subjects from art history. The Ionic fluted columns with the characteristic scroll-like Ionic capitals support a roughly painted pediment shaded in gray in which a skull is embedded wearing the *crown of thorns*, one of the 'Instruments of the Passion' (*Arma Christi*).[12] Bleeps' symbolic language approaches this motif as a mere cultural relic devoid of any substance and mystic potency. The skull is flanked by two stenciled hands with colored red nails whose iconographic source is to be sought in Dürer's famous study for an apostle's hand, *Praying Hands* (circa 1508).[13] Does Bleeps evoke here an ambivalent sexuality, innately in all human beings? Does he isolate the pair of hands to induce a metonymy that stands *pars pro toto* for the most essential instrument of the artistic creativity? Does he make references to the dark impulses lurking behind the visual? The impression of something disturbing and uncontrollable has been enhanced as a sleeping female figure with chained hands occupies the center of the composition. She is embedded in a cobalt blue cloud that set her off and erases other background noises. At the lower end of the painting two half-length standing Madonnas, echoing iconic types of Holy Virgin in Western art, surround the woman and seem to pray for her. But their hands are cut off and replaced by the androgynous ones above them; additionally, their halo is shaped by various digitally reworked and collaged banknotes, directly affixed to the wall surface. If we consider the sleeping woman as the personification of Greece, the land that faces now its most severe debt crisis and is expected to seek another international bail-out agreement in order to meet its financing needs, will then the prayers be proved effective or will her awakening remain a far-fetched dream? In visual terms this sense of danger comes from the obscure and restrained palette, the raw, unschooled drawing, and especially from the cacophonous heterogeneity of the pictorial elements. In short, what is added up cannot be neatly resolved, and this uncertainty fits Bleeps' experience of living in Athens better than anything.

The frequent occurrence of traditional cultural elements in Bleeps' pieces has been predicated on a vibrant relation between a sense of self and a community. He regards folklore as fundamentally appealing because it conjures up a specific discourse on traditional values, group solidarity and political mobilization. Besides, according to Henry Glassie 'At its best, all art, whether folk art or fine art, either engages a process of 'transcendence of consciousness' or leads us 'into an awareness of our position in the cosmos'' (Glassie, 1999, p. 119). Bleeps is especially concerned with the issue of place that has also been scrutinized by the discipline of the phenomenology; phenomenologists focus on the subjective experience and perception of a person's life world. In particular, Christian Norberg-Schulz' thesis on place has influenced the artist's thought and thematic imagery (Norberg-Schulz, 1980). *Place* gained prominence in phenomenological research, architecture and geography through Norberg-Schulz' work on the existence of a 'genius loci,' meaning the spirit of a place. Revelations of traditions and re-collections of disseminated identities in particular, turn out to be powerful critiques of several contemporary rhetorics of domination. The contemporary reinvention of ethnic identity through remembering is of course nothing new, but in Bleeps' work implies a potent political force, in an oblique attempt to understand its dynamics in his own troubled homeland.

Thus, in the piece 'We Lived (Consumed) our Lives; WRONG! So we Changed our Pathway (Lives)' (Image 15) the male figure dressed in a modern, fashionable way contrasts with the old-fashioned, traditional way of life which reflects a remote past. The chronological disparity has been also emphasized through the wooden frame that encloses and isolates the figure from the adjacent scene: the real caned chair, the plastic tablecloth, the painted vase with the flowers, the coffee cup and the glass of water, all attributes relating to a particular ethnic memory. The red cap, component of the Greek guards' (*Evzones*) traditional uniform, the British and American flags depicted in the T-shirt of the man, as well as the black eagle on the plate he holds, the main coat of arms of Prussia, are all well-known symbols that demonstrate the assimilation to the bland, neutral style of a globalized economy and society. To a Westerner, twenty-first society globally seems to be characterized by surface homogenization, by the erosion of public enactments of tradition, by the loss of ritual and historical rootedness. Furthermore, the intrusion of the Prussian emblem into the Seferian verses from the poem 'Denial'[14] invites a comparison between the Prussian dominance over the German states as a result of the Austro-Prussian War in 1866 and Germany's current superior role in the EU since Germanocentric prescriptions for the Eurozone impose conditions on monetary and fiscal policy. Utilizing layers of associations, emotionally resonant metaphors and historical knowledge the picture resists to specific meaning but does not abolish meaning altogether. Seeing all these heterogeneous elements, the viewer has been invited to invent stories in which the pictorial elements become the synecdochic characters. Bleeps gives the viewer a critical apparatus that provides a set of conceptual tools to check against assimilating the other to the self, and to inquire into what is hidden in language and picture, what is deferred by signs, what is repressed, implicit, or mediated. Moreover, it is not accidental that he renders the scene through a folk-art style look: naive drawing style striving for simplicity, planar pictorial modes, distorted shapes defined through outline, not shading, contrast between dark outlines and flat areas of bright colors.[15]

In the 'Greece Next Economic Model' (2011, Image 11) we see a full-length, standing female figure, awkwardly drawn through an anti-naturalistic modeling and bounded by clear outlines. The figure is depicted against a densely painted cobalt blue background, a typical device of Bleeps' compositions. She is dressed in underwear and her body's stance mimics fashion models walking the catwalk. But her disability is obvious: her right leg is amputated and replaced with a wooden pirate-leg, a visual pun that intensifies the painting's message of disillusionment. The sense of the uncanny, typical of Bleeps' idiosyncratic visual idiom, stems not only from the enigmatic distortion of an otherwise fashionable and beautifully proportioned woman, but also from the feeling that we are watched by her: her eyes stare out from the pictorial plane and are looking obliquely at us from a place that is not our place, but in which we are unwillingly and thoroughly enmeshed and implicated. Thus, even if we seek to flee from her unpleasant appearance and her implying message, we are incapable of escaping. Next to the figure the stenciled phrase 'Greece Next Economic Model' refers to the well-known reality show 'Greece's Next Top Model'. Recalling again Crimp's commentaries on the combination between caption and picture, we will agree with him that

> The caption is only one of many expressions of a desire that treats the image with the mechanistic devotion appropriate to a fetish. The obsessive manipulations and alterations of words are the materialization of a reverie. But because desire comes about only in the sphere of frustration the image remains forever at a distance. [...] It is not because this is a particular woman, but because this is no particular woman, that the picture becomes a fetish (Crimp, 2005, p. 25).

The interesting feature of the picture lies in the fact that the coherence as well as the distinction between word and image breaks down, and a hybrid form is produced. The hidden symbolism anticipating the harsh austerity measures which were going to be implemented by the IMF rescue packages politics, serves here as a warning of resistance and as an attempt to involve the viewer. Although this kind of involvement does not mean interactivity, it calls for activity: the activity of thinking.

I would like to conclude this paper by referring to the series 'Playing the trumpet' (2007-2012).[16] In my opinion, the series has a certain interest, not only because it is accompanied by the written command 'Wake Up', an immediate plea to viewers for reflecting upon the implemented financial politics, and against the alienation from their own emotions, creativity and desires, but also because of its implying visual and acoustic twists and interconnections. The pieces display the silhouette of a girl blowing the trumpet, consisting of many polychromatic, stenciled patches that invoke the penetrating sound of the trumpet in a fresh and playful way. The color patches form a visual/oral rhythm that combusts into a tense complexity of the pieces as painted sight and painted sound.[17]

Summarizing, I would like to point out that Bleeps has devised a grand complexity referring to politics and existential deep-felt anxieties out of an expressionist, primitive and at times infantile style. In short, he deploys elements that extend from the early twentieth-century historical Expressionism, American Abstract Expressionism, Conceptual and Outsider art. If by their monumental scale his works demonstrate an ambition to change the world, according to Marx, and to change life, according to Rimbaud, their ephemerality, due to deliberate erasure as vandalism or through weather and the passage of time, metaphorically shows the fragility of the position from which he is critically challenging hegemonic structures. However, Bleeps presents the unwritten history of the city, the lost objects of a fabulated origin, his 'Athens' under erasure, driven out of the official picture, but ready to erupt at any time. Paraphrasing the lyrics of the renowned American musician's song, we would agree that 'the answer my friend is not blowin' in the wind. The answer is written on the walls.'[18]

Chapter 12

Bleeps.gr: A Visual Diary on Public Display

The established motivation for every activity is money. The motivation was never, after all, human beings. In a capitalist system, human beings have learnt to think in terms of equivalence, subjugating their entire lives under the law to give less than what you take as an exchange. Goods follow the arbitrariness of hyper-value. The configuration of desires from consumers gradually installs the power of the status quo. 'I want what you are selling to me because you can convince me that with that I will feel better and more supreme'. In capitalism, if you are not a part of the bourgeoisie, you are just a consumable unit.

We held onto our lives
travelling
through OCHRE trees

Image 11: **Greece next economic model**

Image 12: **Dreaming Safe**

Image 13: **The Bailout Sleep**

Image 14: **Hopeless**

Image 15: **We Lived (Consumed) our Lives WRONG; so we changed our Pathways**

Part 4:

The Revolution Will Not be Analyzed

Chapter 13

Europhile or Eurosceptic?: Gaps in the Narrative and Performances of Panic

Marilena Zaroulia and Philip Hager

> Theirs is a state of anxiety; if it becomes more definite, then it is fear. [...]
> A feeling that suits us better is overdue. It is a question of learning hope (Bloch, 1995, p.3).

After the unclear results of the 6 May 2012 general election, Greece was led to a second round on 17 June, offering a spectacular arena for the expression of the international community's concern: what the mainstream media branded as the most important election since the colonels' downfall (1974) would decide the future of the common European currency and, consequently, the European project. The *Spiegel*'s website headline 'Europe's Future hangs in the balance' (Hawley, 2012) and *The Irish Times'* observation that 'the Greeks vote in our names' (Anon, 2012) are indicative of the discourses that circulated outside the Greek borders, spreading an atmosphere of suspension over Europe about its future.

In this context, Greeks were presented with an oversimplified dilemma: are you for the European Union (EU) or against it? While *Europhile*s proposed to continue the memorandum of austerity, *Eurosceptics* advocated a break with such policies, a proposal that, according to the Europhiles, would directly lead to a Greek Eurozone exit with devastating results for the country and unforeseeable consequences for Europe. The Europhiles were presented as responsible, rational, sensible and guarantors of the country's security and European prospects; the

Eurosceptics were accused of lack of responsibility, naivety, unrealistic thinking and, in short, were considered dangerous for the country's and Europe's future.[1] This Europhile/Eurosceptic opposition underpinned political parties' campaigns, framed national and international media analysis and reproduced the dominant narrative about the Greek crisis, originally articulated by former PM Giorgos Papandreou: 'We have all inherited a boat that is about to sink. A country that has lost its friends' and partners' respect'; a collective response to this emergency is a 'national imperative' (PrimeMinisterGr, 2010).

In his statement, addressing the nation while officially calling for the international community's 'support', Papandreou described the crisis as a 'new Odyssey for Hellenism' and through metaphors of maritime life – 'storm' tormenting the country, the need for a 'safe harbor to rebuild our boat' – suggested that the nation's 'wonderful people' would be able to navigate the difficulties and 'find the route to Ithaca' (PrimeMinisterGr, 2010). Expressing faith in 'this land' he pledged for a future of 'justice, pride and security'. Greek and EU futures were bound together, but could be protected as long as Greece took the necessary steps towards 'emancipation' from practices and ideologies that had historically obstructed its progress. This ostensibly calm, rational but actually emotion-arousing address, delivered from the Eastern border of Europe – the small island of Kastelorizo - set the tone for the account of the crisis.

Using the June elections as our starting point, we aim to study this dominant narrative in its various socio-political, ideological and affective dimensions, arguing that it is solidly founded on the normalizing, Europhile/Eurosceptic hierarchical opposition and limits comprehensive analyzes of the crisis and consequential performances of resistance. This tale of emergency, responsibility and common sense conceals a gaping hole, filled in by 'rational' performances of emotions and panic and perpetuating a problematic interrelation of national and European belonging, articulated through the Eurosceptic/Europhile dichotomy and staged in the Athenian urban fabric.[2] We view Athens not as exceptional but, rather, as exemplary of the European norm (in crisis).

In the realm of signification, the Europhile/Eurosceptic binary operates through a chain of metaphors or metonyms, transforming into new dichotomies of what cultural theorist Sara Ahmed has identified as 'sticky terms', where stickiness can be read both as 'binding' people together but also as 'blockage' (2004, p. 91). We will explore four iterations of the dichotomy, questioning how they contribute to people 'sticking' together and 'sticking to' particular views, while 'blocking' Other attitudes to the crisis: secure/insecure; rational/irrational; sensible/insensible and responsible/irresponsible. We will close the chapter by re-evaluating the Europhile/Eurosceptic opposition beyond fetishization or scepticism. We argue that practices in a city like Athens might pave the way towards a multilayered understanding and experience of Europeanness, where master narratives of panic are subverted by micro-narratives and, significantly, *doings* of hope.

This article analyzes the performative dimensions of discourse and emotion that 'work' on subjects, ideology and urban space. Focusing on examples from the media and the parties' pre-elections campaigns, we discuss what kinds of signs circulate and their complex 'doings' as they retain or augment their 'stickiness' through repetition. Before we discuss such performances of the Europhile/Eurosceptic dichotomy that currently prevents any possibility for genuine dialogue and democratic politics, we consider how it is embedded in a particular ideological framework that lies at the core of contemporary Greek identity. This performative that both 'depend[s] on past histories, at the same time as [it] generate[s] effect' (Ahmed, 2004, p. 13) underpins debates about the country's future in the EU and the way out of the crisis and makes members of the Greek nation 'stick' together while 'blocking' any real possibility of interaction with Europe.[3]

Genealogies: 'Us' versus 'Them'

Since 2010, Greece appears to be moving back to the late 1970s-early 1980s period, when the country's entry to the European Economic Community (EEC) became a battlefield between the right, center and left; by the late 1980s, though, 'the EEC metamorphosed from being a symbol in intra-party competition into becoming a reality in Greek political and economic life' (Verney, 1993, p.132). It is beyond the scope of this article to map in detail how political and popular attitudes towards the EEC/EU shifted in the past three decades but a brief summary of the key moments in the country's process of 'Europeanization' is necessary for an analysis of the current crises. These attitudes were shaped after the fall of the colonels' junta but reflect anxieties that – at a discursive and ideological level – have defined Greek identity since the nation-state's formation in 1830.

The June elections staged in the most obvious way what can be described as the ideological cornerstone of Greek national identity: the hierarchical opposition between 'us' and 'them', Greek and Other.[4] Currently, this tension permeates attitudes towards the non-Greek Other, embodied either by the representatives of the 'troika',[5] or the immigrants 'flooding' urban centers. Performances towards the non-Greek Other determine national belonging, usually in negative terms, through shame, fear or hate. Further, beyond cultural, racial and ethnic definitions, the Other is also identified in ideological and political terms. A new incarnation of cold war rhetorics, where national membership was contested for those with 'deviant' ideological dispositions, namely the communists and communist leaning, is now under way. A key difference is that whereas in its first incarnation, the Other existed both inside (Greek communists) and outside the borders (the iron curtain), in its current form the 'communist Other' exists only within the borders. Such rhetoric employs the panic-inducing narratives and memories of the Cold War in order to reiterate sticky metaphors and delegitimize any form of resistance as Other. In short, this 'us/them' division translates into *who could stick together against whom*, inside the Greek borders.

At the present moment, it is interesting to consider a historical paradox in perceptions of the West, in this case 'Old Europe'. On the one hand, culturally and geopolitically, West has been regarded as 'Other' to Greece; on the other hand, the making of modern Greekness cannot be disassociated from the Western Europeans' influential role. Vangelis Calotychos, in *Modern Greece: A Cultural Poetics* (2003), has shown how the idea of the modern Greek nation was conceived outside its borders and subsequently transplanted to Greece. He acknowledges the philhellenes' instrumental role in branding modern Greekness, based on vague ideals of Hellenism and follows the analysis of modern Greek scholar Stathis Gourgouris, who has compared the phenomenon of philhellenism to 'a similar cultural ensemble constitutive of colonization, i.e. orientalism' (Calotychos 2003, p.53). Calotychos observes that this process of inventing 'the Greek' ultimately deprived modern Greeks of a present identity, for the emphasis was constantly placed on the past and Greece was imagined as an ideal space. This process of identity-formation galvanized a 'discourse of ab-sense' (Calotychos 2003, p.47), a refusal of the present that structured experiences of Greekness and, crucially for this discussion, outlined progressive and traditionalist attitudes, the left and the right and their perspectives on what constitutes Europe.

Since the early 1990s, the EU's growing federalism as well as the conflicts in the Balkans dictated the need for a renegotiation of Greek domestic and international policies, beyond PASOK's 1980s antagonistic, populist approach to EEC, summarized in PM

Andreas Papandreou's aphorism 'Greece belongs to the Greeks'.[6] After the election of Costas Simitis as PASOK's new leader in 1996, the government's paramount objective – soon elevated to a national priority – was the convergence with Western Europe, sealed by the integration in the European Monetary Union. The measures that the government introduced on the way to the early 2000s were summarized under a term that haunted modern Greek politics: modernization. In the late nineteenth century, modernization signified 'the disappearance of self-contained, traditional communities, the transformation of 'subjects' into 'citizens', and more generally the mobilization and inclusion of the majority of the population into the 'imagined national community' (Mouzelis, 1996, p. 218), thus tightening the links between nation and state. In the late twentieth century, modernization acquired a new meaning: neoliberal policies that would align Greece with Western Europe and galvanize an attitude of 'openness to Europe from a position of socio-political and cultural autonomy' (Mouzelis, 1996, p. 225) that would guard national sovereignty while fostering national and transnational financial links.

The country's official entry to the Eurozone in 2002 and the Athens 2004 Olympics emerged as two milestones in this process of modernization and Europeanization. Perceptions of the nation and Athens as its symbolic center shifted. Greece's position was not simply aligned to what was in the past perceived as the Other, the 'Old Europe'; it occupied anew a unique position in Europe, as the origin of European culture. As the Games' Opening Ceremony manifested, Greece was gladly limiting itself to a performance of 'ab-sense' where the focus was placed in past narratives of grandeur that seemed to secure a prosperous future. What had been advocated as the ultimate mission of the politics of the *metapolitefsi*, namely Costantinos Karamanlis' famous 1970s mantra 'we belong to the West', by 2004 was finally elevated to political and ideological orthodoxy; ironically, to be dismantled during the years of his nephew's Costas Karamanlis administration (2004-9).

Nonetheless, amidst this *milieu* of celebration of dominant orthodoxy, there were frictions: at the turn of the 00s, the stock market boom and the ID cards crisis were – in their material, intellectual, ideological, cultural and affective dimensions – precursors of the present crises.[7] 'Ab-sense' dominated the practices and ethics of a new social class that flooded Athens at the turn of the third millennium; what was a gap in politics and present time was disguised as a new lifestyle performing the 'here and now', only to celebrate false affluence, consumerist hedonism and consequential fraud political practices. Athens transformed, bearing all the scars of global late capitalist uneven development, which lay underneath the European convergence mission, while the 'us/them' dichotomy seemed to have disappeared from public discourse.

But when the crisis erupted, Papandreou openly alluded to it: the other was a vague enemy, 'the markets', and 'the ultimate goal is to free the country from any protection or supervision' (PrimeMinisterGr, 2010). Since the first memorandum's approval by the Greek Parliament, the imperative of national sovereignty has been emphasized across the political spectrum, albeit articulated in different ways. The oxymoron permeating the crisis is that all political parties profess defense of the country's independence, which arguably was why the international community's 'support' was first called upon. This Greek state of emergency that follows a decade of 'ab-sense' and shapes the interaction with the European Other/'partner', is not only an economic one that requires certain 'objective' measures. Significantly, it is a socio-political one, challenging the 'democratic consensus', which in turn needs to be *imposed* through state repression cloaked as rationality.

Rational/ Irrational

Neoliberal rationality, Wendy Brown points out, 'renders every human being and institution, including the constitutional state, on the model of the firm and hence supplants democratic principles with entrepreneurial ones in the political sphere' (Brown, 2011, p.47). The neoliberal firm offers a blueprint for identity and community formations, dictating the logic upon which social and political relations are built. In this sense, (neoliberal) rationality 'becomes' a 'natural' human disposition, a 'universal' principle of conviviality. In the pre-election period the question of rationality was closely related to the country's position within or without Europe in the abstract sense of the European unification dream, as opposed to its materialization in the EU structures. In this emerging incarnation of the binary opposition, the Europhiles performed rationality, while Eurosceptics exemplified the irrational. Alexis Papachelas, the editor of *Kathimerini*, calls for a battle 'we must all strive to keep the country on its feet, to keep it in the Western camp, and convince those angry youths that the spark they see is in fact the promise of chaos and blind protest' (2012b). The age-old 'we belong to the West' mantra re-emerges and drives the 'rational' approach, while any critique of European political and economic structures embodies the irrational, the chaotic, and the blind – sticky metaphors that in Papachelas' reasoning stigmatize the youth.

The December 2008 riots mark a turn in a long history of youth Othering, in combination to the demonization of a particular spot in the Athenian urban grid, Exarcheia. There, according to mainstream representations, anarchists, 'known strangers', masked youth and Other troublemakers roam freely, until their next calamitous drift. Such discourses *choose* to overlook the fact that the younger generation were the first victims of the crisis, alongside other vulnerable social groups, 'no-hopers produced by transcendental capitalism and the policies of neo-liberal government. They are the 'refugees of the interior'' (Hage, 2003, p. 21). Any argument about youth *blindness* is undermined when one *looks* at youth unemployment statistics (15-24) rising above the 52% mark in the first term of 2012 (EL.STAT., 2012). Of course it would be reductive to suggest that to be *young* means to be *angry*. The following example presents a different attitude by the youth organization of the conservative party, ONNED.

In an advertisement we watch a couple eating and drinking some of the priciest items in the menu in a glossy restaurant. He is an Alpha-male: he feeds his 'babe', then asking her whether she liked the food to which she responds with sighs. The bill arrives, he looks at it and returns it. The waiter forces back the bill, at which point the girl utters her first words 'Alexis... don't'. Alexis, however, exclaims: 'this is odious, I denounce my debt on my part.' Unavoidably they are thrown out, the door closes behind them and on it we read: 'with his cockiness they will throw us out of Europe'. In the final sequence Alexis apologizes to the girl; he simply wanted to impress her, to deceive her into consent, but miserably failed.

In this, rather shallow, narrative Greece is a dim-witted girl, that is deceived by Alexis Tsipras,[8] an ordinary and not so successful *conman*, and Europe is reduced to a fancy restaurant. Apart from the obvious problematic gender politics and the silencing of the youth experience as described earlier, this TV spot articulates Europe as luxurious Other – a parochial fantasy that eliminates any possibility of a relation in equal terms. Further, a clear right/wrong divide emerges: Alexis makes all the wrong decisions, his attitude is irrational on the basis that he knows *how things are* and chooses to break the rules. The naturalized ethics of the (capitalist) marketplace are closely linked to EU membership: in the same way that the concepts of individual freedom and freedom to own become increasingly indistinguishable; EU membership becomes a marker of freedom, democracy, decency and prosperity. Outside the EU Greece is only a humiliated girl that consented to Alexis' irrational decisions. As it is irrational not to pay a bill at a restaurant, it would be wrong and irrational to renegotiate EU membership frames and challenge its neoliberal consensus that dictates that Greece 'pays the bill'.

ONNED's bluntly populist spot rehearses a punitive politics of shame that dominated public discourses before the June election. Yiannis Pretenderis, a commentator for *Ta Nea*, suggests that Greece should stay in the Eurozone at any cost, because 'it is not a matter of currency or economic policy, but a matter of freedom and democracy' (2012). Pavlos Tsimas, another commentator for the same newspaper, calls for 'restoration of rationality in political discourse [...] not to eliminate differences nor to govern without opposition, but to render differences rational and, therefore, resolvable' (2012b). Papachelas echoes the former PM, describing the Eurozone as 'the lifeboat' on which Greece must stay at all costs: '[i]t would be suicidal to fall into the water just because we felt dizzy on board the ship' (2012b). The naturalization of the crisis as raging storm invites a rational response (staying on board in order to survive), which is the basis of consent to the 'necessary' structural adjustment in the social, political and economic organization of life. All three commentators refuse to consider the possibility of Greece exiting the Eurozone – it is a taboo matter. In this sense the analyzes of the current crises offer a rather restricted view of the Greek problem, promoting readings that are related to the Greeks' irrational behavior for which they must be punished: their suffering will seal stability, democracy and prosperity that the EU 'guarantees'.

Thatcher, David Harvey points out, 'forged consent through the cultivation of a middle class that relished the joys of home ownership, private property, individualism, and the liberation of entrepreneurial opportunities' (2005, p.61). Similarly, as already outlined, consent to Greece's neoliberalization as modernization in the 1990s was forged alongside a new consumerist life-style culture that nurtured a whole generation in a false sense of (debt-driven) prosperity and stability. For Pretenderis, the problem seems to be related to a vague idea of a young generation that 'was happily prepared to live in a bubble that burst. And, now that they have to adapt to lower expectations and levels of prosperity, experience the demanded effort as misfortune' (2012). This argument rehearses and expands attitudes Othering the youth, whereby the 'refugees of the interior' are irrational to lose hope. According to the apologists of neoliberal rationality the fault does not rest with the framing of European integration, but the debt-based life-style of the 1990s that paved the way for the current crisis. Therefore, the rational response is that Greeks did not live up to the challenge of the European project and for this they have to consent to further and more aggressive reforms. Returning to the ONNED campaign: Alexis and the girl clearly do not fit within this refined environment, they cannot live up to the demands of being 'European'. This reading of the crisis refuses to acknowledge its systemic character, the vicious circle of debt-based growth (a prevailing norm in neoliberal capitalism) and austerity.

The consecutive rescue packages and the subsequent austerity measures inflicted a punishment on the Greek people for not being sufficiently European or rational. The austerity further poses a threat on Greeks that if they do not successfully reform and de-regulate themselves, they will lose the 'privilege' of being European. Such narratives speak of the probability of a Greek exit from the Eurozone as an 'accident', a catastrophic development imposed or not prevented by the EU authorities. In Tsimas' 'realistic' assessment of the situation, Germany will let the accident happen and 'with the images of a Greek calamity flooding the Germans' TV screens, they will announce a new euro-politics with the convincing argument that this disaster should not happen again' (2012a). In this reading, the crisis rehearses a punitive spectacle that consolidates shame and panic among the Greeks, while warning other irrational nations, particularly in the 'lazy' European periphery. The tactics of austere fiscal discipline inflicted on Greece by the 'troika' are consistent with the history of the IMF – the institution that proliferated neoliberal rationality around the globe in the last four decades. In the 1970s, amidst the New York City fiscal crisis, US Secretary of the Treasury William Simon outlined what has, by now, become not only the main tactic of IMF intervention, but a hegemonic narrative in globalized capitalism, a rational orthodoxy of the neoliberal project:

> [He] strongly advised President Ford to refuse aid to the city. The terms of any bail-out, he said, should be 'so punitive, the overall experience so painful, that no city, no political subdivision would ever be tempted to go down the same road (Harvey, 2005, p.46).

A bailout or rescue package is, therefore, a spectacle of discipline, whereby the suffering body of the 'rescued' society serves as a marker of failure – a vivid example of the kind of punishment awaiting those who fail to comply with the demands of the 'markets'. In Papandreou's 2010 address from Kastelorizo, the bailout is presented as the 'secure harbor that will allow us to rebuild our boat with solid and reliable materials'. What Papandreou defines as a secure harbor is, in fact, a spectacle of discipline that will inscribe on Greek society a 'new collective consciousness' through which Greeks will reach their modern neoliberal Ithaca – a teleological orthodoxy, a product of the rational outlook. And whereas a harbor is supposed to be a safe place, the IMF-inspired bailout raises all sorts of questions about security.

Secure/Insecure

In another pre-elections TV spot of New Democracy, a man is teaching a class of young children the Eurozone members-states. In this hypothetical scenario of Greece's future, the country has exited the Eurozone – presumably because voters in the crucial, upcoming election had made the wrong choice. When a little girl realizes that the country is not included in this list, she implores the teacher: 'And Greece? Isn't Greece part of the Eurozone? Why?' The teacher is now facing a sea of young children's eyes, looking at him with major disappointment and possibly judging him. He is at a loss for words, he cannot face them, he cannot explain; the teacher is ashamed. The TV spot finished with the slogan 'We don't gamble with our children's future', implying that New Democracy was offering a 'grown up', responsible and secure proposal for Greece's future.

This was one of the party's many slogans that in populist, sentimentalist terms presented the country at a crucial point, at crossroads between destruction and progress, security and insecurity. Since SYRIZA's statement that if the party formed government, they would renegotiate the bailouts' terms – which could upset the fragile Eurozone equilibrium – the two parties that governed Greece since its entry to the EEC in 1981, declared open battle against the coalition of the left. The claim to security or stability was one of the main arguments that they employed, reminding the electorate that a renegotiation of the bailout terms would possibly signify a Greek exit from the Eurozone and subsequently the country's default on its debt. PASOK – attempting to retain a moderate position– emphasized the term 'certainty' in its slogan *'asfalos PASOK'*, which means both 'certainly PASOK' but also a 'secure choice: PASOK'.

But what exactly constitutes security in the present moment? In the nation's macro-narrative, it suggests a vision of a fatherland protecting its people, a hard, masculine land that can defend the space that the citizens inhabit, its feminine core, the motherland. This macro-narrative frames ongoing debates about border controls and immigration after the Dublin Treaty and escalates in what Ghassan Hage (2003) terms 'paranoid nationalism' in the Far Right's practices and rhetoric. In the micro-narrative, that of the city, the 'absence of security' and the rise of criminality have led to clashes between 'soft' and 'hard city' attitudes and the demonization of specific social groups, especially immigrants and anyone supporting them. In January 2011, a group of asylum-seekers aided by activists and leftist groups occupied the Law School in Athens and staged a hunger strike. Mainstream media – ostensibly expressing common sense, though actually articulating the fatherland rhetoric – produced a 'word-for-word' chain, whereby binaries such as legal/illegal, Greek/Other, citizen/*sans papiers* denounced any solidarity with the Other, contestation or resistance to the dominant consensus for security as radical, deviant and, in short, criminal.

Against this backdrop, subsequent performances of resistance – particularly events at Syntagma Square in June 2011 and the riots in February 2012 – were demonized as criminal. Images of Athens as a city in ruins had saturated the national and international media and contributed to the escalation of panic in this 'insecure city', thus dismantling any differentiation between opposition and criminality. This intricate combination of narratives of security and representations of its lack led to particular emotions – hate and fear – sticking to bodies. In Ahmed's theory, emotions operate as part of 'affective economies', whereby 'the more signs circulate, the more affective they become' (2004, p.45). The ensuing panic in the city is produced through the contact with 'sticky' images of criminality, which not only delegitimize resistance but also rationalize the security rhetoric, in its most banal forms during the pre-election campaigns and necessitate tightening the police's grip of the city.

Sensible/Insensible

'[T]o be witnessed in one's failure is to be ashamed; to have one's shame witnessed is even more shaming. The bind of shame is that it is intensified by being seen by others as shame' (Ahmed 2004, p.103). Both TV spots mentioned earlier instigate shame by staging metaphors of Greece's hypothetical exit from the Eurozone, which according to neoliberal rationality is a shameful deed. In the second one, in particular, this feeling is intensified as it is deemed as such by children, the most powerful symbol of the future. The TV spot clearly addressed the viewers' affect, by calling to their responsibility as adults to protect the vulnerable kids. This patronizing representation of the young generation 'in need of protection' combined with a banal version of parental and societal responsibility towards children, reduced to measures for securing the European currency, expose how 'sticky' understandings of right and wrong, secure and insecure are.

Despite rationalist attitudes that disassociate emotion from politics, Thompson and Hoggett argue that emotion, when moderate, might enhance reason and faculties necessary for political decisions. For example, they explain the phenomenon of 'anger voters': 'this emotion motivates them to search out information, and to take a more critical stance towards arguments which they may have previously accepted at face value' (Thompson & Hoggett, 2012, p. 5). Appreciating the affective and emotional dimensions of the present moment does not imply that we should psychoanalyze and thus further naturalize a crisis that must be read mainly in materialist terms. However, we must read emotion as a factor that shapes responses to the crisis and, in some cases, perpetuates it.

Parties' campaigns and the media's surrounding, normalizing arguments, though advocating the 'rational solution', framed as neutral and commonsensical, were deeply driven by emotion. Designed to trigger shame, fear or panic, as first steps towards immediate action, such representations aspired to align the viewers' bodies – the body politic – with the national body, binding them together and making them 'stick to' the country's commitments to Europe. This echoes Papandreou's analogy of the national body to a crew of the 'sinking boat' sticking together, and Antonis Samaras's argument, shortly after New Democracy's electoral victory, that Greece remained 'anchored to the euro', suggesting that the country would 'honor its pledge' (telegraphtv, 2012).

Neoliberal rationality as outlined shapes what Ahmed has criticized as 'a model of social structures that neglects the emotional intensities, which allow such structures to be reified as forms of being' (2004, p.12). The emphasis on resistance and hope that SYRIZA had placed during the lead-up to the elections was condemned as insensible, demagogic populism. Nonetheless, as we have attempted to show, other parties' practices were equally or more populist, in Ernesto Laclau's conceptualization of the term (1979, p.173) as an ideology of 'widespread emotional legitimacy' that can permeate diverse political positions through 'popular democratic interpellations'. While the consensus reifies panic as sense, Eurosceptic rhetoric locates sensibility at the heart of sense. Resistance to the neoliberal barbarity demands a break from 'sensible terrorization' and addresses tangible questions of human dignity and corporeal suffering as foundations for new collective identities and habitats.

In 2003, at the wake of massive public protests against the Iraq war, Jürgen Habermas and Jacques Derrida saluted 'the power of emotion [that] has brought European citizens jointly to their feet' (2003, p. 292). Almost ten years later, the power of emotion underpins citizens' initiatives across the continent, suggestive in names such as *Indignados* or *Aganaktismenoi* that locate indignation at the heart of politics. In Athens, the rise of an affect-based, sensible politics of resistance, which challenges what Jacques Rancière (2006) has termed 'distribution of the sensible' in society, marks a break with the dominant attitude of 'ab-sense' as a refusal of the present and a distanciation from a hegemonic 'national body'; it brings to the surface different collectivities and alignments to others' bodies in the present tense, in the inhabited space that is the city.

Responsible/Irresponsible

In yet another turn, the dichotomy setting the tone for the current crisis distinguishes between responsible and irresponsible citizens and is closely related to the 'ab-sense' of democratic politics that is implied in the neoliberal consensus. Such discourses are evident in Papachelas' writing, where he reads the May election result as a warning to the bourgeois political establishment to '[s]ober up and get your act together' (2012c). The people's vote for either Eurosceptics or anti-Europeans was seen as punitive vote, a chance for the accumulated anger to be vented off the system of the body politic, before they are able to go back and vote on 'the real dilemmas are still ahead' (Papachelas 2012c). Papachelas' question is however, whether the existing political formations and, what is more, the existing political leaders can live up to their historic responsibility. The country's rescue is, in this sense, a matter of expertise and determination to do 'what is right'; a task for 'responsible' politicians.

Papachelas' reasoning is characteristic of the post-political consensus of current forms of liberal democracy that, in Chantal Mouffe's analysis, 'refuses to acknowledge the antagonistic dimension of the 'the political'' (Mouffe, 2005a, p.2). In this sense, Papachelas' call for 'responsible' responses to the crisis reiterates 'commonsensical' narratives of rationality and security, whereby politicians 'have to decide to say or do what is least popular, simply because it is the right thing to do' (2012a). Responsible is, therefore, the individual that will act on the basis of a democratic consensus that offers no space for difference, only for compromise. Mouffe's critique seems pertinent here:

> The mistake of liberal rationalism is to ignore the affective

> dimension mobilized by collective identifications and to imagine the supposedly archaic 'passions' are bound to disappear with the advance of individualism and the progress of rationality (2005a, p. 6).

In a system of governance that aims to eliminate all conflicts, democracy becomes an empty signifier, the vehicle of a neoliberal consensus, whereby the responsible attitude is that of the ever-consenting subject. However, as Kristin Ross points out, in the context of the (neo)liberal state '[t]he term consensus is no longer adequate to describe what is in fact a kind of socializing of people into silence—silence as consent' (Ross, 2011, p.88). The mainstream readings of the current crisis demonstrate this democratic deficit that both Mouffe and Ross expose: there seems to be a discrepancy between democracy as spectacle and democracy as lived experience. Whereas the 'silent majority' seeks to overcome the crisis and return to stability, the 'vocal minorities' read the crisis through what Walter Benjamin calls the 'tradition of the oppressed' for which 'the 'state of emergency' in which we live is not the exception but the rule' (Benjamin, 1999, p.248). Whereas the former inhabits the realm of representation, the latter erupt irregularly in the everyday.

If we are, then, to offer a different perspective on the crisis, it is crucial that we further unpack the discrepancies between representation (the space of the powerful) and the quotidian (the space of the oppressed). Both the hegemonic narratives and the quotidian practices of democracy are played in the urban fabric. But whereas the former outline the citizen as a visitor to the city, the latter claim their *right to the city*, which, as Henri Lefebvre has argued, 'cannot be conceived as a simple visiting right or as a return to traditional cities. It can only be formulated as a transformed and renewed *right to urban life*' (1996, p.158). Consideration of the right to urban life is fundamental in any meaningful analysis of the democratic deficits exposed by the current crises. Edward Soja suggests that 'the spatial order of human existence arises from the (social) production of space, the construction of human geographies that both reflect and configure being in the world' (1989, p.25). Urban space and the social, political and economic relations inhabiting it are at once signatories and products of the organization of space. The right to democratic urban life is, thus, related to the socio-spatial dialectic between the hegemonic narratives of 'responsibility' and the 'irresponsible' practices that occur within the city's micro-narratives.

Claiming the right to urban life, then, consists of claiming urban space from its designated use. If urbanists seek to inscribe hegemonic ideologies on urban space, the citizens' task is to transform it through a democratic politics of conviviality. An example of such an intervention on urban space can be seen in the corner of Navarinou Street and Harilaou Trikoupi Street in Athens. A parking lot that stood there empty was commandeered by the locals in 2009: they planted trees, installed benches, made paths with stones. A formerly fenced and cemented square in the urban matrix was turned into a patch of green. This ongoing intervention raises a series of questions about the sustainability of the contemporary models of urban development. If democracy is indeed, as Brown asserts, 'a politics of resistance' (2011, p.56), then this collectively embodied act of self-organization outside state institutions performs the indeterminacy of democratic politics.

Hage draws a very important distinction between participation at an institutional level and as 'an affective relation to society, an indicator of how much one 'cares'' (2003, p.2). The ongoing political project performed in and through the park gestures to democracy beyond the rational and the sensible and replaces abstract notions of responsibility with collective practices of care, creating a 'social imaginary' that is driven by 'passion'; that is, 'fantasies, desire, all those things that a rationalist approach is unable to understand in the very construction of human subjectivity and identity' (Zournazi, 2001, pp.40-1). The park as an example demonstrates that, as the country goes deeper into recession and the state fails to address the question of democracy in a meaningful way, the citizens' task is to reinvent it. The failure of neoliberal democratic narratives opens up a field of opportunities for *both* the powerful and the oppressed; both for the 'responsible' and the irresponsible'. Hope, if it is to emerge, rests beyond the discursive rationalist dichotomies of neoliberal hegemony in the micro-narratives that make up life in the streets of Athens, the 'spontaneous theater' where 'I become spectacle and spectator, and sometimes an actor' (Lefebvre, 2003, p.8).

Europhile/Eurosceptic: The doers of hope?

Writing amidst the crises of immigration and multiculturalism in the early 00s Australia, Hage identified 'scarcity of hope' as a major consequence of transnational capitalism. As the neoliberal state, he argues, 'withdraws from society […], many people, even those with middle-class incomes […] have begun suffering various forms of hope scarcity' (2003, p.20-1). The performances of panic and gaps in the narrative that we explored, reveal a similar scarcity of hope in 2010s Greece, often cloaked by sticky metaphors: its 'refugees of the interior' are the irrational, dangerous, insensible and irresponsible agents of an attack on the future of Europe. Hope can be read as 'something that one does, […] something that one has' (Hage, 2003, p.10), how one behaves (Hage, 2003, p.25). Hope is an affect, a relational practice and a catalyst of politics. Contemporary Athens appears to be staging absence of hope, a void future should this apocalyptic narrative prevail.

We set out to study a gap in the narrative about the crisis; a gap that is both discursive and affective, perpetuating a society at a state of emergency. This gap corresponds to the 'discourse of ab-sense': it refuses to acknowledge the present while lamenting a glorious past or waiting for a future, which appears to be cancelled. The scarcity and absence of hope in Greek society, we argue, was galvanized by the Europhile/Eurosceptic dichotomy, which both reaffirms this absence of hope and masks this discursive blind spot at a national level, while spreading it across the continent. Although the EU was founded upon the post-war hopes for a 'peaceful, united and prosperous Europe' (Anon, n.d.), its current incarnation emerges as the key factor eliminating any possibility of hope. The Greek paradigm stages a paradox through the Europhile/Eurosceptic dichotomy: instead of situating Greece within a Europe bound in despair, it legitimizes a relation of submission to a politics of hopelessness, by perpetuating a reading of crises as isolated national phenomena, instead of symptoms of the neoliberal pathology that exists elsewhere too. Thus, the dichotomy hides the actual questions the crisis is asking: can or should Europe be reduced to the current system of governance? What is really the object of fetishization or scepticism?

The city is, in the current phase of neoliberal globalization, at the core of its production of space and everyday life, therefore, reductive dichotomies that 'block' the European imaginary also regulate practices in the European city. Accordingly, they inscribe a normalizing spectacle of Europe on its urban settings, which reinstates a politics of ab-sense and an absence of politics. Raising the question of Europe in the context of the city leads to the fundamental objective of our times: if a democratic Europe is to emerge, it will have to happen within the European urban fabric; the right to Europe is interconnected to the right to urban life. And whereas those 'technicians and specialists who 'act' are unaware that their so-called objective space is in fact ideo-logic and repressive' (Lefebvre, 2003, p.183), the urban revolutionary class will need to expose how the rational, secure, sensible, and responsible systems of European governance bleed into its cityscapes through a complex interplay of ideology, discourse, representation and affect.

Who can be this urban revolutionary class? It certainly cannot be reduced to the followers of *any* party of the (neo)liberal political arena or dichotomies that emerge from this system. The crises that have challenged the ostensibly secure European edifice since 2008 have produced ruins in urban, social and political landscapes, which can also be seen as remains at a material, but most significantly, at an embodied dimension. The crisis leaves behind new collectivities that can, potentially, build a new (and temporary) class consciousness: the urban revolutionary class will emerge from the dispossessed and the displaced (either geographically or socially), the urban 'refugees of the interior', the remains of the crisis. In this sense, Greece's state of emergency marks the state of emergence of a new European narrative and a parallel tension: a deeper descent into reductive political practices and discourses of Europeanness or the rise and potentiality of an urban democratic model.

Chapter 14

Remapping Political Trust in the Greek Crisis: Where has it Gone Wrong?

Theofanis Exadaktylos

The idea of political trust as the cohesive factor in the triangular relationship between the government, its agents and the targeted populations is not a novel one (e.g. Hardin 2006). Trust is what brings stakeholders together to the negotiations table in any decision-making or implementation processes. Its absence can only weaken and slow down those processes. Whereas in times of expansion the absence of trust is covered up by profit-making and economic prosperity, during periods of crisis or extreme austerity—as in the case of Greece since 2009—its impact is more noticeable since when the pie shrinks, society becomes a 'zero-sum game between conflicting groups' (Rothstein & Uslaner 2005, p. 46). Decision-making processes then break down, new political measures become confrontational and stakeholders are less keen to cooperate. This is mainly due to the fact that political trust lubricates cooperation in this trilateral relationship (Cook, Hardin & Levi, 2005).

The purpose of this chapter is to engage with the idea of political trust and remap the concept within the context of Greek society in this age of austerity. The main question here is how does the absence of political trust affect the efforts of Greece to exit the crisis and what kinds of factors prevent trust from emerging in policy-making processes? Effectively, this chapter makes an attempt to understand where Greece has gone wrong in this regard. The headline in this effort is that the long-term absence of political trust between social groups, economic partners, and within the political system at large has allowed corruption to become embedded in all social, political and economic processes and part of the psyche of Greek society, to the point that decreasing corruption does not effectively guarantee the increase of political and social trust.

This chapter is built around three empirical key aspects of political trust, i.e. trust in people we know, trust in people we do not know and trust in institutions, following a short theoretical treatment of the concept. It focuses first on the impact on society by looking at grass-roots movements and political mobilization. It continues with the effects on the economy by examining the public sector clientele and the closed-shop professions. Finally, it explores trust in the context of electoral contests, political cooperation and coalition governments. In concluding, the chapter brings all the above together in an effort to remap the idea of political trust in the context of Greece in the age of austerity.

Political trust and the Greek state of play

Trust is one of those highly contested concepts in politics and other social sciences: it is a multifaceted idea that finds expression in many outlets and through many different circuits. Trust can be broken down to trust in people we know, in people we do not know and in institutions (Uslaner, 2005). The focus of this chapter is on the latter. At the same time it is also hard to measure or create an effective index of political trust based on anything but experiments (cf. Glaeser et al., 2000; Hugh-Jones et al., 2011) or on the perceptions of the public of the concept itself in their daily transactions with the political system. Broadly speaking however, the concept of trust follows three main axes: trustworthiness (Levi & Stoker, 2000); incentives and knowledge (Kurzban, 2003); and encapsulating interests across involved parties (Hardin, 2006). All three axes are linked together through confidence-building, collective action and honest brokering. In the realm of policymaking processes, where the stakes are clear and high, this linkage becomes ever more important since it decreases the domination of self-interest (Chong et al., 2001). It can be deduced then that in the absence of high levels of trust the likelihood of free riding increases dramatically; and this incentivizes further corruption.

The mechanisms to curtail this effect are stability of the relationship between stakeholders, repeated interaction among parties (Ostrom & Walker, 2003) and most importantly, clarity of message and rule-compliance by the enforcing authority (Ostrom, 1990). 'Trust is likely to be higher based on information about past behavior and signals and rules about incentives for adversaries to keep their promises' (Exadaktylos & Zahariadis, 2012, p. 9). The measures for building trust in political institutions therefore need to commence at the level of political leadership. If political leaders themselves do not have ways of infusing trust to their constituents either due to non-enforcement or non-compliance, then both the bureaucratic arm of the government and the affected populations receive the wrong message that deviation from the proposed targets or policy actions is normal and desirable. The relations of trust then break down and the system comes to a halt as all parties await the next step.

This situation generates obliviousness alongside resentment that only enhances social and economic problems and feed into the cycle of corruption (Rose-Ackerman, 1999). In turn, this window of opportunity for corruption—or the perceived notions of corruption that develop—comes back to undermine trust in political institutions as the umpires of the social and political system. Therefore, citizens are more prone to seek individual solutions to their predicaments, thus opening the door to further corruption (Exadaktylos & Zahariadis, 2012). At the same time the fluidity of policy-making by not maintaining a stable government line on certain issues, for example, increases conflict between participants, as they expect that the next government in place will either have a different policy or at least reverse the previous one, reducing the likelihood of trusted collaboration. This in consequence, decreases the levels of trust that stakeholders and, political institutions and actors will honor their commitments. In these cases, the signals of commitment are low and political leadership fails to provide impulses of trust building (Exadaktylos & Zahariadis, 2012).

How does Greece fit into this picture? The rudimentary observation to be made simply by looking at Eurobarometer surveys (2003; 2010) is that trust in all political institutions in Greece (government, parties, parliament and courts) has dramatically decreased in some cases more than halved. The current austerity climate certainly does little to help restore the public's trust in political institutions.

Since the start of this enduring crisis in Greece, the stakes across involved parties are substantially high and crystal clear: many of the previously privileged social groups have lost their status or preferential treatment by the government, and their special relationship with society has been called in question. The previous social stratification has markedly changed, altering the hierarchies of groups and other actors across the board on the social ladder.

With savings schemes rolled out across the public services, local government and social welfare, the state itself is eroding. Gaps therefore emerge across the public sector creating discontinuities in which corruption can flourish, especially in cases where there is complete absence of monitoring and enforcement mechanisms. The cuts across the public sector also result in the bureaucratic arm underperforming with no clear signals or guidance by the central government on implementation, intensifying and streamlining—in a paradoxical way—the missing of targets.

The quick shift of the political agenda since the Socialist government took office in 2009 to one of extreme austerity changed the rules of the game in any effort for reform, while the opposition was still bantering with non-austerity promises and novel agendas to a desperate electorate. In trying to save face, the government found itself in a position of frequently changing direction in policy-making to satisfy internal opposition and electorally pivotal social groups, thus complicating the processes for the targeted populations to understand the strategy line. What was valid one day was annulled the following by a different minister or a group of parliamentarians.

Finally, the prior history of lack of commitment by the political leadership in promoting reforms in times of expansion, as well as the sustainability of a clientele-type environment in daily transactions only added to the volatility of the system and to the inability of the government to break the cycle of distrust and corruption that plagued the public sector. And this is the state of play: Greece is at a critical juncture, where the only way should be forward-looking, making a clean break from the practices and norms of the past and understand that the crisis has exposed all those embedded notions of distrust and corruption, that everyone was aware of but willing to place under the carpet, and which had once been concealed behind a façade of prosperity and economic growth. It is time to turn to some illustrative cases to demonstrate the breakdown of trust in Greece across the social, economic and political spheres.

Remapping trust in Greek society

When looking at Greek society at large, the concept of trust in political institutions starts from the very basic level of trusting the government to provide certain services and, undoubtedly, to appropriately manage the public purse. Despite Greece having a long history of tax-avoidance or tax-dodging practices with an extensive shadow economy (Matsaganis & Flevotomou 2010), there is widespread concern about the management of tax money that makes it to the state coffins. There are a few occasions where this concern has emerged across the Greek population.

The first instance was the small-scale social movement 'I won't pay', named after the old theatrical farce by Dario Fo (1974) *'Non si paga! Non si paga!'* where customers in a supermarket arbitrarily agreed to pay only what they could afford to pay from their shopping baskets. Its purpose was to express frustration and mistrust in the negative correlation between tax revenues and quality of public service provision. It started as a social activism group in 2008 that protested and occupied tollbooths around the country allowing free access to passing drivers. The movement claimed that since the motorways were incomplete and hazardous, then users should not be paying a toll fee to the private companies that maintained them. 'I won't pay' claimed to be a grass-roots movement that took decisions collectively among members in open deliberation and shared no political affiliation. During the Indignados unrest in Athens, the movement developed into a nationwide group which confirmed five principles of action: What is revealed is a deep understanding that government authority is not to be trusted and a profound perception of non-responsibility of the public for the state of play in Greece, deepening divisions and demarcating sides.

The movement expanded subsequently into other areas of activity that included not paying bus fares, one-off taxes and VAT rates. At the same time other social groups started using their protest practices, like farmers who started occupying tollbooths in their demands for government subsidies and lower fares for using the motorways. Nonetheless, these types of movements, which presented themselves as movements of civil disobedience or anger against public management, were often caught in the middle of political rows, with government ministers claiming that small opposition protest parties had captured their agendas. Whether this was a coincidence or not, the government has developed a sense of mistrust to such organizations, and the relationship is mutual. Yet, this kind of entanglement has created an atmosphere of suspicion between social groups and the government that brings society in direct conflict with the political elites in a 'spiral of cynicism and disillusionment' (Capella & Jamieson, 1997).

The second occasion is that of the actual Indignados (*Aganaktismenoi* in Greek) movement in Athens. For about two months in 2011, protesters gathered on a daily basis in front of the parliament to protest against austerity and unemployment and to express their anger about corruption, clientelism and the mismanagement of the public finances. Deriving its format from its counterparts in Spain and elsewhere, the movement used the spontaneity of social networks to organize and claimed again no political affiliation, mobilizing the underprivileged and those who had never protested before. The movement transformed itself in the course of these months into a bad imitation of its Spanish relative and has now moved out of their camping site.

Greece has a long history of social struggles and demands since the beginning of the 20th century calling for a just and fair society amongst democratic interludes, a devastating civil war, some authoritarianism and persecution of the left as well as international intervention (overt and covert) in domestic affairs. This kind of history has made Greek social movements more prone to confrontation than other European ones. The Indignados included the younger population that wanted a moral revolution in public life; exasperated by decades of administration that promised the world and delivered very little.

What this movement revealed through the current financial crisis was a fracture of the power differential between citizens and an overprotective Greek state that can no longer sustain a system of governance that benefits certain social groups or that is inscribed within corrupt practices. Yet, interestingly individual members of the movement often came from the old guard in Greek society who benefited immensely from such practices, such as early pensioners, customs workers or urban planning officers. What remains unknown is the precise reason of their protest, whether it was indeed a pure expression of enragement or simply a will to return to the previous state of spoils. Still, there was an unprecedented—by Greek standards—absence of political affiliation or coloring of the movement, which, albeit being its unique and strongest characteristic, perhaps led the movement to be transpired by individualism rather than a collective notion of identity, without actually promoting a coherent set of pragmatic solutions as a counterproposal to austerity. At the same time, in standard populist practice, most—if not all—political forces tried to capitalize on the movement (at times even philander with their social reactions) to obtain ephemeral support and electoral gains, each party attaching its own semantics to the movement.

Remapping trust in the economy

Every economic and financial transaction begins with trust in the institutions that govern it. Hence, reliance on sound regulatory and legal frameworks and in the administrative bodies forms the basis of a nation's economic and financial environment. In remapping trust in the economy, it is essential to make reference to both public and private sectors when looking at Greece, albeit for different reasons: the public sector has been marred by decades of clientelism and favoritism, whereas the private sector was blighted by distortions in the free market economy to protect electorally pivotal professional groups and guilds. When crisis hit home, the fragile balances that held the Greek economy together came down with a crash, bringing to light all of those structural inefficiencies that were well known but also well covered under a veil of artificial prosperity.

The wider public sector in Greece is plagued not only by favoritism and cronyism to the detriment of efficiency and quality assurance (in a similar pattern to the claims of the social groups analyzed in the previous section) but also by a culture of exploitation for short term political gains both by governing and opposition parties. The cases of the liberalization of telecommunications (Pagoulatos & Zahariadis, 2011) and the privatization of Olympic Airways (Featherstone & Papadimitriou 2008) are two classic cases of ineffective public sector reform marred by a spoils system. Attempts at reforming the public sector in Greece have stumbled upon certain idiosyncratic features of the system, such as the salary allowances and the permanency clause for public sector employees (Featherstone, 2011; Lyberaki & Tsakalotos, 2002; Ongaro, 2010, Spanou, 2008). One of the much-needed reforms exposed by the current financial crisis was the requirement to rationalize the public sector salaries to eliminate falsely claimed allowances but also to make sense of the exact cost of the sector to the government.

The story of reforming the public sector is almost as old the modern Greek state itself. The power differentials between the government and its employees that developed inside the highly unionized sector as well as the policy of favoritism (Sotiropoulos, 2004) have made practically any government attempting to tackle the issue—be it of the center-left or the center-right—succumb to pressures to maintain the status quo through long-lasting strikes and political interference. In this case, lack of trust in the political leadership has a strong role to play. Even at the dawn of the financial crisis in April 2008, when the center-right government took a first step towards rationalizing the salaries in the public sector, the General Confederation of Greek Workers (GSEE) reacted so starkly that the government closed the issue for a year. It initiated a new round of dialogue with the central committee of the public sector unions to create a new uniform payroll system for new employees, including a discussion about reviewing the permanency clause for the public sector workers (*To Vima*, 2009). Yet, it pulled back again under the weight of public sector strikes and left the matter unstirred until a few months later, when a new plan for eliminating all allowances for new employees was brought forward. After the center-left government took office in November 2009, the public sector unions assumed and 'trusted' that the incoming government would not tamper with their *acquis* since many of the trade union leaders were party members.

To the surprise of the unions however, and given the burden of the crisis on public finances, one of the very first pieces of legislation that the center-left government brought forward was the creation of a new uniform payroll system for public sector workers. The proposed bill included a salary freeze and reductions in all allowances and compensation forms, becoming a personal bet for the prime minister, who made a public commitment to tackle high-salaried civil servants saying he would 'not tolerate any more scandalous favoritism, acquired benefits for the few, (…) the shadow economy and corruption in the public sector' (*Ta Nea*, 2010). Yet, once again the measures were pushed back for another year in light of contradictory independent reports by consultancy firms and international organizations on the state of play in the expenditures on salaries of the public sector. Eventually halfway measures were adopted that did not actually add any value to the reforms, favoring established elites.

What this case reveals is a strong lack of leadership on behalf of consecutive administrations, who under the pressure by a highly unionized public sector that represents more than 750 thousand workers were not able to initiate, let alone implement any significant measures. There seems to be a strong misunderstanding of the tractability of the issue but also an inability to generate trust among stakeholders (in this case, the government's own bureaucrats) about the intentions and the end goals of the proposed reforms that changed at consecutive iterations of the negotiation processes. The delay in designing, deliberating, approving and implementing the measures led to austerity fatigue in the public sector, which in the absence of political trust piloted a prolonged reaction by the public sector workers.

A similar pattern can be observed when dealing with reforms in the private sector. The most significant obstacle to the functioning of a free market economy is artificial distortion of the market via closed-shop professions, in other words, certain categories of professions that contain a number of restrictions and criteria for entering and exiting of businesses. The issue in Greece has been a long-standing obstacle to reform and in fact, there are a number of legal acts that legitimize anticompetitive regulations for specific groups that provide public services (Featherstone, 2011), such as lawyers and notary publics, medical professionals or owners of public-utility trucks. One interesting case is that of the taxi-license owners who can either be self-employed or can hire drivers to operate the taxis and can collectivize their individual vehicles into associations.

Following a series of directives on liberalizing services by the European Union, the Greek government found itself under pressure since the early 2000s to open up some closed-shop professions. Specifically for the taxi-license holders, a first draft of legislation was put forward in 2001 (*in.gr*, 2001). Nonetheless, the government succumbed to pressures from the license holders unions and withdrew the measures in haste, sending one more signal of mistrust to stakeholders or rather, of trust of the administration inertness. The current crisis brought such issues back into focus and led the Greek government to bring forward a bill opening up about 150 of those professions that could generate a medium-term GDP increase of 13.5% (IOBE, 2010). Yet, the list of professions tallied a whopping 340 categories. Though initially received in a positive way by the Confederation of Transport Unions on issues of eliminating distortions and creating jobs, and by the taxi-drivers' union on protecting employees' insurance rights, the taxi-license owners were firmly opposed to the bill.

Owners entered a long-term strike that created polarization across social groups and political parties. The strike took place at the peak of the holiday season affecting the tourism industry by blocking access to sights, airports and harbors as well as highways. The prolonged strike heavily impacted the already flimsy social trust and solidarity to the point that other professional groups initiated lawsuits against the taxi-license holders.

Despite the intensification of the political debate between government and opposition, all parties called for considering the damage to the economy amidst the tourist season and encouraged participation in a constructive dialogue. Yet, the lack of political trust led this particular group to even doubt the legitimacy of the proposed bills. The controversy was such that the Council of State intervened to rule in favor of the proposed legislation arguing that freedom of profession is a constitutional right, thus opening up the way to liberalize more closed-shop professions. Nonetheless, and as more professional groups are affected in bulk by the crisis, there is a need to remap political trust in between professional groups but also with the government. Tarnished by the lack of clear signals and determination by consecutive governments to go ahead with the liberalization of closed-shop professions, there was high uncertainty and volatility in future plans. This increased the levels of mistrust in the ability of the state and the political leadership to provide concrete solutions to yield concrete results. At the same time, the professional guilds managed to manipulate electoral cycles to their favor forcing the administration to frequently abandon any reforms or, much like in the case of the public sector, to adopt halfway measures with little or no value.

The case of political trust within the economy shows the absence of communication links across affected groups as well as of any notion of social responsibility. More importantly, the government as a political institution suffered a severe blow to its trustworthiness by failing to create reciprocity among stakeholders and by being captured by other political entities and professional agents. This was not a novelty for Greece, yet the crisis by exposing the depth of all those structural rigidities in the Greek economy intensified a certain type of adverse trust in maintaining the status quo rather than moving forward; and that makes remapping political trust in the economy quintessential for the success of any economic measures.

Remapping trust in the political system

The absence of trust within society and within the economy as discussed in the previous sections is bound to have a significant impact on the political system itself, at the basis of which lies political trust. In this facet we have the association of political trust with political corruption and exploitation of the system for political benefits. As a matter of fact, the political system incorporates aspects of political trust already analyzed in the context of trust in society and economy. Greece, despite being considered among the developed western nations, still has remnants of underdevelopment (some would argue due to a long-term Ottoman rule, e.g. Mouzelis (1978)) that created, by Weberian standards, a sultanistic type of governance. This in turn has solidified an underdog culture within the Greek populace. Yet, the country itself, despite the alternation of political regimes (monarchies, dictatorships and intermittent democratic rule) never managed to break away from this model and to disassociate itself from past political and economic elites. No matter the paradox of this statement, one cannot miss the fact that feudalism, political and party oligarchy, and a clientelistic mutual understanding between the political elites and the masses (i.e. the electorate) holds steady since the beginning of the modern Greek state. A type of Greek-style parliamentary system was developed within the framework of this clientelistic perception of political life that allows the concentration of power to parties, rather than specific individuals.

Mouzelis and Pagoulatos (2003) name this phenomenon one of 'partitocracy', rather than democracy, one where power is not in the hands of the people but rather in the hands of extremely powerful parties. This is now an integral feature of the Greek parliamentary reality that has transformed political parties into mechanisms of capturing voters for their own benefit and with an intriguing two-way character: on the one hand parties are keen to maintain their power in government and on the other a great share of the voters trust them in maintaining the status quo and in providing them with favors that will allow them to exploit the state apparatus to their benefit.

In other words, the gap of political trust within the political system is immense. Citizens cannot trust that their elected governments have answers to the social, economic and foreign affairs problems that are (a) viable and applicable and (b) targeting the heart of the matter. On the contrary, there seems to be a type of paradoxical trust: citizens do believe in the failure and the political comfort of their elected governments, namely that they will not interfere with the *acquis* and they will not meddle with the established interests. Therefore, consecutive Greek administrations touched the problems only in a superficial manner for a range of decades, cunningly shifting the blame for the situation to previous administrations and the responsibility to tackle the issues to the forthcoming ones. A type of morphostasis, as Margaret Archer (1995) would argue, was developed in this way. The socioeconomic ideal types that the Greek political structures reproduced remained highly unchanged—with the odd modification here and there to go with the times. Instead of having the very opposite of morphogenesis (Archer, 1995) that introduces new socioeconomic norms of behavior, the basic operating framework of the Greek social and political system did not change: in effect, any innovations that were introduced in the Greek public administration never accounted for the exigencies of the Greek context but they were rather badly imported models with minimum implementation. This resulted in the emergence of public administration monstrosities that allowed the systemic structures to be reproduced intact in most cases.

The success of any reform is based above all (but not solely) in the ability of the political leadership to instill a sense of trust through their actions. The absence of trust on behalf of the stakeholders in the leadership's ability to track the problems down, to bring forward viable solutions and to fully implement any measures is a significant factor in the failures of the Greek reform programs during the crisis. Nevertheless, at the same time, there was a sense of trust that self-interested pork-barrel politics oriented governments to secure the *acquis* of certain social groups and the favorable market distortions for the professional guilds. In turn, these groups were acting like cliques, manipulating the political system and intensifying those structural deficiencies. In the context of the current crisis, the socio-political system came face-to-face with the accumulation of very long-term structural rigidities. Even at this phase of hard line austerity policy and fiscal discipline, the model of protecting special or electorally pivotal social and professional groups remains deeply rooted in the social context and the political system at large.

The long-standing tax evasion practices that continue even during the crisis reveal that even if there is ever a government with the political will to promote reforms, it is bound to stumble upon non-compliance by its own citizens. The enduring favoritism and cronyism as well as the appropriation of public property have truly established the inadequacy of public administration mainly through electoral promises and the electorate's threat of withdrawing electoral support. The capturing of political agents shattered any notion of trust among social groups and political institutions and therefore any reforms efforts against deeply established interests were bound to fail.

Yet, a large share of Greek society is placing the blame largely on corruption; a phenomenon that plagues the political system. However, trust becomes more important than honesty in an odd way: trust does not increase with the removal of dishonest leaders or bureaucrats and with their replacement with new governing elites. If the mentality amongst citizens remains the same, then most likely, the electorate will treat these new elites in the same clientelistic way. What helps instead is the change of cultural paradigms that embed within their definitions the notion of trust in public policymaking. Otherwise, even if society becomes less corrupt this does not presuppose the increase of political trust levels. The point is that trust begets honesty in public life; decreased levels of corruption do help, but this change cannot be governed by the politics of fear but rather by the politics of building strong social and political links across social actors and the leadership.

Post-election blues: what's in it for Greece?

Remapping political trust in Greece in the context of the financial crisis and austerity is a difficult task that gets enhanced by international intervening variables. For example, since the beginning of the debt crisis in Greece, the arrival of the monitoring committees of the European Union, the European Central Bank and the International Monetary Fund as well as the high pressures at the European level for quick implementation of socially harsh measures and cuts across the board, alongside the heightened attention (and the often misguided interpretations) by the international media acted against the domestic generation of trust or social agreement on the nature of the crisis and the ways to tackle it. Therefore things are not as simple as they may look in the first place for the remapping of political trust.

Between May and June 2012, Greece underwent two rounds of elections; the May election was called to replace the cooperation government led by a non-elected prime minister. The June election was called upon inconclusive results and failed coalition negotiations from the one in May. In any case, what both electoral contests reveal is quite important to determine what's in it for Greece in the near future. Primarily, they exposed the deep fragmentation of the political system as a result of the prolonged period of crisis and austerity. At the same time they also brought to light a significant polarization of the electorate relating to the breakdown of trust across social groups. The outcome of both contests was one that signaled the willingness of Greece to remain part of the European structures and which at the same time sent a powerful message to the political establishment domestically: the electorate desired cooperation at different levels not only to overcome the crisis but also to build a safer future for the country. Concurrently, there was a strong momentum against more austerity that the elected government cannot overlook and which could become a potential threat for the success of future reforms. In other words, a new equilibrium of consensus needs to be established.

When regarding the outcome of the vote a number of dimensions need to be considered. The era of majority single-party governments is formally over and the type of governments that will emerge in the immediate future should be ones that build on cross-party cooperation. Perhaps those two rounds of elections in 2012 demonstrate how the politics of fear may operate; yet, the support for the radical left opposition that grew stronger allows for the argument that a share of the population was not afraid of the unknown. At the same time the rise of extreme right-wing parties that solidified over time is a phenomenon that should not be taken light-heartedly. This begs the conclusion that the state of play in Greece is one of deep economic recession and pessimism; the people feel they have nothing more to lose. In addition, it exposes new cleavages that have emerged within the political system and society—most notably between the center and the periphery, and young versus old in terms of voting preferences and experiences of the crisis.

The question remains whether the coalition government(s) will be able to take advantage of the new setting and create a political environment conducive to trust-building and trust-development. Can political trust return to the core of the system? Achieving consensus is a difficult task, let alone in a country that has no prior history of political consensus or at least by the standards of comparison against hallmarks of consensus politics like the Netherlands. The looming divide could easily become one between consensus as the lowest common denominator for policy-making and efficiency or effectiveness of public policy itself. In other words, the minimum standards agreed between government partners will not necessarily guarantee the achievement of the set goals or the implementation of reforms.

Coalition governments certainly tend to represent different strata of the electorate in a more proportional way—yet this cannot be coagulated without consensus and trust. Consensus models of democracy are based after all on sharing of power, with political minorities formally included in the process, and decentralization of government. In Greece, despite the move towards a coalition based on consensus, the political system remains majoritarian. The winning party or 'coalition of parties' exercises virtually limitless power within the political system since it maintains an absolute majority in parliament. At the same time, it is effectively still creating winners and losers as the two camps have now been clearly demarcated: pro-bailout and anti-bailout. The evident lacuna ahead concerns the capacity of coalition governments to actually create a system of fairness across social groups with an embedded notion of trust.

Finally, despite Greece being under international scrutiny, any complications in re-establishing trust in political institutions are more likely to come from within. The determining factor here is the tolerance of the population for continued favoritism and cronyism. Trust can re-enter the equation if the electorate treats the 'new' political elites in a way different from the one of the previous decades. Certainly, the absence of demand for such practices by the electorate can turn the political system away from clientelism. This was the cornerstone of all evil in Greece, but sincere effort and trust in political leadership is quintessential to achieve a clean break from the past. If trust cannot be remapped on the Greek landscape the danger of entanglement in the never-ending spiral of politics succumbing to specific social, economic and political interests and agendas remain.

Chapter 15

Live your Myth in Greece: The Mythology of Crisis

Zacharoula Christopoulou

This paper is an attempt to analyze the discourse surrounding the Greek financial crisis as founded on an illogical and moralistic rhetoric, overtly lacking in rational analysis of facts. The reliance on imaginary constructs in order to explain reality makes one uneasy as it opens up once again the unsettling issue of political myth and its historical repercussions. I will not attempt to analyzing a phenomenon as vast and complex as the financial crunch and its particular instantiations in the Greek context as it is beyond my expertise. The focus is not on investigation of recession, but discursive analysis of the political /mass media rhetoric and the use of mythopoeic devices in that discourse. My aim is to point out that the language used to present the crisis through political and mass media channels resorts to the illogical, thereby weakening scientific explorations and decreasing the population's ability to understand and evaluate the facts. The recession is not in itself a myth. Nevertheless, it has been surrounded by mythological language and presented as a fatal disaster.

Mythology and Greece have been interrelated concepts since the advent of Classical education. In 2005 the Greek Ministry of Tourism launched an advertising campaign with the motto 'live your myth in Greece'. The campaign's TV advert showed children playing on beautiful beaches, people happily enjoying Greek sun under the shadow of ancient temples, a man swimming alongside a mermaid. The message of the commercial was that when someone comes into contact with the Greek land, they come closer to the ancient Greek frame of mind. By breaking the confines of ordinary, rationalistic thought, they are able to view their life within the fantastic context of myth. The mythical is an antidote against the mundane. It is connected to the Greek territory, which on its own occupies a space in fictional discourse. Obviously, the idea that a life in the land of myths can transform one's life into something different is a myth in itself. However, everyone is ready to consent to a bit of fiction in an advert.

As opposed to advertising, the use of fiction in political and social affairs is less innocent and more disquieting to witness. Consider for example a subsequent campaign launched some years later by the Greek government. It addressed the Greek citizens with the purpose to convince them to accept austerity measures and a surrender of national sovereignty, all in the name of that huge debt that suddenly came to light and apparently caught the ruling political parties unaware. Hence, the Socialist government's pre-election slogan 'there is money' quickly transformed after the election to 'we are facing bankruptcy', without anyone in the media really asking difficult questions like how was the deficit created, when, by whom and how it was possible for the political elite not to have any prior knowledge. However, all these considerations were overridden by a discourse dictating the need to accept an austerity that would 'restructure' the country and would deter an impending financial collapse. What was needed was not a rational analysis of the available data, but a *story* that would justify drastic policy reforms that would promote loss of work rights, huge cuts in salaries and dismantling of the welfare state.

The Oxford Dictionary defines myth as 'a traditional story, either wholly or partially fictitious, providing an explanation for or embodying a popular idea concerning some natural or social phenomenon or some religious belief or ritual'. The second meaning of the word is: 'a widely held [...] story or belief; a misconception; a misrepresentation of the truth' (Oxford, p.

1876). These definitions reflect our popular conceptions of myth as both a fictitious creation of the past, as well as a discredited notion of the present. Part of its unreliability is the fact that it is the result not of empirical analysis but of imagination. According to Claude Lévi-Strauss mythical thinking characterizes primitive thought and is a way of understanding the universe. Therefore myth, in the anthropological sense is a tale that gives holistic explanations to phenomena as well as the illusion of complete understanding. For the mythical mind 'if you don't understand everything, you don't explain anything.' This mode of thought is contrary to the scientific thought that proceeds gradually in the quest for explanations by methodically resolving parts of a greater question. Therefore mythical thinking gives the comforting impression of absolute knowledge, whereas scientific thought can actually provide real mastery over man's surroundings (1978, p. 16-17).

This tendency of mythical thought to override the true causes of events with a fictional narrative might explain why it was discredited as a foundation of thought by both the philosophers of Classical Greece and the Enlightenment. Robert L. Fowler points out that in fifth century Greece the critical examination of the inherited modes of thought led to a distinction between the imaginary and the factual, between *mythos* and *logos* as conflicting categories: 'What we call the Greek myths were a powerful cultural institution which came into focus as a problem and/or a target of criticism in both historiography and philosophy as a result of the work of Herodotus and contemporary philosophers' (2011, p. 65-66). The outcome of the criticism was a stricter definition of these terms. In fact, the original meaning of both words was 'speech'. The semantic progress of the term *logos* to designating verifiable discourse and *mythos* to its opposite can be traced in Plato according to Luc Brisson. Furthermore, by applying the internal criterion of the discourse's development Brisson discerned an additional level to the *mythos/logos* opposition: that of narrative and argumentative discourses. A narrative is a story that connects arbitrarily its several parts in order to give an account of events 'as they are supposed to have happened, without giving an explanation' whereas, argumentative discourse follows 'a rational order [...] according to rules aiming at making the conclusion necessary'. In other words, relating a narration is to strive for 'emotive fusion', whereas argumentation aims at rational agreement (Brisson, 2004, p. 19-25).

The philosophers of the Enlightenment exalted the critical mind of the Greek thinkers. According to the Encyclopédie, Greek philosophy pursued the truth based on evidence and freed the human mind from the restrictions of authority and superstition (Gay, 1966, p. 73). The intellectuals of the Enlightenment advanced the notion that with reason as a driving force the human race was progressing from imaginative and irrational thinking to a final triumph of reason. The historians of the movement saw classical historiography as a prime example of emancipation from fable, indicating a linear evolution from the primitive and mythical thought to a civilized and rational one. Peter Gay has further illustrated how the term 'mythical thinking' encompasses diverse intellectual functions. Mythical thinking does not clearly distinguish the categories part and whole, subjective and objective and thus could easily leap into the most extraordinary connections. Mythical thinking is the main characteristic of all ancient religions: 'they were not reasoned about; they did not require proof and hence could not be disproved' (1966, p. 90-91). Also, as Gay points out the mythopoeic mind is, on the whole, hostile to history' (1966, p. 91-92). Enlightenment admonished the cultivation of a new type of intellectual life, one that is worthy of free citizens. One could be able to impact on one's own course of life by freeing oneself from the limitations of a thought that does not allow rational estimation of events and the factors that influence it. One could base one's reflections on deductions made from evidence and not inferences made according to a given fictional explanation. These are the ideological precincts we all ascribe to today, regardless of the fact that the project of the Enlightenment project has been criticized for embracing the actual mythical mechanisms it verbally rejects (Horkheimer and Adorno, 2002, p.11-12). Contrary to our assumptions of rationality prevailing in contemporary thought, in more than one instance the embrace of irrationality is evident: the field of political myth is one of these instances.

Peter Gay's remarks on the nature of mythical thought are very insightful regarding the function of political myth: essentially it is worth noting the dismissal of the necessity of proof in an assumption, as well as the aversion to historical interpretation. Political myth employs the aforementioned intellectual mechanisms in order to create tangible explanations of a political situation and promote an ideological agenda. The reason that myth is used instead of argumentation is either insufficient proof for the claims made or evidence pointing to the contrary of a claim. A myth that is partially based on events and partially on fiction and contextualized within an emotionally charged narrative can easily persuade of its authenticity. According to Henry Tudor, by having practicality at its core, myth can offer an easy way of codifying a complicated situation. Both a scientist and a mythmaker can equally offer explanations for the same issue. The difference between them is that the scientist - for example the historian- will lay out his sources and the process of the deduction of her conclusions whereas the mythopoeic mind will only offer a story of origins and a narration of how something came about, which only requires plausibility. The importance is placed in vindicating a certain situation and supporting a particular course of action, and not on knowledge for knowledge's sake (1972, p. 121-124). The gravest danger lurking within political myth is the characteristic Levi-Strauss had discerned into mythical thinking in general: the illusion of total knowledge. Total knowledge, has two serious prerogatives: firstly, it cannot be refuted and secondly, all its actions are justified. This is why political myth is the favorite child of totalitarianism.

The relevance of 'myth' in examining the discourse surrounding the Greek financial crisis becomes evident when one analyzes the dominant political discourse in terms of its uses of mythopoeic devices and contexts. The propagation of myth in this case, has to do with the fact that the political and media narrative does not only focus on a specific subject. On the contrary, it attempts to offer a holistic explanation of the economic crunch ingrained in a moralistic and racist discourse that reinforces polarities. Examples of this will be provided further down. The reference to 'mythology of the financial crisis' in the chapter title implies that in the Greek case there is not only a single myth at work, but a system of interrelating myths attempting a simplistic interpretation of a very complex historical phenomenon: the results of the global financial crisis on the Greek economy.

The following examples demonstrate how the mythology surrounding the Greek crisis unfolded and what its major components are. In the Greek case the narrative begins with a shock, a few weeks after the October 2009 elections. Naomi Klein has already demonstrated the power of shock and awe into pushing forward any agenda that the public would have otherwise rejected (2007, p. 6-21). The new Prime Minister George Papandreou warned that the Greek deficit is bigger than the previous government had stated and that the country is in 'intensive care'. The disaster seemed imminent, unless drastic measures were to be taken immediately. The news was coupled with the Prime Minister's references to corruption and unreliability that needs to be tackled (Skai, 2009). Although this might have been a valid comment, it remains vague both regarding the reference as well as the actions taken. Corruption was never identified with specific individuals, groups, or businesses, but remained a general motto that was attached to the concept of crisis. The government does not publicize a logistical report presenting details on the accumulation of debt, nor how it came about to be so much higher than the previous government's estimation. Surprisingly, there is not a single mention of the credit crunch that had started in 2007, bringing down Lehman Brothers and several other banks in the US and sparking a domino effect worldwide. Nor is any reference made to the deficit that the consequent bail out of the Greek banks created. The Greek crisis hence was singled out of any wider historical context and any reference to actual data. Instead, the government and media discourse handled it as an isolated incident, caused by general concepts such as corruption and ineffectiveness, without founding these references in an analysis of empirical data. Thus, from the outset the crisis is framed within a narrational background and not an argumentative one. According to the rules of political myth, instead of an explanation the public is given a story, which only needs to be plausible to be effective. As it is not based on evidence, the story could neither be proved nor disproved. The aim of the narrative was to focus on supporting a future agenda for the country, not the importance of a deep and exact knowledge of the facts.

The grand announcement by the Prime Minister was of course not enough. The mythology, in order to engage the public sentimentally needed to rely on some key elements of *mythopoeia* one of which is its religious character. Myths have invariably been connected to religious and moral thinking. Political myth is no exception; however it needs to make sure that these characteristics have a secular coating. The main components of the mythology in question are: the fear of an impending total annihilation (sometimes reminiscent of millennium movements), the absence of alternatives and the narrative's moralistic character.

From the outset of the Greek crisis the public have been terrorized with dystopian images in case the country defaults. In February 2010 the Finance Minister George Papaconstantinou, speaking in Brussels, compared the course of the Greek economy to that of the Titanic (Brown, 2010). Although he added that he would do his best to avoid hitting the iceberg, he had already semiologically connected Greece with catastrophe. The statement became a self-fulfilling prophecy, as it sparked an immediate fall of Greek bonds and caused increasing uneasiness in the markets.

Since then, the country's media commenced a daily bombardment with fantasies of disaster in case the government follows any other route to that of accepting an EU and IMF bailout. No other alternative is explored or even discussed, at least in mainstream media. The tale of impending disaster has become convincing because of its constant repetition, but also because of its carriers. The two interrelated myths of catastrophe and fatality were supported by 'experts' of all kinds in newspaper articles and broadcast round tables. Their story was supported in virtue of their status, not of their arguments. The imagery of annihilation was best summarized in the interim Prime Minister's televised address to the Greek public, before a new package of legislation, drawn according the terms dictated by international lenders, was brought to the Greek Parliament. In February 2012 Mr. Lucas Papademos stated if the lawmakers do not back the bill then: 'a disorderly default would set the country on a disastrous adventure'. He added: 'it would create conditions of uncontrolled economic chaos and social explosion' and that 'the country would be drawn into a vortex of recession, instability, unemployment and protracted misery and this would sooner or later lead the country out of the euro' (Papachristou & Robinson, 2012). This speech uses fear in order to warn against any divergence from the solutions offered, as well against any attempt at exploring alternatives. It appeals to emotion and imagination, rather than logic. Again, any reference to data and evidence, or historical equivalents is absent in favor of an already well-established imagery of an impending end constructed by the media.

Another interesting component of the mythology of crisis is its moralistic character. Departing from Sorel's definition of ideology, Tudor comments that a political myth can be a single key doctrine through which a system of heterogeneous beliefs is interpreted (1972, p. 121). The key doctrine in the Greek crisis is the corrupt nature of the Greeks, which is dogmatically propagated as the sole reason for Greece's downfall. Borrowing heavily from religious discourse, this belief asserts that the financial crisis is a result of an innate vice of the Greek population. Consequently, suffering is presented as an unavoidable outcome of that 'original sin'. As we have seen, from the very beginning George Papandreou had connected the Greek crisis with corruption. Additionally, the newspaper *Eleftheros Typos* revealed in January 2011 that the deputy Prime Minister Theodoros Pangalos had stated in a speech at the University of Oxford in May 2010 that all Greeks are corrupt. He added that politicians don't go out in the streets seeking for voters. On the contrary, corrupt citizens go the politicians' offices asking for favors (Logotheti, 2011). In October 2010 Jean-Claude Jüncker, prime minister of Luxembourg and president of the Eurogroup said in the Irish Times that he knew that 'one of the main Greek characteristics is corruption' and that the Greek Prime Minister stated that he is governing a country of corruption (Marlowe, 2010). With public accusation of the Greeks from their own leaders, Greek and international media added daily stories supporting the claims of 'secret dishonesty' and enumerating the excesses of the troubled country. Again, the discourse remains an abstract generality and never focuses on specific examples. Claude Jüncker refers to corruption as a 'Greek characteristic' generalizing the behavior of some people with an inherent national quality. Such generalizations from individual behavior to national characteristics once again display the distinctiveness of mythical thought. Tudor reminds us that according to Ernst Cassirer, this is 'the law of the leveling and extinction of specific differences. Every part of the whole is the whole itself; every specimen is equivalent to the entire species' (1953, p. 91-92). Political myth, especially racism has used this device in the past. The individual difference is lost under the supposed major characteristics of the group. In this mode of thought, the crime of a certain individual is ascribed to his entire 'race' or the victory in a war might make individual citizens feel proud, although they were not part of the fighting army (1972, p. 130-131). This law of 'leveling and extinction' is explicitly at play in the mythology of the Greek crisis.

The myth of natural corruption gave birth to another myth, that of the vile pariah of the European family. Indicative of this is the initial statement from Jean-Claude Trichet. Referring to Greece, he claimed in November 2009 that particular sinners on the boundaries of the Eurozone were 'very close to losing their credibility' (Evans-Pritchard, 2009). Talking of sinners, Trichet barely disguises the use of religious terminology in order not to engage with evidence. Of course media can take the development of the myth further. There are countless articles and news broadcasts warning that Greece's shortcomings jeopardize world economy (for example see Economist, 2010; Chapman, 2011). One could not explore all in such a limited space, so I will refer only to two of them, which I consider characteristic. The first one is the UK show on Channel 4 'Go Greek for a week', broadcast in November 2011, which juxtaposed the lives of hard working British taxpayers to that of the supposed lazy, money-squandering Greeks. The premise of the show is to present the lives of a British hairdresser, a bus driver and a doctor in relative terms with their Greek counterparts. However, this comparison relies on selective use of data and coarse generalizations. It is interesting that in the opening of the show the speaker lays out that it will help the viewers 'understand how Greece got into the terrible mess that is threatening us all', immediately presenting Greeks as the biggest danger in world economy. Although reality TV is like that, the show reinforces polarities by visualizing a stereotype of British diligence versus Greek corruption and idleness.

Along these lines is the second example, from the German magazine *Focus*, whose edition on 22 February 2010 issue showed on the cover Venus de Milo holding up a middle finger and was entitled: 'Cheater of the Euro family'. In the magazine, the article '*Die Griechenland-Pleite*' explains that Greece is in the brink of financial ruin, threatening to bring down Germany with it. According to the authors, for many years the European Union had thrown money at Greece and now the Germans feel it is their right as sponsors to cut off the money supply. Bribery, corruption and tax evasion is second nature to the Greeks. In order to become 'good Europeans' they need to change profoundly. The Greeks have behaved as true members of the honorable Euro-family, when in fact they were fraudsters. Although admittedly many countries manipulated their accounts in order to join the Euro, only the Greeks failed to abide by the requirements of the single currency. Now the Greek economy threatens healthy economies, like the German one, whereas the Greeks don't feel guilty. Hence it is European Union that needs to prepare itself for an emergency financial help to Greece (Berbalk & Borst, 2010). In short, the article presents Greeks as immature cheats whereas Germany and other EU countries are presented as supervisors and guarantors of European stability.

Of course the stereotype is not limited to the Greeks. Other countries threatening the 'honorable' Eurozone are named: Spain, Portugal, Italy and Ireland. The countries that are 'similar to Germany' are not named, but it could be deduced that they are Northern European. In other words, Greece fits into the wider context of a negative imagery including all the European South (see also Economist, 2008; Von Reppert-Bismarck, 2008). Although there is not a single country in Europe not in debt, or one that can boast innocence of corruption, the countries of the South, and especially Greece, are put to the stand and accused as a threat to the global financial stability. The Southerners' laziness is perceived as innate, exactly as the Northerners' work ethic. As often in history, scapegoats were sought in order to alleviate interest from the true causes of a crisis, though in this case maybe it is better to speak of scapePIGS. The fact that the term PIGS was coined in order to describe the European South, and spread throughout the media like wildfire, went largely unchallenged for issues of discrimination, or even racism. A mode of thinking that supposes that a specific group of people has genetically imparted virtues and another one hereditary vice is a racist one, Tudor points out when discussing the myth of the Aryan race (1972, p. 103). The idea of Northern superiority is not new. According to Henry Hatfield it arose out of 'Nordic renaissance' of the mid-eighteenth century, which favored the blond and blue eyed as exceptional. These myths in turn fed the intellectual armory of Nazism (1960, p. 203-213). A myth cannot grow if it doesn't appeal to an already existent ideology. And the fact that the myth of the South European inferiority was so easily accepted testifies to the fact that racist myths survive in the background of European societies and come to the fore in periods of crisis, like the current one. In the context of the financial crunch, by singling out and vilifying a particular group, one prepares the ground for its financial extermination and additionally reassures the rest of the world that the calamity will never reach its doorstep.

For decades we have been witnessing the vilification of the Arabs. Now we are witnessing the defamation of the Mediterranean Europe. Generalizations based on arbitrary assumptions have created a negative imagery of Southern laziness and corruption without ever bringing any sort of factual proof into the discussion. The bailouts are presented as donations from the strong to the weak, not loans given with interest and burdensome terms. The suffering due to austerity is seen under of the prism of a protestant ethic of a fall from grace. Pain and punishment are accepted as atonement for the inherent vices of the people of debt-ridden countries. However, it has not been made apparent yet that by acquiescing to the extermination of an entire country due to financial problems, one is in fact accepting the death penalty as proper punishment for debts.

Due to the toll the recession has had on Greek society, it is difficult for the myth of the vile Greeks to be sustained. Medecins du Monde has declared Athens as a 'city in humanitarian crisis' since November 2010 (Medecins du Monde, 2010). According to the Ministry of Public Order and Citizen Protection, the suicides have increased by 37% amounting to 3,124 since the beginning of the crisis (Ta Nea, 2012). Additionally, the figures show a dramatic increase in malnourished children (Hadjimatheou, 2012). As the negative portrayal of the Greek population could not be propagated in the face of hardship, a new myth is now taking form, that of the weak sufferer of a calamity equal to a fatal natural disaster. People are now portrayed as struggling underneath something large and untamable. Any action to alleviate suffering is impossible; Greeks have to silently bear their sorrows, waiting for the next loan, while their country is pawned away.

The revival of myth in popular discourse should not pass unnoticed. It testifies to an abandonment of reason in favor of irrationality. The Greek land is once more immersed in myths, not made of tradition and poetry, but manufactured in order to serve certain ends. Roland Barthes saw in mythmaking a dynamic of distortion: '*myth hides nothing*: its function is to distort, not to make disappear' (2000, p.121). The mythology developed currently is possibly useful for distorting the true causes of the financial crisis. Therefore, it conveniently diverts attention from considerations of the culpability of the markets, unregulated banking, or the structural defects of a European single currency. One should be aware that with the commencement of the Greek crisis in 2009 a new chapter opened up in European History: the triumph of *mythos* over *logos,* of fiction over argumentative discourse. The introduction of a manufactured mythology that overrides historical facts is indicative of the beginning of a new phase of political affairs. The vilification of certain nations, the promotion of the infallibility of central, unelected leadership and the justification of financial extermination can bring only one thing to mind: totalitarianism.

Chapter 16

Anti-Conclusions: The 'uprising' will not be analysed

Myrto Tsilimpounidi

This concluding chapter presents the deeply ambiguous project of engaging with a social reality that is emergent, contested, and that resists singular 'readings'. While people are on the streets, and while the implications of ever increasing policy changes are as yet unknown, analysis can at best seem like conjecture. Academic analysis tends to take a longer view: demanding the perspective of time in order to seem conclusive or viable. What this brief piece does is suggest that we need to question the very notion of viable or conclusive analysis about times of sudden social change. It raises such questions without entirely abandoning faith in the potential for theories to be productive in a moment in which categories of meaning are revealed to be precarious.

At the same time it resists the tendency to reduce social phenomena, lived realities and embodied subjectivities to mere numbers. As demonstrated in the latter chapters of Judith Butler and Athena Athanasiou's book *Dispossession: The Performative in the Political* (2013), there is an insidious relationship between the ways 'crisis' has been problematized and schematized as 'fiscal' or 'political', and therefore its cures are managerial. If, however, the 'crisis' erodes the distinctions between social and economic spheres, then the conditions of crisis necessitate new ways of responding with new tools of analysis. These tools must begin to take into account the intersecting and multiple ways people are becoming dispossessed of material wealth, and of the loss of stature promised by education and employment as precarity becomes the status quo. However, as the preceding chapters demonstrate, national identity is also (importantly) being called into question in light of the ways crisis affects the interplay of national/EU interests.

What connects the contributors is not a political or ideological position, but rather a commitment to the production of knowledge through empirical investigation. Yet, rather than presenting their findings as absolute – especially since social conditions are constantly shifting – this combination of academic with activist and artist perspectives demonstrates the need for including the discourses of reflection, action, and creativity in the ways we approach 'crisis'. It no longer seems appropriate for intellectuals to take positions based on teleological understandings of social change. By this, I mean the propensity of social scientists to engage out-dated theories and apply them to current situations in order to make their claims. Such a view does not make account of the radical shifts needed in our language when investigating the slippery concepts of 'change', which can, after all, refer to 'positive' or 'negative' transformations.

This concluding idiosyncratic manifesto attempts to capture the fragments of two prevailing concerns that sit beneath the thematic sections of the book: the role of the academic/public intellectual in the milieu of austerity; and what it means to engage with theory in the era of crisis. These related concerns are explored through a single image, captured at a top university in Athens in December 2011 during a conference dedicated on 'finding ways to exit the crisis'.

The image tells a story of the serious minds hard at work attempting to define the symptoms of a social catastrophe. What is evident in the photograph is the clusters of intellectuals, officials and policy-makers whose backs are turned to the writing on the wall. The slogan reads 'the uprising will not be analysed'. It points towards the urgent social and political project of the near future: how to engage those in power with the radical voices

Image 16: **The uprising will not be analysed.** Photo: Author's own.

of the streets, whose expressions may be messy and uncomfortable, but whose audibility is growing. Or even, how do we challenge the structures of oppression and domination which dictate who the powerful elites and the experts are on the first place? As Žižek asks 'how should we read the signs of this rage?' (2012, p. 128). For him, the 'signs' are not to be sought in historical or contextual studies, but are reflections of emerging futures. He suggests that in this milieu, academic analysis should seek to balance between 'reading the signs from the hypothetical future and maintaining the radical openness of that future' (2012, p. 129).

This claim for radical openness while at the same time eagerly engaging with the signs of dissent in the present highlights certain tensions within the hegemonic narratives of knowledge production. The three problems of the academy begin with the problem of representation. In the age of protest and revolt, in which democracy is being challenged, acts of resistance and rupture make claims (in public space) that 'we' are not to be represented by politicians, that the notion of representability in politics needs to be re-examined; and that, by extension, all claims to 'represent' should be opened to scrutiny. It is in this light that this chapter seeks to draw attention to the shadows cast by academic representations of 'crisis'. There is a need now to abandon the theoretical towers of abstraction and engage with the resisting bodies on the streets, only their act of standing there together opens up new spaces for negotiation, or as Athanasiou & Butler suggest 'the very practice of stasis creates both space for reflection and a space for revolt' (2013, p. 150).

The second related problem is that analysis can seek to make truth claims based on one theoretical position or another. One research lens can be applied to a 'problem' with a certain result, while another might destabilise that argument. At the same time, I am cognizant of the illusion of stability in describing or evoking a particular moment in time. Thus, truth claims in political philosophy or socially engaged research need to be understood as contingent. Finally, I seek to disabuse the notion of the academy as having a curative function, as if by defining 'problems' we can propose solutions. Such a view does not allow for the power of counter-narratives (often the 'unwelcome' voice of activists or protesters who disrupt the well-constructed statements of the 'privileged academics'). As in the picture above, the stark simplicity of slogans can serve to undermine the hegemonic language of social science with its urgency, impropriety and occasionally, humour.

Having said that, I would like to return to a wider concern about the place of academics and public intellectuals in the project of imagining our collective way through and between the losses of certainty the crisis has made inevitable. In the case of Athens, academic freedoms have been prized since the University was the centre-point of the 1973 uprising against the Junta. Universities were spaces of asylum until 2012, when a law passed which allowed law enforcement officers to enter university grounds. This symbolic retraction of a law that exemplified academic freedoms has resulted in several high profile attacks on places of learning. What is even more worrying is the sense that radical opposition will not be tolerated; and that since the civil service is being squeezed that the right to education is being eroded. In other words, this is not an easy journey through celebratory stops of protest and uprising, but rather a delicate and reflexive exercise. To put it differently, rather than celebrating (or critiquing) the uprising of the faceless multitude, the urgent task is to engage with the space of reflexivity that the individual untold stories open up.

Žižek makes reference to the messiness of the genesis of protests in a range of contexts (2012, p. 58). His recent work in *The Year of Dreaming Dangerously* seems to highlight the gap between the sterility of studies that seek symptoms to diagnose and propose cures and the counterclaim that social movements lack focus. Rather, there is the need for public intellectuals to engage in imagining in different ways. This demands a reworking of disciplinary affiliations, new networks of solidarity and different terms, if we are to develop productive academic responses to the era of austerity. 'Our inability to imagine alternatives, or to imagine that alternatives can work, may tell us more about the power of the present system than about the alternatives themselves' (Ferrell, 2009, p. 76). Or, as Graeber puts it, the 'revolution over common sense is more strategically important than ever before' (2012, p. 167). In other words, there is a call for action and a battle over the systemic received notions of what comprises society, who belongs and who does not belong and according to what criteria have consistently been understood through the hegemonic narratives of capitalism and its powerful playmates class and race.

In reflecting on the place of imagination, self-expression and collective cultural creation as an embodied means of engaging with the current milieu of change, Appadurai calls for a view of imagination as a popular, social and collective fact, with a split character.

> On the one hand, it is in and through the imagination that modern citizens are disciplined and controlled—by states, markets, and other powerful interests. But is it is also the faculty through which collective patterns of dissent and new designs for collective life emerge (2000, p. 6).

Following Appadurai, if the imagination is the realm which produces and sustains the totalities of the status quo, then as Graeber suggests it is now more crucial than ever to start the revolution of the common sense, to engage in subversive ways of imagining and redefine our vocabularies through action.

Thus, in conclusion, the manifesto I would propose is firstly, to encourage people to 'read the signs', and move towards a critical ability to be radically open: this includes being transparent about the ambiguity (emotionally and intellectually) of debating the 'future' of contested concepts such as 'nations', national identities, and belonging. Secondly, work towards a transformative imagination that can both destroy fixed understandings, paradigms and narratives as well as forge new possibilities. Finally, engage collaboratively, across disciplinary borders, in order to explore more deeply what discourses can be employed in the project of 'remapping crisis'.

As a final point, I recall an argument of Immanuel Wallerstein that genuine revolutionary moments, even if they seem to take place in one country, are always worldwide in scope (cited in Shukaitis, Graeber & Biddle, 2007, p. 26). While the cases and analyses in this volume talk to instances, effects and affects of the Greek Crisis in Athens, there are obvious links to be made with dissatisfaction and dissent, protests and revolts in squares and streets elsewhere in the world, from Tahrir Square to Syntagma Square, from Zucotti Park to Gezi Park. As we imagine the possibilities of a world in transition, the academy has a role to play. The uprising, thus, will not be analyzed it will (hopefully) transform our ways of seeing, understanding and imagining social worlds.

Notes to chapters

Foreword:

1 Plato, *Laches or Peri andreias*, 195a.

Notes to Chapter 1:

1 This is a broad categorisation of municipalities and smaller communities of the Attiki region –apart from the Municipality of Athens that forms a category of its own– following their social composition and its transformation between 1971 and 1991. The traditional high status or working class areas contain municipalities that had a clear social profile in 1971, which remained rather unchanged, like *Palaio Psychico* or *Keratsini* respectively. New high status areas were considered those where upper-middle or working class groups gathered more recently and where the overall population increase is also more recent, like *Marousi* or *Ano Liosia*. The intermediate category contains socially mixed and middle middle-class areas where both the overall population and the social profile did not change considerably during that period, like *Dafni* or *Kallithea*. A map of Athenian municipalities according to this categorization in Maloutas (1997).

2 The central municipality accounted for 35,7% of the metropolitan population in 1951 against 17,3% in 2011 (http://www.statistics.gr/portal/page/portal/ESYE/PAGE-census2011).

3 For a discussion of the increasing presence of higher occupational categories in working class areas, see Maloutas (2004) and Leal (2004) for an analysis of the same phenomenon in Madrid.

4 See Leontidou (1986: 97) for data concerning 1961 to 1981, and EKKE-ESYE (2005) for 1991 to 2001.

5 The classification of census tracts in map 1 was produced

using a combination of multivariate analyses of their social profile, which is detailed in Maloutas (2007, 751-4).

6 'Antiparochi' is a way of promoting housing production on a very small scale; it brings together a small landowner and a small building firm in a joint venture to realise a unique operation, usually limited to just one apartment building. Its great success in the 1960s and 1970s was mainly due to preferential tax reliefs and to the reduced solvency needed by the builder to realise the operation.

Notes to Chapter 3:

1 The level difference between the level of the surrounding area of the entrance of the building of the old palace and the level of the square of the Unknown Soldier- that used to be at the same level before the construction of the monument- is almost 7 meters in height. In addition to those changes the main entrance of the building was moved from the side facing the square to the side facing Amalias Avenue enhancing the disconnection from the square.

2 Perhaps the only exception to this tendency is the 'emo' group that was gathering at the square in the 00s. However, 'emos' were a social category commonly tied to music, fashion and 'emo' subculture and had mainly apolitical stances.

3 Kaloudis writes in 2000 that 'the majority of Greeks are now strong supporters of democratic principles' and 'view their democracy as legitimate' (2000, p. 83).

4 BBC News. 2008. In pictures: Greek riots. *The Guardian.* [online] Available at: <http://news.bbc.co.uk/2/hi/in_pictures /7770189.stm>. [Accessed 6 June 2012]. Also a number of alternative media and hundreds of users of social media used the same picture and videos with the title 'Merry Christmas from Athens' in order to celebrate the event: Mysterrr. 2008. *Merry Christmas from Athens 2008 (with*

ringtone link). [online] Available at: <http://www.youtube.com/watch?v=NOkbeb1WBqQ>. [Accessed 7 June 2012].

5 Ta Nea Online. 2008. 'The Lighting of the Christmas Tree at Syntagma'. [online] Available at: <http://www.tanea.gr/ellada/article/?aid=4492389>. [Accessed 5 June 2012]; Aspro Provato. 2009. 'A Beloved Mayor'. *Aspro Provato.* [blog] 8 February. Available at: <http://asproprovato.blogspot.gr/2009/02/blog-post_8199.html>. [Accessed 5 June 2012].

6 This image did not make it to headlines around the world.

7 In Greek they are referred to as *kinima aganaktismenoi.*

8 'Traditionally' refers to the history of Greek movements but also to contemporary urban conflicts.

9 Smith, H. 2011. Greek Police Face Investigation After Protest Violence. *The Guardian.* [online] 1 July 2011. Available at: <http://www.guardian.co.uk/world/2011/jul/01/greek-police-investigation-protest-violence>. [Accessed 16 May 2012].

10 Amnesty International. 2011. *Tear Gas Fired as Greek Police Clash with Athens Protesters.* Available at: <http://www.amnesty.org/en/news-and-updates/tear-gas-fired-greek-police-clash-athens-protesters-2011-06-29>. [Accessed 10 May 2012].

11 Some indicative video material recording the extensive police violence and tactics: PALAVIARIS30, 2011. 'Chemicals at Syntagma Metro Station' [video online] 29 June 2011. Available at: <https://www.youtube.com/watch?v=2xR_ME-XYZM>. [Accessed 12 June 2012]; RealDemocracyGr, 2011. 'Junta at Syntagma Square'. [video online] 29 June 2011. Available at: <https://www.youtube.com/watch?v=S20_JuaX8gg>. [Accessed 12 June 2012].

12 Ethnos.gr. 2011. Interview: Theodoros Pagalos. The Black Market Traders Want the Return to Drachma. *Ethnos.gr.* [online] Available at: <http://www.ethnos.gr/article.asp?catid=22767&subid=2&pubid=63097052>. [Accessed 12 June

2012].

13 Sky.gr. 2011. Reactions to the Siege of Parliament from *Aganaktismenoi*. [online]. Available at: <http://www.skai.gr/news/greece/article/171043/adidraseis-gia-tin-poliorkia-tis-voulis-apo-aganaktismenous-/>. [Accessed 20 June 2012].

14 14 Act (noun) 1 ***a***: the doing of a thing ***b***: something done voluntarily, 2 a state of real existence rather than possibility, 3: the formal product of a legislative body, 4: the process of doing, 5: a formal record of something done or transacted 6: one of the principal divisions of a theatrical work, 7: ***a***: one of successive parts or performances ***b***: the performer or performers in such an act ***c***: a performance or presentation identified with a particular individual or group ***d***: the sum of a person's actions or effects that serve to create an impression or set an example, 8: a display of affected behaviour".

15 Mouffe distinguishes between antagonism and agonism as antagonism is the relation in which the two conflicting sides are enemies who do not share any common ground while in agonism the conflicting parties recognise the legitimacy of their opponents, although acknowledging that there is no rational solution to their conflict (Mouffe, 2005b).

16 Indicative of elitism could be the fact that since the reconstitution of democracy in 1974 two members of Karamanlis family (Konstantinos G. Karamanlis in 1974 and 1978 and Konstantinos A. Karamanlis in 2004 and in 2007) and two members of Papandreou family (Andreas Papandreou in 1981, 1985 and 1993 and George Papandreou in 2009) were prime ministers of the country. Konstantinos G Karamanlis was also in office in 1955, 1958 and 1961 and George Papandreou (the elder) in 1944, 1963 and 1964.

17 This refers also to the critique of movements, acts and occupations in different Athenian public spaces as well as the critique of the recent global occupy movements.

Notes to Chapter 4

1 PASOK: The Panhellenic Socialist Movement was founded in 1974. It was in Government when Greece agreed in an economic rescue plan with IMF and EU, which led to a series of austerity measures. PASOK participates in a coalition Government with New Democracy and the Democratic Left, which has been formed since the elections of 2012.

2 http://parkingparko.espivblogs.net/

Notes to Chapter 5

1 Suicide has indeed become the last option for some hit hardest by the crisis. In a most public way, a retired pharmacist shot himself on Syntagma Square, in front of the Parliament, on April 4th 2012. In his suicide note he said: 'I see no other solution than a decent ending before I start looking in the garbage to feed myself' (quoted in Smith, 2012).

2 This is a countrywide initiative organised by the Archdiocese of Athens, the Dioceses of Greece and Skai, the Greek TV and radio channel. The campaign wants to provide food to soup kitchens organised by the Church. In cooperation with twenty big supermarket chains, customers are asked to leave some of their purchased food products at designated areas in the supermarket as a donation to the soup kitchens (Skai News, 2012a).

Notes to Chapter 8

1 The terms are encountered often but none of them really prevailed for the simple reason that they did not describe the practice sufficiently. The term hip-hop graffiti is also not adequate because graffiti precedes the advent of hip-hop by ten years, before their parallel presence and frequent overlap in the 80s. Subsequently, graffiti and hip-hop went their separate ways and while many graffiti writers related to hip

hop, the rest and most possibly, the majority, had no particular or no contact at all with it.

2 Neumayer, K., 2010.

3 See <http://www.graffiti.org/faq/graf.def.html>. [Accessed 30 March 2013].

4 See Graffiti 'Invasion' in Greece. 05 Oct 2008. <http://www.youtube.com/watch?v=xfDeI99IW28>. [Accessed 30 March 2013].

5 In many cases writers face direct imprisonment and or have to pay large amounts of money

6 An analogous tradition probably exists with the Greek Right.

7 Austin, J. 2001. *Taking the Train: How Graffiti Art Became an Urban Crisis in New York City*. New York: Columbia University Press.

8 The same atmosphere is described in Schmidlapp, D., Phase II, 1996. *Style: Writing from the UnderGround*. Viterbo, Italy: Stampa Alternativa and IGTimes.

9 Chalfant, H. & Prigoff, J. 1987. *Spraycan Art*. London: Thames and Hudson.

10 Various Authors. 2010. *Akataliptes Mountzoures*. Athens: Grammi 500 Press.

11 This can be seen in an episode of 'Beautiful World' Episode 18. Omorfos Kosmos.

12 Various Authors. 2011. *Outsiders Magazine*. Athens: self released.

13 Various Authors. 2012. *Dopamine Magazine*. Athens: self released.

14 Various Authors. 2012. *Pisa ('Tar') Magazine*. Thessaloniki and Athens: self released.

15 As above.

16 As above.

17 From a conversation with Jnor, Athens, June 2012.

18 I would like to thank Alie, Abort, Jnor, Tomy and Tuiyo for sharing information.

Notes to Chapter 9

1 For more on *Pisa![tar],* see the blog. Available at: <www.pisazine.blogspot.gr>. [Accessed 30 March 2013].

2 'Communities of practice': a term developed by the cognitive anthropologists Jean Lave and Etienne Wenger. As E. Wenger argues 'a community of practice is not merely a community of interest—people who like certain kinds of movies, for instance. Members of a community of practice are practitioners. They develop a shared repertoire of resources: experiences, stories, tools, ways of addressing recurring problems—in short a shared practice'. Available at: <http://www.ewenger.com/theory/index.htm>. [Accessed on 30 March 2013].

3 See Lefebvre, H. 1996. *Writings on Cities.* Translated by E. Kofman & E. Lebas. Oxford: Blackwell.

Notes to Chapter 10

1 Hall et al. (1978, p. 9-10) argue that statistics are largely respected because are considered to be 'hard facts', but they also 'have an ideological function… everything depends on how statistics are interpreted and then on how these interpretations are reported'.

2 These 'discussions' between artists and viewers should not be seen through the traditional face-to-face exchange framework, as they are never immediate. As Kelly Harris (2006, p.104) argues, 'the way in which these 'conversations' take place is more gradual: it operates as a seeping into one's consciousness'.

3 Andrea Mubi Brighenti, based on the idea of the plurality of publics, is critical of the prefixes 'counter-' or 'subaltern-' when he argues that 'just like the public does not belong to the state or any formal institution, it does not belong to any specific social group either' (Brighenti, 2010a, p. 19). Instead, he counterproposes the term 'non-public publics', noting

that this should not be perceived as a negative notion.

4 According to Michael Warner (2003, p. 88), 'publics are lacking any institutional being'. Thus, (counter)publics should be distinguished from any specific social groups or entities.

5 The degree of public interaction with the dominant public sphere in the case of political wall writing is substantially higher in comparison with other forms of wall writing (e.g. NY graffiti, street art).

6 For Warner (2003, p. 10), the choice of oneself to be part of a public, either as addressee or receiver, is influenced by certain social and ideological motives.

7 Echoing Iveson (2009), Brighenti (2010a, p. 38) argues that the city should be studied along with the media. He is critical of the genuineness of face-to-face interaction and notes that 'urban spaces are saturated with mediations and prolongations'.

8 It is not surprising that even the mainstream coverage of the Greek crisis focuses on wall writings. Thus, political graffiti writers take advantage of this fact by identifying those places that would potentially permit the widest possible circulation of their views. For instance, see the articles 'Protest Graffiti Art in Athens' in *Time* and 'Spray Paint and Foment: Street Art from Athens' in *Bloomberg*; and the documentary 'The wake up call' by Kostas Kallergis. <http://www.time.com/time/photogallery/0,29307,2099542,00.html> <http://www.bloomberg.com/slideshow/2012-06-19/spray-paint-and-foment-street-art-from-athens.html#slide1> [Accessed 20 September 2012]; And <http://thewakeupcall.gr/> [accessed 15 November 2012].

9 At this point, it is important to address how the notions of 'space' and 'place' are conceptualized here. According to Cresswell, 'space has been in distinction to place as a realm without meaning… when humans invest meaning in a

portion of space and then become attached to it in some way it becomes a place' (2002, p. 10). For him, the notion of place 'combines the spatial with the social - it is 'social space''(1996, p. 3).

10 According to Jackson (1989, p. 3), this 'preferred reading' is not imposed directly but rather tenderly, by becoming 'unquestioned', 'natural' and 'common sense'.

11 Cresswell studies a type of graffiti that is known as 'Hip-Hop style' (also frequently cited as 'Signature' or 'New York style' graffiti) and is not by definition political. This is why he argues that graffitists' actions are transgressive rather than resistant. 'Transgression, in distinction to resistance', Cresswell suggests (1996, p. 23), 'does not, by definition, rest on the intentions of actors but on the results - on the 'being noticed' of a particular action'.

12 Although being relatively safe and efficient practice, those who write graffiti with political content are at much more risk to get caught and penalized, as opposed to other types of wall writing, such as signature graffiti.

13 According to Iveson (2007, p. 144), graffiti should not be considered to be 'private address', since graffitists, as they write-address their messages, do not draw a dividing line between desired and wider audiences.

14 The 'Re-think Athens' architectural competition, launched in May 2012, is the most widely advertised and indicative of this trend. According to the competition's program, one of the central roads in Athens, namely Panepistimiou Avenue, is about to be transformed into a pedestrian area. Even though the need for interventions are crucial, many oppositional views concerning the intensions behind the competition are already voiced, claiming that it is a par excellence gentrification project whose purpose is to establish a specific 'clean' image in Athens centre (see also Leontidou, 2012, p. 301). The Institute of Greek Architects

(SADAS) rejected to advertise this competition since, as they reported, it is poorly scientifically grounded and its main goals are still vague.

15 The 45 year-old teacher and trade unionist Savvas Metikidis committed suicide on 21st of April 2012. Just fifteen days earlier (on 4th of April) a similar event shocked Greek society, when the 77 year-old pensioner Dimitris Christoulas shot himself at Syntagma square, because he did not want to 'find [him]self fishing through garbage cans for [his] sustenance', as he wrote in his suicide note. The suicides fuelled by debt and its consequences in Greece have dramatically increased since the begging of the crisis and resulted to several rallies with main slogan 'We won't get used to death'.

Notes to Chapter 11

1 Poster, M. ed. 1988. *J. Baudrillard Selected Writings*. Stanford: Stanford University Press.

2 See Foucault, M. 1977. What is an Author? In D.F. Bouchard, ed. *Language, Counter Memory, Practice: Selected Essays and Interviews.* Ithaca: Cornell University Press; and Barthes R. 1984. La Mort de l' auteur. In *Le Bruissement de la langue*. Paris: Seuil.

3 At this point I would like to express my great indebtedness to curatorial consultant Andreas Fakis (Studio 4) who made me familiar with Bleeps' works. His comments were of much help to draw my attention to the artist and to the better understanding of his purposes.

4 On the notion 'false normativity' as a return to the verities of tradition (in art, religion, family, etc.), see Habermas, J. (1998).

5 Mouffe contends that the 'agonistic' struggle is the core of a vibrant democracy; it is the very configuration of power relations around which a given society is structured; it is a

struggle between opposing hegemonic projects that can never be reconciled rationally. In relation to the consequences of the agonistic model applied to the visualizing of the public space Mouffe states that the most important consequence is that this model challenges the widespread conception that, albeit in different ways, informs most visions of the public space conceived as the terrain where consensus can emerge. For the agonistic model, on the contrary, the public space is the battleground where different hegemonic projects are confronted, without any possibility of final reconciliation. Her radical democratic project differs significantly from the conceptualization of the public space as space of deliberation and consensus. See Mouffe (2007).

6 See the video *'bleeps.gr video I'*. Available from <http://bleeps.gr/main/category/videos>. Accessed 20 May 2012.

7 Of special interest is also Slavoj Žižek's standpoint that illustrates the aforementioned problematic: 'There are two main stories about the Greek crisis in the media: the German-European story (the Greeks are irresponsible, lazy, free-spending, tax-dodging etc, and have to be brought under control and taught financial discipline) and the Greek story (our national sovereignty is threatened by the neoliberal technocracy imposed by Brussels). When it became impossible to ignore the plight of the Greek people, a third story emerged: the Greeks are now presented as humanitarian victims in need of help, as if a war or natural catastrophe had hit the country. While all three stories are false, the third is arguably the most disgusting. The Greeks are not passive victims: they are at war with the European economic establishment, and what they need is solidarity in their struggle, because it is our struggle too' (2012, p. 13).

8 On the notion of systemic crisis, see David M. Kotz, (2009).

'A systemic crisis occurred at the end of the 1920s, when an earlier liberal form of capitalism went into crisis following the stock market collapse of 1929. Another developed in the mid-1970s, as the regulated form of capitalism of the post-World War II decades stopped working effectively. In both cases, the crisis was followed by a thorough restructuring of capitalism. Today it appears that we are entering another systemic crisis, this time of the neoliberal form of capitalism that dates to the late 1970s/early 1980s' (2009, p. 2).

9 Crimp's 'Pictures' in the art magazine X-TRA is a reprint of the original essay written in the catalogue published on the occasion of the exhibition with the same title. The exhibition organized by Crimp himself was held at the Artists Space in New York in 1977 (September 24-October 29). On show were not paintings but pieces of multimedia art focused on the theme of representation.

10 See Morell (2010). On the notion of the cognitive economy, see also Hardt (2010).

11 The caption 'The Bailout Sleep' is not integrated into the piece on the wall, instead, it has been added to the image posted on Bleeps' website. This particular practice reflects the above-mentioned notion on the common wealth whose nature is social and reproducible such that it is increasingly difficult to maintain exclusive control over it.

12 *Arma Christi* are seen as arms in the sense of heraldry, and also as the weapons Christ used to achieve his conquest over Satan; These may include the ladder, crown of thorns, hammer, nails, spear, dice, scourge, rod and sponge, column where scourged, robe, cock for Peter's denial, and pincers for removing the nails. For Jesus' Passion in Christian symbolism and iconography see A.N. Didron (1969). For the iconographical sources and analysis of religious motifs and symbols detected in Bleeps' work I am deeply indebted to Athanasios Paliouras, professor emeritus of the Faculty of

History and Archaeology of the Philosophical School, University of Ioannina.

13 The artwork with the original title *Betende Hände* is stored at Albertina Museum Graphische Sammlung in Vienna Austria.

14 Giorgos Seferis (1900–1971) was a renowned Greek poet, and 'Denial', one of his most famous poems, was published in his collection *Turning Point* (*Strophe*) in 1931.

15 There is such a rich bibliography about the stylistic characteristics of the folk art that it is not possible to list all publications. The following have been among the most important in my thinking: Zdunić, D. 1981. *Primitive Painting. An Anthology of the World's Naive Painters*. Zagreb: Spektar; Bihalji-Merin, O. 1959. *Modern Primitives: Masters of Naïve Painting*. New York: Harry N. Abrams; Gardner, A.T.E. 1961. *101 Masterpieces of American Primitive Painting From the Collection of Edgar Willam and Bernice Chrysler Garbisch*. New York: The Metropolitan Museum of Art. ; Dasnoy, A. 1970. *Exégèse de la peinture naive*. Bruxelles: Laconti.

16 The 'Wake Up' series is on display on Bleeps' website, available at <www.bleeps.gr> .

17 Historically, the seeking of equations between particular hues and musical notes has played an important role in the artistic creativity of the 20th century beginning with Kandinsky's early search for musical analogies to his abstract paintings. Wagner's operatic vision of a *Gesamtkunstwerk* and Scriabin's composition *Promethée* of 1910 (which incorporated a color organ) gave the synesthetic haze a spectacular body. After World War I the down to earth rhythms of jazz became important to painters as disparate as Matisse, St. Davis, Bearden, and Mondrian. See a very informative article on the history of the painting-music affair by Cooper, H. (2005). An Eye for an Ear: Art and Music in the Twentieth Century. *Artforum*. 43(10): pp. 310-15.

18 I am referring of course to the singer and songwriter Bob Dylan and to the song *Blowin' in the Wind* written in 1962 and released on his album *The Freewheelin' Bob Dylan* in 1963.

Notes to Chapter 13

1 By Euroscepticism, we do not refer to the regressive forces that have historically stalled aspects of Greek political life and returned to prominence due to the crisis, combining critique against the EU memoranda with nationalist propaganda and racist arguments, offering no proposal for the country's future. We view such insular positions defined by strong hostility towards anything non-Greek and adding to the paranoid state of emergency as *anti*-European. Nonetheless, mainstream media present Euroscepticism and anti-Europeanism as synonymous, thus legitimizing dominant Europhile attitudes.

2 Panic here means exaggerated reactions, disproportional to the cause, perpetuated through arguments of crisis, anxiety, hostility and threat. Although we are not referring to 'moral panic' explicitly, Stanley Cohen's understanding of the term as manifestation of 'condensed political struggle to control the means of cultural reproduction' (2011, p. xxxv) is useful: panic is not an abstract sentiment that emerges among people, but the product of the interrelation between power, ideology and representation at a time of crisis.

3 Commentators often refer to Europe and the EU as synonymous, thus excluding a number of countries that are still at the periphery of the EU, yet geographically are within the borders of Europe.

4 Certainly, this is not solely a Greek phenomenon, as the tension between identity and difference constitutes the nation. In the Greek paradigm, it can be argued that the Others historically have been the Balkans, the Muslim East and Western Europe.

5 The term 'troika' refers to the guarantors of the bailout packages: EU, IMF and ECB.

6 PASOK: Panhellenic Socialist Movement.

7 In the late 1990s the stock market attracted investment, which rapidly spread from the private sector to households. As the stock market grew, so did speculation, which in turn led the stock market bubble to burst, leaving a large number of investors in debt (Close, p. 290-291). During the same period, government proposed the removal of religious affiliation from ID cards, which was until then compulsory for all citizens. The church of Greece responded with massive protests claiming that 'the measures struck at the heart of Greek identity', while the government 'was anxious to demonstrate Greece's western European credentials' (Clogg, 2002, p. 236-237).

8 Leader of SYRIZA, a coalition of left wing parties and groups that gained momentum in the May elections and is currently opposition party in the Parliament.

References

Adorno, T.W. & Horkheimer, M. 1997. *Dialectic of Enlightenment*. Translated by J. Cumming. London: Verso.

Ahmed, S. 2004. *The Cultural Politics of Emotion*. Edinburgh: Edinburgh University Press.

Alex B. 2012. Spanish Commuters Say 'I'm not Paying' to Fare Hikes. *France 24*. [online] Available at <http://observers.france24.com/content/20120119-spain-commuters-say-yo-no-pago-not-paying-fare-hikes-public-transport-debt-crisis>. [Accessed 01/04/2012].

AMHS. 2011a. Statement of the Assembly of Migrant Hunger Strikers, [online] 23 January, Available at: <http://hunger-strike300.espivblogs.net/2011/01/23/statement-of-the-assembly-of-migrant-hunger-strikers/>. [Accessed on 20/11/2012].

AMHS. 2011b. Press Release Decision of the Assembly of Migrants on Hunger Strike. *Allilmap*. [online] 28 January, Available at: <https://allilmap.wordpress.com/>. [Accessed on 20/11/2012].

AMHS. 2011c. Announcement to the Society. *Allilmap*. [online] 30 January. Available at: <https://allilmap.wordpress.com/>. [Accessed 20/11/2012].

AMHS. 2011d. Announcement of the Hunger Strikers. *Allilmap*. [online] 5 February, Available at: <https://allilmap.wordpress.com/>. [Accessed 21/11/2012]. (In Greek).

AMHS. 2011e. Decision of the Assembly of Migrant Hunger Strikers. *Diktio*. [online] 14 February. Available at: <http://diktio.org/node/705>. [Accessed 21/11/2012]. (In Greek).

Amnesty International. 2012. *Police Violence in Greece*. London: Amnesty International.

Anderson, B. 1991. *Imagined Communities*. London: Verso.

Andrews, R. 2005. Shoplifting as Social Commentary. [online] 25 August. Available at <www.wired.com/culture/lifestyle/news

/2005/08/68609>. [Accessed 15/9/2010].

Andronikidou, A. & Kovras, I. 2012. Cultures of Rioting and Anti-Systemic Politics in Southern Europe, *West European Politics.* 35(4): pp. 707-725.

Anonymous. 2012. The Moment of Truth. *Irish Times.* [online] 14 June. Available at: <http://www.irishtimes.com/newspaper /opinion/2012/0614/1224317876339.html>. [Accessed 12 Aug 2012].

Anonymous. n.d. The History of the European Union. *Europa.* [online] Available at: <http://europa.eu/about-eu/eu-history/index_en.htm>. [Accessed 12 August 2012].

Antzoletos, A. 2011. Migrants Settled in the Law School. *Skai.* [online] 24 January. Available at: <http://www.skai.gr/news /greece/article/161315/metanastes-egatastathikan-sti-nomiki-sholi/>. [Accessed 16/12/2012]. (In Greek).

Appadurai, A. 2000. Grassroots Globalization and the Research Imagination. *Public Culture.* 12(1): pp.1-19.

Arapoglou, V.P. 2004. The Governance of Homelessness in the European South: Spatial and Institutional Contexts of Philanthropy in Athens. *Urban Studies.* 41(3): pp. 621-640.

Arapoglou, V., Kandylis, G., Kavoulakos, G., & Maloutas, T. 2009. The New Social Geography of Athens: Ethnic Diversity and Urban Conflicts. *Synchrona Themata.* 107: pp. 57-66. (In Greek).

Arapoglou, V.P. & Maloutas T. 2011. Segregation, inequality and marginality in context: the case of Athens. *The Greek Review of Social Research,* Special Issue. 136(c): pp. 135-155.

Arapoglou, V.P. & Sayas, J. 2009. New facets of urban segregation in Southern Europe: Gender, migration and social class change in Athens. *European Urban and Regional Studies.* 16(4): pp. 345-362.

Archer, M. 1995. *Realist Social Theory: The Morphogenetic Approach.* Cambridge: Cambridge University Press.

Asen, R. 2000. Seeking the 'Counter' in Counterpublics.

Communication Theory. 10(4), pp. 424-446.

Avramidis, K. 2012. 'Live your Greece in Myths': Reading the Crisis on Athens' Walls. In A.M. Brighenti, ed. *Regards on Crisis in Europe*. [online] Available at: <http://www.professional-dreamers.net/_prowp/wp-content/uploads/Avramides-Reading-the-Crisis-on-Athens-walls-fld.pdf>. [Accessed 30 March 2013].

Balestrini, N. & Moroni, P. 1988. *Die goldene Horde. Arbeiterautonomie, Jugendrevolte und bewaffneter Kampf in Italien*. Berlin: Assoziation A.

Barthes, R. 1972. *Le Degré zero de l' écriture. Nouveaux Essais critiques*. Paris: Editions du Seuil.

Barthes, R. 1977. *Image, Music, Text*. Translated by S. Heath. London: Fontana Press.

Barthes, R. 2000. *Mythologies*. Translated by A. Lavers. London: Vintage Books.

Bastéa, E. 2000. *The Creation of Modern Athens - Planning the Myth*. Cambridge: Cambridge University Press.

BBC. 2012. Greek Unrest after Pensioner Suicide Beside Parliament. *BBC News*. [online] 5 April 2012. Available at <www.bbc.co.uk/news/world-europe-17620421>. [Accessed 6/6/2012].

Belting, H. 2005. Image, Medium, Body: A New Approach to Iconology. *Critical Inquiry* 31(2), pp. 302-319.

Benford, R. & Snow, D. 2000. Framing Process and Social Movements. *Annual Review of Sociology*. 26(1): pp. 611-639.

Benjamin, W. 1999. Theses on the Philosophy of History. *Illuminations*. Translated by H. Zorn. London: Pimlico, pp. 245-255.

Benjamin, W. 2006. *Berlin Childhood Around 1900*. Cambridge: Harvard University Press.

Berbalk, O. & Borst, S. 2010. Die Griechenland-Pleite. *Focus*. [online] 22 February. Available at: <http://www.focus.de/finan zen/news/staatsverschuldung/wirtschaft-die-griechenland-

pleite_aid_482498.html>. [Accessed 12 December 2012].

Bhabha H. 1994. *The Location of Culture*. London: Routledge.

Bion, W.R. 1961. *Experiences in Groups and Other Papers*. London: Tavistock Publications.

Bion, W.R. 1962. *Learning from Experience*. London: Heinemann.

Blaug, R. 2002. Engineering Democracy. *Political Studies*. 50: pp. 102-116.

Blaug, R. & Schwarzmantel, J. 2001. Introduction: Democracy—Triumph or Crisis?. In: *Democracy: A Reader.* Edinburgh: Edinburgh University Press, pp. 2-44.

Bloch, E. 1995. *The Principle of Hope*. Translated by N. Plaice. Boston: MIT Press.

Brenner, N., Peck, J., & Theodore, N. 2009. Neoliberal Urbanism: Moments, Relations, Mutations. *SAIS Review*, 29(1): pp. 49-66.

Brenner, N., Peck, J., & Theodore, N. 2010a, Variegated Neoliberalization, Geographies, Modalities, Pathways. *Global Networks*. 10(2): pp. 182–222.

Brenner, N., Peck, J., & Theodore, N. 2010b. After Neoliberalization? *Globalizations*. 7(3): pp. 327-345.

Brighenti, A.M. 2010a. The Publicness of Public Space: On Public Domain. *Quaderni del Dipartimento di Sociologia e Ricerca Sociale*, no.49, Trento: Universitá di Trento.

Brighenti A.M. 2010b. At the Wall: Graffiti Writers, Urban Territoriality, and the Public Domain. *Space and Culture*. 13(3): pp. 315-332.

Brisson, L. 2004. *How Philosophers Saved Myths: Allegorical Interpretation and Classical Mythology*. Translated by C. Tihanyi. Chicago: The University of Chicago Press.

Brook, R. & Dunn, N. 2011. *Urban Maps: Instruments of Narrative and Interpretation in the City*. Farnham: Ashgate.

Brown, M. 2010. Greek Bonds Fall as Minister Compares Task to Steering Titanic. *Bloomberg* [online] 15 February. Available at: <http://www.bloomberg.com/apps/news?pid=munievents&sid=aePtdgh9zsCI>.

[Accessed on 18 December 2012].

Brown, W. 2011. We Are All Democrats Now… In: G. Agamben et al., eds. *Democracy in What State?* New York: Columbia University Press, pp. 44-57.

Brubaker, R. & Cooper, F. 2000. Beyond 'Identity'. *Theory and Society*. 29(1): pp. 1-47.

Butler, J. & Athanasiou, A. 2013. *Dispossession: The Performative in the Political*. Cambridge: Polity.

Calhoun, C. 2011. Series Introduction: From the Current Crisis to Possible Futures. In: C. Calhoun & G.M. Derluguian, eds. *Business as Usual: The Roots of the Global Financial Meltdown*. New York: New York University Press, pp. 9-42.

Calotychos, V. 2003. *Modern Greece: A Cultural Poetics*. Oxford: Berg.

Capella, J.B. & Jamieson, K.H. 1997. *Spiral of Cynicism: The Press and the Public Good.* Oxford: Oxford University Press.

Casey, E.S. 2004. Public Memory in Place and Time. In: K.R. Phillips, ed., *Framing Public Memory.* Tuscaloosa: The University of Alabama Press. pp. 17-44.

Casey, E.S. 2007. Public Memory in the Making; Ethics and Place in the Wake of 9/11. In: G. Caicco, ed. *Architecture, Ethics, and the Personhood of Place.* Lebanon: University Press of New England. pp. 69-90.

Cassirer, E. 1953. *Language and Myth*. Translated by S.K. Langer. New York: Dover Publications.

Certeau, M. de. 1980. On The Oppositional Practices of Everyday Life. *Social Text*. 3 (Autumn): pp. 3-43.

Certeau, M. de., 1988. *The Practice of Everyday Life*. Translated by S. Rendall. Berkeley: University of California Press.

Chaffee, L.G. 1993. *Political Protest and Street Art: Popular Tools for Democratization in Hispanic Countries*. Westport: Greenwood Press.

Chapman, J. 2011. Playing with Fire: IMF Chief Warns Failure to Get Grip on Greek Crisis Threatens Global Economy. *Mail*

Online. [online] 18 June. Available at: <http://www.dailymail.co.uk/news/article-2004962/Greece-bailout-IMF-chief-warns-Greek-crisis-threatens-global-economy.html>. [Accessed on 18 November 2012].

Cheliotis, L.K. & Xenakis, S. 2011. Crime, Fear of Crime and Punitiveness. In L. K. Cheliotis & S. Xenakis, eds. *Crime and Punishment in Contemporary Greece: International Comparative Perspectives*. Bern: Peter Lang AG, pp. 1-43.

Cheliotis, L.K. & Xenakis, S. 2010. What's Neoliberalism Got to Do With It? Towards a Political Economy of Punishment in Greece. *Criminology & Criminal Justice.* 10(4): pp. 353-373.

Chimienti, M. & Solomos, J. 2011. Social Movements of Irregular Migrants, Recognition, and Citizenship. *Globalizations.* 8(3): pp. 343-360.

Chmielewska E. 2008. The Wall as Witness-Surface. *Lo Squaderno* 08: pp. 24-29.

Chomsky, N. 1967. The Responsibility of Intellectuals. *New York Review of Books,* 23 February.

Chong, D., Citrin, J. & Conley, P. 2001. When Self-interest Matters. *Political Psychology.* 22 (September): pp. 541-70.

Clarke, N., Barnett, C., Cloke, P. & Malpass, A. 2007. Globalising the Consumer: Doing Politics in an Ethical Register. *Political Geography.* 26(3): pp. 231–249.

Clarke, S. 2001. From Aesthetics to Object Relations: Situating Klein in the Freudian Uncanny. *Free Associations.* 8: pp. 547-561.

Clogg, R. 2002. *A Concise History of Greece*. 2nd ed. Cambridge: Cambridge University Press.

Cloke P., May J., & Johnson, S. 2010. *Swept-Up Lives: Re-envisioning the Homeless City.* Oxford: Wiley- Blackwell.

Close, D.H. 2002. *Greece Since 1945: Politics, Economy and Society.* London: Pearson.

Cook, K.S., Hardin, R. & Levi, M. 2005. *Cooperation Without Trust?* New York: Russell Sage.

Cohen, S. 2011. *Folk Devils and Moral Panics.* 3rd ed. London: Routledge.

Communiqué. 2008a. Intervention Against Rising Prices. [online] 31/05/2008. Available at <https://athens.indymedia.org/front.php3?lang=el&article_id=873169>. [Accessed 30/01/2013].

Communiqué. 2008b. Robin Hoods hit Greek Supermarket. [online] 5/9/2008. Available at <www.nowpublic.com/world/robin-hoods-hit-greek-supermarket#ixzz1lzLlMLqq>. [Accessed 31/3/2012].

Communiqué. 2009. Crisis, I'm having a crisis... [online] Available at <http://athens.indymedia.org/front.php3?lang=el&article_id=979877>. [Accessed 22/06/2012].

Communiqué. 2010a. On the Expropriation of a Supermarket in Thessalonica. [online] Available at <http://athens.indymedia.org/front.php3?lang=el&article_id=1184313>. [Accessed 01/04/2012].

Communiqué. 2010b. What are we Waiting for? [online] Available at <http://athens.indymedia.org/front.php3?lang=el&article_id=1225991>. [Accessed 01/04/2012].

Communiqué. 2010c. Taking up Responsibility – Supermarket Arson in Thessalonica. [online] Available at <http://athens.indymedia.org/front.php3?lang=el&article_id=1168628>. [Accessed 01/04/2012].

Communiqué. 2011a. Expropriation at a Supermarket in Peristeri. [online] Available at <http://athens.indymedia.org/front.php3?lang=el&article_id=1363667>. [Accessed 01/04/2012].

Communiqué. 2011b. Let's take back all that belong to us. [online] Available at <http://athens.indymedia.org/front.php3?lang=el&article_id=1386152>. [Accessed 01/04/2012].

Communiqué. 2011c. We Welcome 2012 with Rage and Class Consciousness. [online] Available at <http://athens.indymedia.org/front.php3?lang=el&article_id=1366431>. [Accessed 22/06/2012].

Communiqué. 2012. Charity: The Alibi of Barbarism. [online] Available at <http://athens.indymedia.org/front.php3?lang=el&article_id=1384705>. [Accessed 01/04/2012].

Converse, P.E. & Pierce, R. 1986. *Political Representation in France.* Cambridge: Belknap Press.

Crimp, D. 2005. Pictures. *X-TRA.* 8(1): pp. 17-30.

Cresswell, T. 1996. *In Place - Out of Place: Geography, Ideology and Transgression.* Minneapolis: University of Minnesota Press.

Cresswell, T. 2004. *Place: A Short Introduction.* Oxford: Blackwell.

Cronin, A.M. 2008. Urban Space and Entrepreneurial Property Relations: Resistance and the Vernacular of Outdoor Advertising and Graffiti. In A.M. Cronin & K. Hetherington, eds. *Consuming the Entrepreneurial City: Image, Memory and Spectacle.* New York: Routledge. pp. 65-84.

Crozier, M., Huntington, S.P. & Watanuki, J. eds. 1975. *Trilateral Commission Task Force Report no 8: The Crisis of Democracy.* New York: New York University Press.

Dalakoglou, D. 2012. Beyond Spontaneity: Crisis, Violence and Collective Action in Athens. *City: Analysis of Urban Trends, Culture, Theory, Policy, Action.* 16(5): pp. 535-545.

Dama, G. 2011. Lives Below Zero. *Enet,* [online] 8 March, Available at: <http://www.enet.gr/?i=news.el.article&id=257380>. [Accessed 21/11/2012]. (In Greek).

Danto, A. 1986. *The Philosophical Disenfranchisement of Art.* New York: Columbia University Press.

David, B. & Wilson, M. eds. 2002. *Inscribed Landscapes: Marking and Making Place.* Honolulu: University of Hawaii Press.

Deleuze, G. & Guattari, F. 2005. *A Thousand Plateaus. Vol. 2.* Minneapolis: University of Minnesota Press.

DeVerteuil, G., May, G. & von Mahs, J. 2009. Complexity not collapse: Recasting the Geographies of Homelessness in a 'Punitive' Age. *Progress in Human Geography.* 33(5): pp. 646-66

DIMAR. 2011. DIMAR Statement Regarding the Settling of Migrants in the Athens Law School. *Dimokratikiaristera.*

[online] 25 January, Available at: <http://www.dimokratikiaristera.gr/epikairotita/katalogos-deltion-graf-typou/901-2011-01-25-12-21-32>. [Accessed on 15/12/2012]. (In Greek).

Dingley, J.C. & Mollica, M. 2007. The Human Body as a Terrorist Weapon: Hunger Strikes and Suicide Bombers. *Studies in Conflict and Terrorism*. 30(6): pp. 459-492.

Douzinas, C. ed. 2007. *Adieu Derrida.* London: Macmillan.

Drucker, J. 1998. *Figuring the Word: Essays on Books, Writing, and Visual Poetics*. New York: Granary Books.

Druckman, J.N. 2001. On the Limits of Framing Effects: Who Can Frame? *Journal of Politics*. 63(4): pp. 1041-66.

Economides, S. & Monastiriotis, V. 2009. *The Return of Street Politics? Essays on the December Riots in Greece.* London: The Hellenic Observatory, The London School of Economics.

Economist. 2008. Ten Years on, Beware a Porcine Plot. *The Economist* [online] 5 June. Available at: <http://www.economist.com/node/11496844?story_id=11496844>. [Accessed 3 December 2012].

Economist. 2010. Acropolis Now. *The Economist.* [online] 29 April. Available at: <http://www.economist.com/node/16009099>. [Accessed 3 December 2012].

Economou, D. 1988. Land and Housing System. In T. Maloutas & D. Economou, eds. *The Problems of Welfare State Development in Greece.* Athens: Exandas, pp. 57-114 (In Greek).

EKKE. [National Centre for Social Research] – ESYE. [National Statistical Service of Greece]. 2005. *Panorama of Greek census data 1991-2001.*

Eleftherotypia. 2008. Generations of Rage and Uprising. *Enet.* [online] Available at <www.enet.gr/?i=news.el.article&id=109044>. [Accessed 1 April 2012].

Ellermann, A. 2010. Undocumented Migrants and Resistance in the Liberal State. *Politics & Society*. 38(3): pp. 408-429.

EL.STAT. [Hellenic Statistical Authority, formerly titled ESYE]. 2013. *Population Census 1951, 1961, 1971 and 1981.* [online]

Available at: <http://dlib.statistics.gr/portal/page/portal/ESYE/categoryyears?p_cat=10007862&p_topic=10007862>. [Accessed 24 February 2013].

EL.STAT. [Hellenic Statistical Authority]. 2012. *Press Release – Labour Force Survey* (LFS) (1st Quarter 2012). Available at: <http://www.statistics.gr/portal/page/portal/ESYE/PAGE-themes?p_param=A0101&r_param=SJO01&y_param=2012_01&mytabs=0>. [Accessed 12 Aug 2012].

Enet. 2011 Papoutsis' Friendship Attack towards the Law School Migrants. *Enet.* [online] 4 February. Available at: <http://www.enet.gr/?i=news.el.politikh&id=248274>. [Accessed 21 December 2012]. (In Greek).

Entman, R.M. 1993. Framing: Toward Clarification of a Fractured Paradigm. *Journal of Communication*. 43(4): pp. 51-58.

Ethnos News. 2012. Three Suicides every Second day in Greece of Crisis. *Ethnos News* [online] 12 January. Available at <www.ethnos.gr/article.asp?catid=22768&subid=2&pubid=63601823>. [Accessed 25 May 2012].

EuroHealthNet. 2011. Policymakers in EU States and Institutions Need to Act now for Mental and Physical Wellbeing in National and EU Policies. *Briefing document, PR/2011/12.* [online] 8 July. Available at <http://eurohealthnet.eu/sites/eurohealthnet.eu/files/press-release/PR-2011-12.pdf>. [Accessed 6/6/2012].

European Election Database. 2012. Elections Greece. *Norwegian Social Science Data Services*. [online]Available at <http://www.nsd.uib.no/european_election_database/country/greece>. [Accessed 29/5/2012].

Eurostat. 2012a. Euro Area Unemployment Rate. 155/2012. *Eurostat.* [online] 31 October. Available at <http://epp.eurostat.ec.europa.eu/cache/ITY_PUBLIC/3-31102012-BP/EN/3-31102012-BP-EN.PDF>. [Accessed 5/11/2012].

Eurostat. 2012b. Consumer price levels 98/2012. *Eurostat.* [online] 22 June. Available at <http://epp.eurostat.ec.europa.eu

/cache/ITY_PUBLIC/2-22062012-AP/EN/2-22062012-AP-EN.PDF>. [Accessed 6/11/2012].

Evans-Pritchard, A. 2009. Greece Tests the Limit of Sovereign Debt as it Grinds towards Slump. *The Telegraph*. [online] 22 November. Available at: <http://www.telegraph.co.uk/finance/comment/ambroseevans_pritchard/6630117/Greece-tests-the-limit-of-sovereign-debt-as-it-grinds-towards-slump.html>. [Accessed 12 November 2012].

Exadaktylos, T. & Zahariadis, N. 2012. Policy Implementation and Political Trust: Greece in the Age of Austerity. [conference] 2nd EPSA Conference, Berlin, 21-23 June 2012.

Fagence, M. 1977. *Citizen Participation in Planning*. Oxford: Pergamon Press.

Fakiolas, R. 2003. Regularising Undocumented Immigrants in Greece: Procedures and Effects. *Journal of Ethnic and Migration Studies*. 29(3): pp. 535-561.

Fazel, M. & Silove, D. 2006. Detention of Refugees. *British Medical Journal*. 332(7536): pp. 251–252.

Featherstone, K. 2011. The Greek Sovereign Debt Crisis and EMU: A Failing State in a Skewed Regime. *Journal of Common Market Studies*. 49(2): pp. 193-217.

Featherstone, K. & Papadimitriou, D. 2008. *The Limits of Europeanization: Reform Capacity and Policy Conflict in Greece*. Basingstoke: Palgrave Macmillan.

Ferrell, J. 2009. Against Method, Against Authority… For Anarchy. In R. Amster, A. DeLean, L.A. Fernandez, A.J. Nocella II, & D. Shannon, eds. *Contemporary Anarchist Studies: An Introductory Anthology of Anarchy in the Academy*. New York: Routledge, pp.73 -81.

Fishman, R. 1987. *Bourgeois Utopias: The Rise and Fall of Suburbia*. New York: Basic Books.

Flash. 2011. Today's Interviews (radio excerpts): Anna Dalara. [online] 26 January. Available at: <http://www.flash.gr/press-releases>. [Accessed 16/11/2012]. (In Greek).

Flynn, D. & Kyriakidou, D. 2008. Riots Rock Greece. *Reuters*. Available at <www.reuters.com/article/2008/12/09/us-greece-shooting-idUSTRE4B601720081209>. [Accessed 28 March 2012].

Foster, H. 1992. Subversive Signs. In C. Harrison & P. Wood, eds. *Art in Theory 1900-1990: An Anthology of Changing Ideas*. Oxford: Blackwell, pp. 1065-1066.

Foster, H. 1998. Introduction. In H. Foster, ed. *The Anti-Aesthetic: Essays on Postmodern Culture*. New York: The New Press, pp. ix-xvii.

Foucault, M. 1990. Qu'est que ce la critique. *Critique et Aufklärung: Bulletin de la société française de philosophie*, 84ème année, 2, Avril-Juin.

Foucault, M. 2004. *Society Must Be Defended*. Harmondsworth: Penguin.

Fowler, R. L. 2011. Mythos and Logos. *The Journal of Hellenic Studies*. 131. pp. 45-66.

Fraser, N. 1990. Rethinking the Public Sphere: A Contribution to the Critique of Actually Existing Democracy. *Social Text* 25/26. pp. 56-80.

Freud, S. 2003. *The Uncanny*. Edited by N. Royle, Translated by A. Strachey. London: Penguin.

Friedman, M. 1996. A Positive Approach to Organized Consumer Action: The "Buycott" as an Alternative to the Boycott. *Journal of Consumer Policy* 19(4): pp. 439-451.

Frisby, D. 2002. The Metropolis as Text: Otto Wagner and Vienna's 'Second Renaissance'. In N. Leach, ed. *The Hieroglyphics of Space: Reading and Experiencing the Modern Metropolis*. London: Routledge, pp. 15-30.

Froggett, L. 2002. *Love, Hate and Welfare: Psychosocial Approaches to Policy and Practice*. Bristol: Policy Press.

Fujita, K. 2012. Conclusion: Residential Segregation and Urban Theory. In T. Maloutas and K. Fujita, eds. *Residential Segregation in Comparative Perspective. Making Sense of*

Contextual Diversity. Farnham: Ashgate, pp. 285-322.

Fundamental Rights Agency. 2011. Coping with a Fundamental Rights Emergency: The Situation of Persons Crossing the Greek Land Border in an Irregular Manner. [online] Available at <http://fra.europa.eu/sites/default/files/fra_uploads/1500-Greek-border-situation-report2011_EN.pdf>. [Accessed on 2/12/2012].

Gardiner, M. 2001. *Critiques of Everyday Life*. New York: Routledge.

Gay, P. 1966. *The Enlightenment: An Interpretation. The Rise of Modern Paganism*. London: Weidenfeld and Nicholson.

Gell, A. 1985. How to Read a Map: Remarks on the Practical Logic of Navigation. *Man*. 20(2): pp. 271-286.

Gibson J.J. 1986. *Ecological Approaches to Visual Perception*. Boston: Houghton Mifflin.

Gitlin, T. 1980. *The Whole World Is Watching: Mass Media in the Making and Unmaking of the New Left*. Berkeley: University of California Press.

Glaeser, E.L., Laibson, D.I., Scheinkman, J.A. & Soutter, C.L. 2000. Measuring Trust. *Quarterly Journal of Economics*. 115(3): pp. 811-846.

Glassie, H. 1999. *Material Culture*. Bloomington: Indiana University Press.

Goehr, L. 2005. Art and Politics. In J. Levinson, ed. *The Oxford Handbook of Aesthetics*. Oxford: Oxford University Press, pp. 471-85.

Golden Dawn. 2011. The Lunatics who Carried them Should Take them in their Homes. *Efenpress*. [online] 25 January. Available at: <http://www.efenpress.gr/2011/01/blog-post_4994.html>. [Accessed 2 February 2012]. (In Greek).

Gonos G., Mulkern V., & Poushinsky, N. 1976. Anonymous Expression: A Structural View of Graffiti. *Journal of American Folklore*. 89(351): pp. 40-48.

Graeber, D. 2012. Revolution at the Level of Common Sense. In F.

Campagna, & E. Campiglio, eds. *What We Are Fighting For: A Radical Collective Manifesto*. London: Pluto Press, pp. 165 – 175.

Habermas, J. 1989. *The Structural Transformation of the Public Sphere: An Inquiry into a Category of Bourgeois Society*. Translated by T. Burger & E. Lawrence. Cambridge: MIT Press.

Habermas, J. 1998. Modernity: An Incomplete Project. In H. Foster, ed. *The Anti-Aesthetic: Essays on Postmodern Culture*. New York: The New Press, pp.1-15.

Habermas, J. 1992. Further Reflections on the Public Sphere. In C. Calhoun, ed. *Habermas and the Public Sphere*. Cambridge Massachusetts: MIT Press, pp. 421-462.

Habermas, J. & Derrida, J. 2003. February 15, or What Binds Europeans Together: A Plea for a Common Foreign Policy Beginning in the Core of Europe. *Constellations*. 10(3): pp. 291-297.

Hadjimatheou, C. 2012. The Greek Parents too Poor to Care for their Children. *BBC*. [online] 10 January. Available at: <http://www.bbc.co.uk/news/magazine-16472310>. [Accessed 3 January 2013].

Hage, G. 2003. *Against Paranoid Nationalism: Searching for Hope in a Shrinking Society*. Melbourne: Merlin.

Hall, S., Critcher, C., Jefferson, T., Clarke, J., & Roberts, B. 1978. *Policing the Crisis: Mugging, the State, and Law & Order*. London: Macmillan.

Hardin, R. 2006. *Trust*. Cambridge: Polity Press.

Hardt, M. 2010. Two Faces of Apocalypse: A Letter from Copenhagen. *Polygraph: An International Journal of Culture & Politics*. 22: pp. 265-274.

Hardt, M. & Negri, A. 2009. *Commonwealth*. Cambridge: Belknap Press.

Harris, K. 2006. Graffiti as Public Pedagogy: The Educative Potential of Street Art'. In J. Kincheloe & K. Hayes, eds. *Metropedagogy: Power, Justice and the Urban Classroom*.

Rotterdam: Sense Publishers, pp. 97-111.

Harvey, D. 2005. *A Brief History of Neoliberalism.* Oxford: University Press.

Harvey, D. 2008. The Right to the City. *New Left Review.* 53: pp. 23–40.

Hatfield, H. 1960. The Myth of Nazism. In H.A. Murray, ed. *Myth and Mythmaking*. New York: George Braziller, n.p.

Hauer, D. 2005. Wir wollen Alles – Supermärkte und Bäckereien Einige Anmerkungen zum Thema Aneignung. Presentation at 'Eigentum und Diebstahl. Schwarzfahren für die Revolution?' of *Kritik + Praxis*, Berlin. [online] 1 April 2004. Available at <www.labournet.de/diskussion/arbeit/aktionen/aneignung1.html>. [Accessed 1 November 2011].

Hawley, C. 2012. Greece Votes on Sunday: Europe's Future Hangs in the Balance. *Der Spiegel*. [online] Available at <http://www.spiegel.de/international/europe/outcome-of-greece-vote-may-determine-future-of-euro-a-839104.html>. [Accessed 12 August 2012].

Hekman, S. 2000. Beyond Identity: Feminism, Identity and Identity Politics. *Feminist Theory*. 1(3): pp. 289-308.

Hénaff, M. & Strong, T. eds. 2001. *Public Space and Democracy*. Minneapolis: University of Minnesota Press.

Henley, J. 2012. Greece's Cut-Price Potato Movement Shows Greeks Chipping in'. *The Guardian.* [online] 27 March. Available at <www.guardian.co.uk/world/2012/mar/27/greece-breadline-potato-movement-eurozone-crisis>. [Accessed 25 May 2012].

Hill, J. 1998. *The Illegal Architect*. London: Black Dog.

Hill, R.C. & Fujita, K. 2003. The Nested City: Introduction. *Urban Studies*. 40(2): pp. 207-217.

Hill, R.C. & Kim, J.W. 2000. Global Cities and Developmental States. *Urban Studies,* 37(12): pp. 2167-2198.

Hobsbawm, E.J. 2001. *Bandits*. London: Abacus.

Hoggett, P. 2006. Pity, Compassion and Solidarity. In S. Clarke, P.

Hoggett & S. Thompson, eds. *Emotion, Politics and Society.* Houndmills: Palgrave Macmillan, pp.145-161.

Hook, D. 2005. Affecting Whiteness: Racism as Technology of Affect. *International Journal of Critical Psychology*. 16: pp. 74-99.

Hopper, E. 2003. *Traumatic Experience in the Unconscious Life of Groups*. London: Jessica Kingsley Publishers.

Horkheimer, M., & Adorno, T. 2002. *The Dialectic of Enlightenment: Philosophical Fragments*, Stanford: Stanford University Press.

Hugh-Jones, D., Katsanidou, A. & Riener, G. 2011. Intergroup Conflict and the Media: An Experimental Study of Greek Students After the 2008 Riots. *International Journal of Conflict and Violence*. 5(2): pp. 325-44.

Huysmans, J. 2000. The European Union and the Securitization of Migration. *Journal of Common Market Studies*. 38(5): pp. 751-777.

Inflation EU. 2012. Inflation as Measured in CPI Greece 2008. [online] Available at <www.inflation.eu/inflation-rates/greece /historic-inflation/cpi-inflation-greece-2008.aspx>. [Accessed 6 June 2012].

Ingold, T. 2007. *Lines: A Brief History*. London: Routledge.

Ingold, T. & Vergunst, J. eds. 2008. *Ways of Walking: Ethnography and Practice on Foot.* Aldershot: Ashgate.

in.gr. 2001. Setting the Taxis in order plans the Ministry of Transport. *in.gr.* [online] 15 January. Available at: <http:// archive.in.gr/news/reviews/article.asp?lngReviewID=491097 &lngItemID=205945>. [Accessed 15 July 2012]. (In Greek).

IOBE. 2010. *The Greek Economy 4/10*: *Quarterly Report 62*. [online] Available at: <http://www.iobe.gr/media/elloik/IOBEGreek4 10.pdf>. Accessed 10 December 2012.

Iskander, N. 2007. Informal Work and Protest: Undocumented Immigrant Activism in France 1996-2000. *British Journal of Industrial Relations*. 45(2): pp. 309-334.

Iveson, K. 2007. *Publics and the City*. Oxford: Blackwell.

Iyengar, S. 1991. *Is Anyone Responsible?* Chicago: University of Chicago Press.

Jacks, B. 2006. Walking the City: Manhattan Projects. *Places*. 18(1): pp. 68-75.

Jackson, P. 1989. *Maps of Meaning: An Introduction to Cultural Geography*. London: Routledge.

Jameson, F. 1998. Postmodernism and Consumer Society. In H. Foster, ed. *The Anti-Aesthetic: Essays on Postmodern Culture*. New York: The New Press, pp. 131-34.

Jameson, F. 1992. The Deconstruction of Expression. In C. Harrison & P. Wood, eds. *Art in Theory 1900-1990: An Anthology of Changing Ideas*. Oxford: Blackwell, pp. 1074-1080.

Jasper, J.M. 2004. A Strategic Approach to Collective Action: Looking for Agency in Social- Movement Choices. *Mobilization*. 9(1): pp. 1-16.

Kaejane, G., 2011. Seven Key Words on the Madrid-Sol Experience, 15M. [online] *Madrilonia*.

Available at: <http://madrilonia.org/2011/05/seven-key-words-on-the-madrid-sol-experience-15m/>. [Accessed 5 December 2011].

Kaloudis, G. 2000. *Modern Greek Democracy, The End of a Long Journey?* Lanham: University Press of America.

Kandylis, G. & Kavoulakos, K. 2011. Framing Urban Inequalities: Racist Mobilization Against Immigrants in Athens. *The Greek Review of Social Research*. 136(c): pp. 157-176.

Kanngieser, A. 2008. The Productivity of Disruption. In D. Grindon, ed. *Aesthetics and Radical Politics*. Cambridge: Scholars Publishing, pp. 1-26

Karathanasis, P. 2010. Walls as 'Contested Spaces': Aesthetics and Urban Landscape in Athens. In K. Giannakopoulos & G. Giannitsiotis, eds. *Contested Spaces in the City*. Athens: Alexandreia, pp. 315-348 (In Greek).

Karyotis, G. 2011. The Fallacy of Securitizing Migration: Elite Rationality and Unintended Consequences. In G. Lazaridis, ed. *Security Insecurity and Migration in Europe.* Aldershot: Ashgate, pp. 13-30.

Karyotis, G. 2012. Securitization of Migration in Greece: Process, Motives and Implications. *International Political Sociology*. 6(4): pp. 390-408.

Karyotis, G. & Patrikios, S. 2010. Religion, Securitization and Anti-Immigration Attitudes: The Case of Greece. *Journal of Peace Research*. 47(1): pp. 43-57.

Keenan, H. 2011. Street Art and the Sovereign's Imagination. *Street Art in Israel,* Tel Aviv Museum of Art. Available at <http://www.tau.ac.il/~kenaan/pub.html>. [Accessed 30 January 2013].

Kentikelenis, A., Karanikolos, M., Papanicolas, I., Basu, S., McKee, M. & Stuckler, D. 2011. Health Effects of Financial Crisis: Omens of a Greek Tragedy. *The Lancet*. 378(9801): pp. 1457-1458.

KKE. 2011. Statement of the Press Office Regarding the Presence of the Migrants in the Law School. *KKE.* [online] 25 January. Available at: <http://www.kke.gr/anakoinoseis_grafeioy_typoy/>. [Accessed 13 December 2012]. (In Greek).

Klein, N. 2007. *The Shock Doctrine: The Rise of Disaster Capitalism*. London: Penguin Books.

Knox, P. & Pinch, S. 2006. *Urban Social Geography,* Harlow: Pearson.

Kokkino. 2011. Legal the 250 of the Law School, Illegal the 250 of the 'Siemens case'. [online] 26 January, Available at: <http://www.kokkino.org/index.php?option=com_content&view=article&id=1985:-250-250-siemens&catid=31&Itemid=53>. [Accessed 21 December 2012]. (In Greek).

Kotz, D.M. 2009. The Financial and Economic Crisis of 2008: A Systemic Crisis of Neoliberal Capitalism. *Review of Radical Political Economics*. 41(3): pp. 305-317.

Kurzban, R. 2003. Biological Foundations of Reciprocity. In E. Ostrom & J. Walker, eds. *Trust and Reciprocity: Interdisciplinary*

Lessons from Experimental Research. New York: Russell Sage, pp.105-127.

Laclau, E. 1979. *Politics and Ideology in Marxist Theory*. London: Verso.

Laclau, E. & Mouffe, C. 1998. Hearts, Minds and Radical Democracy: An Interview of Ernesto Laclau and Chantal Mouffe by Dave Castle. [Online] Available at: <http://www.redpepper.org.uk/hearts-minds-and-radical-democracy/>. [Accessed 19 May 2012].

Lathra. 2011. Solidarity to the 300 Hunger Strikers. [online] Available at: <http://www.lathra.gr/en/2010-03-30-15-29-56/397-300>. [Accessed 13 December 2012]. (In Greek).

Lavenex, S. 2001. Migration and the EU's New Eastern Border: Between Realism and Liberalism. *Journal of European Public Policy*. 8(1): pp. 24-42.

Layton, L. 2006. Racial Identities, Racial Enactments, and Normative Unconscious Processes. *Psychoanalytic Quarterly*. 75(1): pp. 237-269.

Layton, L., Hollander, N.C., & Gutwill, S. eds. 2006. *Psychoanalysis, Class and Politics: Encounters in the Clinical Setting*. London: Routledge.

Leal, J. 2004. Segregation and Social Change in Madrid Metropolitan Region. *The Greek Review of Social Research*. 113: pp. 81–104.

Lees, A. 1985. *Cities Perceived. Urban Society in European and American Thought, 1820-1940.* Manchester: Manchester University Press.

Lees, L., Slater, T., & Wyly, E. 2008. *Gentrification*. London: Routledge.

Lefebvre, H. 1991. *The Production of Space*. Oxford: Blackwell.

Lefebvre, H. 1996. *Writings on Cities.* Translated by E. Kofman & E. Lebas. Oxford: Blackwell.

Lefebvre, H. 2003. *The Urban Revolution*. Translated by R. Bonano. Minneapolis: University of Minnesota Press.

Lefebvre, H. 2008. *Critique of Everyday Life, Volume I.* London: Verso.

Leibfried, S., & Zürn, M. eds. 2005. *Transformations of the State?* Cambridge: Cambridge University Press.

Leontidou, L. 1986. In Search of Lost Labour: The Urban Sociology of Post-war Greece. *The Greek Review of Social Research.* 60: pp. 72-109.

Leontidou, L. 1990. *The Mediterranean City in Transition.* Cambridge: Cambridge University Press.

Leontidou, L. 2012. Athens in the Mediterranean 'Movement of the Piazzas': Spontaneity in Material and Virtual Public Spaces. *City: Analysis of Urban Trends, Culture, Theory, Policy, Action.* 16(3): pp. 299-312.

Levi, M. & Stoker, L. 2000. Political Trust and Trustworthiness. *Annual Review of Political Science.* 3(June): pp. 457-507.

Lévi-Strauss, C. 1978. *Myth and Meaning.* London: Routledge.

Lewisohn, C. 2008. *Street Art: The Graffiti Revolution.* London: Tate Publishing.

Loehwing, M. & Motter, J. 2009. Publics, Counterpublics, and the Promise of Democracy. *Philosophy and Rhetoric.* 42(3): pp. 220-41.

Logotheti, E. 2011. Pagkalos: Oi Polites Diaftheiroun Tous Politikous. *Real.* [online] 4 January. Available at: <http://www.real.gr/DefaultArthro.aspx?page=arthro&id=36046&catID=1>. [Accessed 19 November 2012]. (In Greek).

Low, S.M. & Lawrence-Zúñiga, D. eds. 2003. *The Anthropology of Space and Place: Locating Culture.* Malden: Blackwell.

Lyberaki, A. & Tsakalotos, E. 2002. Reforming the Economy Without Society: Social and Institutional Constraints to Economic Reform in post-1974 Greece. *New Political Economy.* 7(1): pp. 93-114.

Malkoutzis, N. 2011. Young Greeks and the Crisis. The Danger of Losing a Generation. *Frederich Ebert Siftung International Policy Analysis.* [online] September 2011. Available at <http://

library.fes.de/pdf-files/id/ipa/08465.pdf>. [Accessed 6 June 2012].

Maloutas, T. 1997. La Ségrégation Sociale à Athènes. *Mappemonde*. 4(97): pp. 1-4.

Maloutas, T. 2000. Urban Growth and Dominant Housing Systems in post-war Athens. In T. Maloutas, ed. *Social and Economic Atlas of Greece*. Athens-Volos: EKKE-University of Thessaly Press, pp. 28-29.

Maloutas, T. 2004. Segregation and Residential Mobility. Spatially Entrapped Social Mobility and its Impact on Segregation in Athens. *European Urban and Regional Studies* 11(3): pp. 195-211.

Maloutas, T. 2007. Segregation, Social Polarisation and Inequality in Athens During the 1990s: Theoretical Expectations and Contextual Difference. *International Journal of Urban and Regional Research*. 31(4): pp. 733-758.

Maloutas, T. & Karadimitriou, N. 2001. Vertical Social Differentiation in Athens. Alternative or Complement to Urban Segregation? *International Journal of Urban and Regional Research*. 25(4): pp. 699-716.

Maloutas, T. & Alexandri, G. (forthcoming) La gentrification dans les villes non gentrifiables? Rénovation urbaine et changement des structures sociales dans le center d'Athènes. In C. Rhein and E. Préteceille, eds. *Gentrification, transformations des quartiers populaires et couches moyennes; notion unique, processus pluriels*, Paris: La Découverte, n.p.

Maloutas, T., Arapoglou, V.P., Kandylis, G., & Sayas, J. 2012. Social Polarisation and Desegregation in Athens. In T. Maloutas & K. Fujita, eds. *Residential Segregation in Comparative Perspective: Making Sense of Contextual Diversity*. Farnham: Ashgate, pp. 259-286.

Mansbridge, J.J. 1980. *Beyond Adversary Democracy*. Chicago: The University of Chicago Press.

Mantanika, R. & Kouki, H. 2011. The Spatiality of a Social Struggle in Greece at the Time of the IMF. *City: Analysis of*

Urban Trends, Culture, Theory, Policy, Action. 15(3-4): pp. 482-490.

Marlowe, L. 2010. Euro Zone Chief Says Currency too Strong. *The Irish Times*. [online] 9 October. Available at: <http://www.irishtimes.com/newspaper/finance/2010/1009/1224280699632.html>. Accessed 19 November 2012).

Mason, P. *Why it's Kicking Off Everywhere: The New Global Revolutions*. London: Verso.

Massey, D. 2005. *For Space*. London: Sage Publications.

Matsaganis, M. & Flevotomou, M. 2010. Distributional Implications of Tax Evasion in Greece. *Hellenic Observatory Papers on Greece and Southeast Europe, GreeSE Paper* No. 31. London: The Hellenic Observatory, LSE.

May, J., Cloke, P., & Johnsen, S. 2005. Re-phasing Neoliberalism: New Labour and Britain's Crisis of Street Homelessness. *Antipode*. 37(4): pp. 703-730.

McGregor, J. 2011. Contestations and Consequences of Deportability: Hunger Strikes and the Political Agency of Non-citizens. *Citizenship Studies*. 15(5): pp. 597-611.

McKee A. 2005. *The Public Sphere: An Introduction*. Cambridge: Cambridge University Press.

Medecins du Monde 2010. Athens, a City in Humanitarian Crisis. *MdM Greece*. [online] Available at <http://www.mdmgreece.gr/en>. [Accessed 20 November 2012].

Migrants' Forum in Crete. 2011. Press Release: Statement of the Migrants' Forum in Crete. *Hunger Strike 300*. [online] 26 January. Available at: <http://hungerstrike300.espivblogs.net>. [Accessed 13 November 2012]. (In Greek).

Migratory Alliance. 2011. Statement of Solidarity to the Migrant Hunger Strikers. *Hunger Strike 300*. [online] 31 January. Available at: <http://hungerstrike300.espivblogs.net>. [Accessed 13 November 2012]. (In Greek).

Mitchell, D. 2003. *The Right to the City: Social Justice and the Fight for Public Space*. New York: Guilford Press.

Ministry of Education. 2011. Statement of the Minister of Education Regarding the Occupation of the Athens Law School. *Ministry of Education* [online] 25 January. Available at: <http://www.minedu.gov.gr/publications/docs/dt_dhlwsh_ypoyrgoy_110125.doc>. [Accessed 13 November 2012]. (In Greek).

Moravsik, A. 2002. In Defence of the "Democratic Deficit". *Journal of Common Market Studies*. 40(4): pp. 603-634.

Mouffe, C. 2000. Deliberative Democracy or Agonistic Pluralism. In C. Neuhold & G. Hafner, eds. *Reihe Politikwissenschaft/ Political Science Series* 72. Vienna: Institut fur Höhere Studien (IHS)/Institute for Advanced Studies, pp. 1- 17.

Mouffe, C. 2005a. *On the Political*. London and New York: Routledge.

Mouffe, C. 2005b. Some Reflections on an Agonistic Approach to the Public. In B. Latour & P. Weibel, eds. *Making Things Public, Atmospheres of Democracy.* Cambridge: ZKM/Center for Art and Media Karlruhe and MIT, pp. 804-807.

Mouffe, C. 2007. Artistic Activism and Agonistic Spaces. *Art & Research. A Journal of Ideas, Contexts and Methods.* 1(2): pp. 1-6.

Mouzelis, N. 1978. *Modern Greece: Facets of Underdevelopment*. Michigan: Holmes & Meier.

Mouzelis, N. 1996. The Concept of Modernization: Its Relevance for Greece. *Journal of Modern Greek Studies.* 14(2): pp. 215-27.

Mouzelis, N. & Pagoulatos, G. 2003. Civil Society and Citizens' Identity in Post-war Greece. *Greek Political Science Review*. 22: pp. 5-29. (In Greek).

Nelson, T.E., Clawson, R.A. & Oxley, Z.M. 1997. Media Framing of a Civil Liberties Conflict and Its Effect on Tolerance. *The American Political Science Review*. 91(3): pp. 567-583.

Neumayer, K. 2010. The Origin of Graffiti and Street Marking: Signs in Transition from Fordism to Postfordism. [conference]. *Public Space and the Challenges of Urban Transformation in Europe: Politics and Culture*. 10-11 November. Vienna, Austria.

Nikolaidou, S. 1993. *The Social Organisation of Urban Space.* Athens: Papazisis Publications. (In Greek).

Norberg-Schulz, C. 1980. *Genius Loci: Towards a Phenomenology of Architecture.* New York: Rizzoli.

Norton, A. 2001. Writing Property and Power. In M. Hénaff & T. Strong, eds. *Public Space and Democracy.* Minneapolis: University of Minnesota Press, pp. 189-200.

Oikologoi Prasinoi. 2011. Migrant Hunger Strike: In the 21st century Europe, no Second Class People are Allowed. *Ecogreens.gr* [online] 25 January. Available at: <http://www.ecogreens-gr.org/cms/index.php?option=com_content&view=article&id=1718:-21-2-&catid=11:rights &Itemid=27>. [Accessed 13 November 2012]. (In Greek).

Ongaro, E. 2010. *Public Management Reform and Modernization: Trajectories of Administrative Change in Italy, France, Greece, Portugal and Spain.* Cheltenham: Edward Elgar Publishing.

Ostrom, E. 1990. *Governing the Commons: The Evolution of Institutions for Collective Action.* New York: Cambridge University Press.

Ostrom, E. & Walker, J. eds. 2003. *Trust and Reciprocity: Interdisciplinary Lessons for Experimental Research.* New York: Russell Sage.

Pagoulatos, G. & Zahariadis, N. 2011. Politics, Labor, Regulation, and Performance: Lessons from the Privatization of OTE. *Hellenic Observatory papers on Greece and Southeast Europe, GreeSE Paper.* 46. London: The Hellenic Observatory, LSE.

Pamphlet. 2011. 3..2..1.. Go. Athens: Independent Publication.

Pamphlet. 2012. Expropriations in Supermarkets. *Independent Publication.* [online] Available at <http://athens.indymedia.org/front.php3?lang=el&article_id=1386152>. [Accessed 1 April 2012].

Panourgia, N. 2011. Hot Spots: Beyond the "Greek Crisis", The Squared Constitution of Dissent. [online] Available at: <http://culanth.org/?q=node/438>. [Accessed 11 January

2012].

Papachelas, A. 2012a. Lessons from our Elders. *Ekathimerini.* [online] Available at: <http://www.ekathimerini.com/4dcgi/_w_articles_wsite3_1_08/05/2012_441256>. [Accessed 12 August 2012].

Papachelas, A. 2012b. Wanted: Captain and Compass. *Ekathimerini.* [online] Available at: <http://www.ekathimerini.com/4dcgi/_w_articles_wsite3_1_16/05/2012_442423>. [Accessed 12 August 2012].

Papachelas, A. 2012c. Too Little Too Late? *Ekathimerini.* [online] Available at: <http://www.ekathimerini.com/4dcgi/_w_articles_wsite3_1_20/05/2012_442989>. [Accessed 12 August 2012].

Papachristou, H. 2012. One in Five Greeks Unemployed, Half of all Youth. *Reuters.* 12 April. [online] Available at <www.reuters.com/article/2012/04/12/us-greece-unemployment-idUSBRE83B0GO20120412>. [Accessed 6 June 2012].

Papachristou, H. & Robinson, M. 2012. It's Bailout or Chaos, PM Papademos Tells Greece. *Reuters.* [online] 11 February. Available at: <http://www.reuters.com/article/2012/02/12/greece-idUSL5E8DB0V420120212>. [Accessed 3 December 2012].

Papagiannis, K. 2011. The 237 Migrant Hunger Strikers: 'We are Determined to go to the End'. *Avgi.* [online] 30 January. Available at: <http://www.avgi.gr/ArticleActionshow.action?articleID=596138>. [Accessed 13 November 2012]. (In Greek).

Pautz, H. & Kominou M. (2012). Reacting to 'Austerity Politics': The Tactic of Collective Expropriation in Greece. *Journal of Social Movement Studies.* (11)3: pp. 103-110.

Peck, J. 2010. Zombie Neoliberalism and the Ambidextrous State. *Theoretical Criminology.* 14(1): pp. 104-109.

Petrucci, A. 1993. *Public Lettering: Script, Power, and Culture.* Translated by L. Lappin. Chicago: University of Chicago Press.

Pile, S. 2005. *Real Cities: Modernity, Space and the Phantasmagorias of City Life*. London: Sage.

Plato. 1956. *Laches or Peri Andreias*, 195a. Athens: Hetaireia Papyros.

Posner, R. 2002. *Public Intellectuals: A Study in Decline*. Cambridge: Harvard University Press.

Pretenderis, Y. 2012. The Drachma Party. *Ta Nea*. [online] Available at: <http://www.tanea.gr/opinions/all-opinions/article/4725825/?iid=2>. [Accessed 12 August 2012].

PrimeMinisterGr (2010). PM's Statement from Kastelorizo. [online]. 23 April. Available at <http://www.primeminister.gov.gr/english/2010/04/23/prime-ministers-statement/>. [Accessed: 12 August 2012].

Rancière, J. 2006. The Distribution of the Sensible. *The Politics of the Aesthetics*. Translated by G. Rockhill. London: Continuum.

Reuters. 2008. "Robin Hoods" Steal at the Store, Give to the Poor? 4/9/2008. Available at <http://in.reuters.com/article/2008/09/04/us-robinhoods-idINN0430484720080904>. [Accessed 30 March 2013].

Ritzaelou, M. 2009. The Robin of Poor Who are Rich in Action. *Ethnos*. [online] Available at <http://www.ethnos.gr/article.asp?catid=22768&subid=2&pubid=2448825>. [Accessed 4 June 2012].

Rodriguez, N. 1996. The Battle for the Border: Notes on Autonomous Migration, Transnational Communities, and the State. *Social Justice*. 23(3): pp. 21–37.

Rose-Ackerman, S. 1999. *Corruption and Government: Causes, Consequences and Reform*. Cambridge: Cambridge University Press.

Ross, K. 2011. Democracy for Sale. In: Giorgio Agamben et al., eds. *Democracy in What State?* Translated by W. McCuaig. New York: Columbia University Press, pp. 82-99.

Rothstein, B. & Uslaner, E.M. 2005. All for All: Equality, Corruption and Social Trust. *World Politics*. 58(1): pp. 41-72.

Rudig, W. & Karyotis, G. Forthcoming. Who Protests in Greece:

Mass Opposition to Austerity, 2010. *British Journal of Political Science*, n.p.

Saïd, E. 1996. *Representations of the Intellectual. The 1993 Reith Lectures* London: Vintage.

Sassen, S. 1991. *The Global City: New York, London, Tokyo*. Princeton: Princeton University Press.

Savra. 2008. Athens Phantome gegen die Teuerung. *Infopartisan.net.* [online] Available at <http://www.trend.infopartisan.net/trd0908/t330908.html>. [Accessed 19 April 2012].

Scheufele, D.A. 1999. Framing as a Theory of Media Effects. *Journal of Communication*. 49(1): pp. 103-122.

Schumpeter, J.A. 2010. *Capitalism, Socialism and Democracy*. London: Routledge.

Segal, H. 1973. *Introduction to the Work of Melanie Klein*. London: Hogarth Press.

Segal, H. 1991. *Dream Phantasy and Art*. Hove: Brunner-Routledge.

Segal H. 2007. Papers on Bion. In N. Abel-Hirsch, ed. *Yesterday, Today and Tomorrow*. Hove: Brunner- Routledge.

Segre, S. 2011. On Weber's and Habermas' Democratic Theories: A Reconstruction and Comparison. *Logos Journal.* [online] Available at: <http://logosjournal.com/2011/fall_segre/>. [Accessed 10 June 2012].

Sennet, R. 2004. *The Uses of Disorder: Personal Identity and City Life.* Athens: Tropi Publications.

Shaw, D., Newholm, T. & Dickinson, R. 2006. Consumption as Voting: An Exploration of Consumer Empowerment. *European Journal of Marketing*. 40 (9/10): pp. 1049-1067.

Shorter Oxford English Dictionary. 2002. *On Historical Principles, Vol.1.* Oxford: Oxford University Press.

Shukaitis, S., Graeber, D. & Biddle, E. 2007. *Constituent Imagination: Militant Investigations, Collective Theorizations.* Oakland: AK Press.

Silove, D., Steel, Z. & Waters, C. 2000. Policies of Deterrence and the Mental Health of Asylum Seekers. *Journal of the American Medical Association*. 284(5): pp. 604–611.

Simeant, J. 1994. Immigration and Social Movements. The Specificity of Undocumented Migrants Mobilizations. [conference]*Communication at the IPSA Congress.* 21-25 August. Berlin.

Skai News. 2009. "Stin Entatiki" I Oikonomia. *Skai News* [online] 9 December. Available at: <http://www.skai.gr/news/finance/article/133100>. [Accessed 30 November 2012]. (In Greek).

Skai News. 2012a. Together We Can. *Skai News* [online] Available at <www.skai.gr/news/greece/article/189420/antigrafotouoloi-mazi-boroume-ekstrateia-tou-skai-me-stoho-ti-diatirisi-tis-koinonikis-sunohis>. [Accessed 30 May 2012]. (In Greek).

Skai News. 2012b. The 'Potato Movement' is Spreading. *Skai News* [online] Available at <www.skai.gr/news/greece/article/196404/to-kinima-tis-patatas-exaplonetai>. [Accessed 21 March 2012].

Smart, L. 2004. *Maps that Made History: The Influential, the Eccentric and the Sublime*. Toronto: Dundurn Press.

Smith, H. 2011. Greek Woes Drive up Suicide Rate. *The Guardian* [online] 18 December 2011.Available at <www.guardian.co.uk/world/2011/dec/18/greek-woes-suicide-rate-highest>. [Accessed 6 June 2012].

Smith, H. 2012. Greek Man Shoots Himself over Debts. *The Guardian*. [online] 04 April 2012. Available at <www.guardian.co.uk/world/2012/apr/04/greek-man-shoots-himself-debts>. [Accessed 7 June 2012].

Smith, N. 1987. Gentrification and the Rent Gap. *Annals of the Association of American Geographers*. 77(3): pp. 462-465.

Smith, N. 1996. *The New Urban Frontier: Gentrification and the Revanchist City*. Routledge, London.

Solidarity Initiative. 2011a. Press Release: The Hunger Strike Is Starting Tomorrow. *Hunger Strike 300.* [online] 24 January.

Available at: <http://hungerstrike300.espivblogs.net/2011/01/24/press-release-the-hunger-strike-is-starting-tomorrow/>. [Accessed 15 November 2012].

Solidarity Initiative. 2011b. Press Release. Group of Lawyers for the Rights of Migrants and Refugees. *Hunger Strike 300.* [online] 26 January. Available at: <http://omadadikigorw-nenglish.blogspot.co.uk/2011/01/solidarity-initiative-with-300-migrants.html>. [Accessed 15 November 2012].

Solidarity Initiative. 2011c. Solidarity to the Hunger Strike of the 300 Migrant Workers *Hunger Strike 300.* [online] 11 February. Available at: <http://hungerstrike300.espivblogs.net/about/>. [Accessed 15 November 2012]. (In Greek).

Sotiropoulos, D. 2004. Southern European Public Bureaucracies in Comparative Perspective. *West European Politics*. 27(3): pp. 405-22.

Soja, E. 1989. *Postmodern Geographies: the Reassertion of Space in Critical Social Theory*. London: Verso.

Souliotis N., Maloutas, T. & Sayas, J. Forthcoming. Mega-projects, Neoliberalization and State Capacities: Assessing the Medium-term Impact of the 2004 Olympic Games on Athenian Urban Policies, *Environment and Planning C*, n.p.

Spanou, C. 2008. State Reform in Greece: Responding to Old and New Challenges. *International Journal of Public Sector Management*. 21(2): pp. 150-73.

Staeheli, L.A. 2009. Political Geography: Democracy and the Disorderly Public. *Progress in Human Geography.* 34(1): pp. 67-78.

Star. 2011. Ragousis: '20 Percent Deduction of Party Funding'. *Star.gr.* [online] 2 March. Available at: <http://www.star.gr/Pages/Politiki_Oikonomia.aspx?art=56158&artTitle=ragkousis_20_kato_i_chrimatodotisi_ton_kommaton>. [Accessed 13 November 2012). (In Greek).

Stara, A. 2009. Urban Fictions with the Office for Subversive Architecture. In S. Chaplin & A. Stara, eds. *Curating*

Architecture and the City. London: Routledge, pp. 233-245.

Stavridis, S. 2011. Communities of Crisis, Squares in Movement. Working Paper No.6. *ProfessionalDreamers*. [Online] Available at: <http://www.professionaldreamers.net/_prowp/wp-content/uploads/Stavrides-Communities-of-crisis-fld.pdf>. [Accessed 5 March 2012].

Stocker, T.L., Dutcher, L.W., Hagrove, S.M., & Cook, E.A. 1972. Social Analysis of Graffiti. *Journal of American Folklore*. 85(338): pp. 356-366.

Stolle, D., Hooghe, M. & Mitcheletti, M. 2005. Politics in the Supermarket: Political Consumerism as a Form of Political Participation. *International Political Science Review*. 26(3): pp. 245-269.

Synaspismos. (2011) Statement of the Press Office Regarding the Migrant Hunger Strike. *Syn.gr* [online] 25 January. Available at: <http://www.syn.gr/gr/keimeno.php?id=21877>. [Accessed 15 November 2012]. (In Greek).

Ta Nea. 2010. George Papandreou: 'Our Efforts will be Worthwhile'. *Ta Nea* [online] 13 March. Available at: <http://www.tanea.gr/ellada/article/?aid=4564717>. [Accessed 5 March 2013). (In Greek).

Ta Nea. 2012. Stoixeia tis EL.AS: Dramatiki Auksisi Stis Autoktonies Logo Krisis. *Ta Nea* [online] 22 November. Available at: <http://www.tanea.gr/ellada/article/?aid=4769785>. [Accessed 3 January 2013]. (In Greek).

Tarrow, S. 1992. Mentalities, Political Cultures and Collective Action Frames. In A.D. Morris & C. McClurg Mueller, eds. *Frontiers in Social Movement Theory*, New Haven: Yale University Press, pp. 174-202.

Telegraphtv. 2012. Antonis Samaras: Greek People are Staying 'Anchored with the Euro'. [online]. 17 June. Available at: <http://www.youtube.com/watch?v=8vo3aQUybW8&feature=youtu.be#_blank>. [Accessed: 12 August 2012].

The Thieves' Thieves. 2010. On the Expropriation of a

Supermarket in Thessalonica. *Indymedia Athens*. [online] Available at <https://athens.indymedia.org/front.php3?lang=el&article_id=1184313>. [Accessed 30 May 2012]. (In Greek).

Thessalia News. 2012. Supermarket Besieged for Food. *Thessalia news*. [online] Available at <http://thessalianews.gr/index.php?option=com_content&view=article&id=9103:souper-market-volos&catid=43:municipality&Itemid=30>. [Accessed 30 May 2012]. (In Greek).

Thompson, S. & Hoggett, P. eds. 2012. *Politics and the Emotions: The Affective Turn in Contemporary Political Studies*. London: Continuum.

Tilley, C. 1994. *A Phenomenology of Landscape: Place, Paths and Monuments*. Oxford: Berg.

Tilly, C. 1995. *Popular Contention in Great Britain, 1758-1834*, Cambridge: Harvard University Press.

To Vima. 2009. Two-speed Salaries in the Public Sector Starting in 2010. *To Vima*. [online] 20 March. Available at: <http://www.tovima.gr/finance/finance-news/article/?aid=260267>. [Accessed on 05 March 2013].

To Vima. 2011. Andreas Loverdos: Order for Vigilance in Military Hospitals and Private Clinics Regarding the Flu. *To Vima*. [online] 14 February. Available at: <http://www.tovima.gr/society/article/?aid=384349>. [Accessed 13 November 2012]. (In Greek).

Triandafyllidou, A. 2009. Greek Immigration Policy at the Turn of the 21st Century: Lack of Political Will or Purposeful Mismanagement? *European Journal of Migration and Law*. 11(2): pp. 159-178.

Tsilimpounidi, M. & Walsh, A. 2010. Painting Human Rights: Mapping Street Art in Athens. *Journal of Arts and Communities*. 2(2): pp. 111-122.

Tsimas, P. 2012a. Fukushima in the Aegean. *Ta Nea*. [online] 9 June. Available at: <http://www.tanea.gr/opinions/all-opinions/article/4728174/?iid=2>. [Accessed 12 August 2012].

Tsimas, P. 2012b. Our 18th Brumaire. *Ta Nea.* [online] 16 June. Available at: <http://www.tanea.gr/opinions/all-opinions/article/4730139/?iid=2>. [Accessed 12 August 2012].

Tudor, H. 1972. *Political Myth*. London: Pall Mall.

TVXS. 2012. Migrants Organised Against Racist Attacks. *TVXS.* [online] 20 November. Available at: <http://tvxs.gr/news/ellada/oi-metanastes-organonontai-apenanti-stis-ratsistikes-epitheseis>. [Accessed 15/11/2012). (In Greek).

UNHCR. 2010. Submission by the United Nations High Commissioner for Refugees for the Office of the High Commissioner for Human Rights' Compilation Report – Universal Periodic Review: Greece. *UNHCR.* [online] Available at <http://www.unhcr.org/refworld/pdfid/4cd8f2ec2.pdf>. [Accessed 16 November 2012].

Union of Salaried Technicians. 2011. All Workers, Greek and Migrant, Against Poverty, the Consequences of the Economic Crisis and Imperialist Wars. [online] 8 February. Available at: <http://www.somtechnik.gr/Texty/anakoin/smt_metanastes_Feb11.htm>. [Accessed 15 November 2012). (In Greek).

Uslaner, E.M. 2005. Trust and Corruption. In J.G. Lambsdorff, M. Taube & M. Schramm, eds. *Corruption and the New Institutional Economics*. London: Routledge, pp. 76-92.

Verney, S. 1993. From the 'Special Relationship' to Europeanism: PASOK and the European Community, 1981-89. In R. Clogg, ed. *Greece 1981-89: The Populist Decade*. London: Macmillan, pp. 131-53.

Von Reppert-Bismarck, J. 2008. Why Pigs Can't Fly. *Newsweek* [online] 28 June. Available at: <http://www.thedailybeast.com/newsweek/2008/06/28/why-pigs-can-t-fly.html>. [Accessed on 3 January 2013].

Vradelis, S. 2010. Desperate Housewives Empty a Supermarket in Kaisariani. *Ta Nea.* [online] 10 March. Available at <http://www.tanea.gr/ellada/article/?aid=4564389>. [Accessed 30 May 2012].

Vradis, A. 2011. Termination of the Spatial Contract. In C. Giovanopoulos & D. Mitropoulos, eds. *Democracy Under Construction: From the Roads to the Piazzas*. Athens: A-synecheia Editions, pp. 211-218. (In Greek).

Wacquant, L. 2008. *Urban Outcasts: A Comparative Sociology of Advanced Marginality*. Cambridge: Polity Press.

Wacquant, L. 2009. *Punishing the Poor: The Neoliberal Government of Social Insecurity*. Durham: Duke University Press.

Walsh, A. & Tsilimpounidi, M. 2012. The Disappearing Immigrants: Hunger Strike as Invisible Struggle. *Journal of Theory in Action*. 5(2): pp. 82-103.

Warner, M. 2002. *Publics and Counterpublics*. Cambridge: MIT Press.

Wittgenstein, L. 2001. *Tractatus Logico-Philosophicus*. Translated by D.F. Pears & B. McGuinness. London: Routledge.

Xenakis, S. 2011. Organised Crime and Political Violence. In L.K. Cheliotis & S. Xenakis, eds. *Crime and Punishment in Contemporary Greece: International Comparative Perspectives*. Bern: Peter Lang AG, pp. 241-287.

Xenakis, S. 2012. A New Dawn? Change and Continuity in Political Violence in Greece. *Terrorism and Political Violence*. 24(3): pp. 437-464.

Žižek, S. 2012. *The Year of Dreaming Dangerously*. London: Verso.

Zournazi, M. 2001. Hope, Passion and the New World Order. Mary Zournazi in Conversation with Chantal Mouffe and Ernesto Laclau. *Contretemps*. 2: pp. 39-44.

Zukin, S. 1995. *The Cultures of Cities*. Oxford: Blackwell.

Index

Contemporary culture has eliminated both the concept of the public and the figure of the intellectual. Former public spaces – both physical and cultural – are now either derelict or colonized by advertising. A cretinous anti-intellectualism presides, cheerled by expensively educated hacks in the pay of multinational corporations who reassure their bored readers that there is no need to rouse themselves from their interpassive stupor. The informal censorship internalized and propagated by the cultural workers of late capitalism generates a banal conformity that the propaganda chiefs of Stalinism could only ever have dreamt of imposing. Zer0 Books knows that another kind of discourse – intellectual without being academic, popular without being populist – is not only possible: it is already flourishing, in the regions beyond the striplit malls of so-called mass media and the neurotically bureaucratic halls of the academy. Zer0 is committed to the idea of publishing as a making public of the intellectual. It is convinced that in the unthinking, blandly consensual culture in which we live, critical and engaged theoretical reflection is more important than ever before.